Scott Foresman - Addison Wesley
MATH

Problem Solving Masters

Grade 3

Scott Foresman - Addison Wesley

Editorial Offices: Menlo Park, California • Glenview, Illinois
Sales Offices: Reading, Massachusetts • Atlanta, Georgia • Glenview, Illinois
Carrollton, Texas • Menlo Park, California

http://www.sf.aw.com

ISBN 0-201-31270-0

Contents

Chapter 8: Using Geometry

Chapter 9: Multiplying and Dividing

Chapter 10: Fractions and Customary Linear Measurement

Chapter 11: Decimals and Metric Linear Measurement

Chapter 12: Measurement and Probability

Overview

Problem Solving Masters provide a variety of problem solving opportunities designed to complement the lessons in the student edition.

For Learn lessons, these masters provide a wealth of additional problems, employing the skills acquired up to that point in the course. Some masters provide interdisciplinary connections and others include problems that require students to first choose a strategy from the following list:

Use Objects/Act It Out, Draw a Picture, Work Backward, Look for a Pattern, Guess and Check, Solve a Simpler Problem, Use Logical Reasoning, Make an Organized List, and Make a Table.

For the Analyze Strategies and Analyze Word Problems lessons, the masters are in the form of a **Guided Problem Solving** worksheet. These worksheets lead students through the four-step Problem Solving Guide: *Understand, Plan, Solve,* and *Look Back.* The problem used on the worksheet is one of the problems from the "Practice and Apply" or "Problem Solving and Reasoning" sections of the student edition. To encourage students to map out the problem solving steps and solve a problem on their own, the Guided Problem Solving Masters include an additional problem similar to the one being analyzed (under the section *Solve Another Problem*).

The four steps of the Problem Solving Guide are described below.

The **Understand** step asks questions about the *question* in the problem and the data provided.

The **Plan** step maps out a problem-solving strategy or approach. At times the worksheet suggests a particular strategy or approach. Other times the worksheet offers students choices of strategies, methods, or operations.

The **Solve** step prompts students to do the computation and then answer the question.

The **Look Back** step allows students to reflect on their answers and the strategy they used to solve the problem. It also encourages the students to consider the reasonableness of their answers.

The Guided Problem Solving master on the next page can be used to assist students in solving any problem as they complete the four steps of the Problem Solving Guide.

Name _____

GPS **PROBLEM** _____

━━ **Understand** ━━

━━ **Plan** ━━━━━━

━━ **Solve** ━━━━━

━━ **Look Back** ━━

© Scott Foresman Addison Wesley 3

Name _____

Reading Pictographs

Science Your class has been studying rare birds and you find this pictograph in an encyclopedia. It shows how many of each kind of bird are still alive.

Use the pictograph to answer each question.

Name of Bird	Number Reported
Echo parakeet	⟋
Kestrel (Mauritius)	⟋ ⟋
Parakeet (Mauritius)	⟋ ⟋
Cuban ivory billed woodpecker	⟋ ⟋ ⟋
Pink pigeon	⟋ ⟋ ⟋ ⟋ ⟋
Magpie robin	⟋ ⟋ ⟋ ⟋ ⟋

⟋ = 4 birds

1. Which is the rarest bird? _____

2. Which two birds are equally rare?

_____

3. For which bird are there only 16 left?

_____

4. For which bird are there only 6 left? _____

Bill counted the birds he saw in his back yard one day. Use the information to answer each question.

Robin	⟋ ⟋
Blue jay	⟋ ⟋ ⟋
Wren	⟋ ⟋ ⟋ ⟋

⟋ = 10 birds

5. How many blue jays did Bill see? _____

6. Which type of bird did Bill see the least? _____

7. How many more wrens than blue jays did Bill see? _____

Reading Bar Graphs

Social Studies Your principal took a survey to learn more about how students and teachers get to school. The principal used the results of the survey to make this report.

Use the bar graph to answer each question.

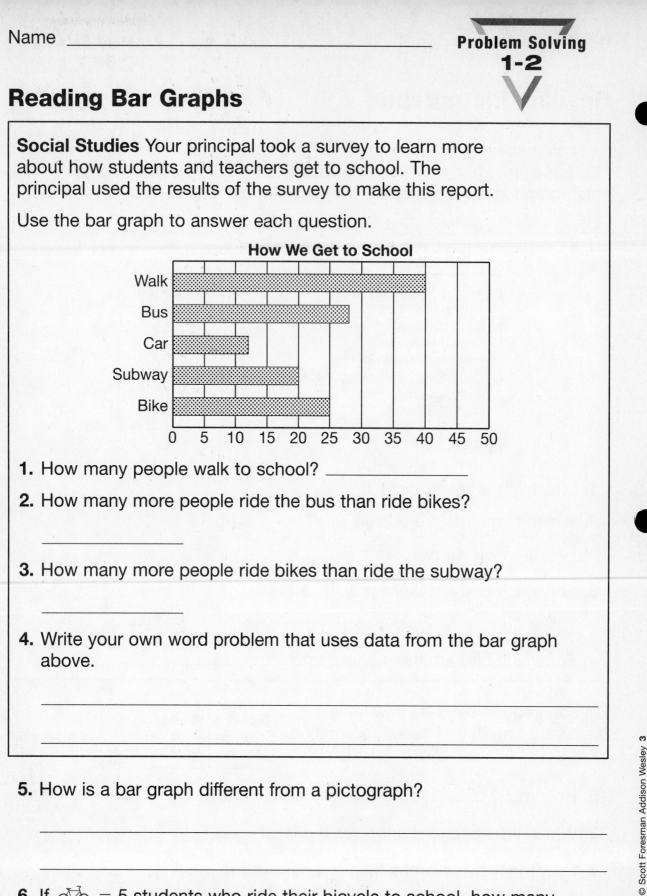

How We Get to School

1. How many people walk to school? _____

2. How many more people ride the bus than ride bikes?

   _____

3. How many more people ride bikes than ride the subway?

   _____

4. Write your own word problem that uses data from the bar graph above.

   _____

   _____

5. How is a bar graph different from a pictograph?

   _____

   _____

6. If 🚲 = 5 students who ride their bicycle to school, how many symbols show 15 students?

   _____

Name _____

Reading Line Graphs

Science Lampreys are fish whose eyes grow bigger after they're born. This line graph shows how long it takes for the eyes to be full-grown.

Use the line graph to answer each question.

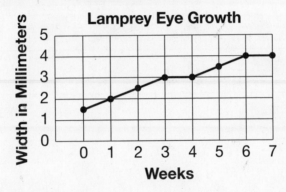

1. Are the lampreys' eyes larger or smaller than 1 millimeter when they are born?

   _____

2. Are the eyes larger or smaller than 2 millimeters when the lamprey is 2 weeks old? How do you know?

   _____

3. The eyes of a full-grown lamprey are 4 millimeters wide. How long does it take for the eyes to be full-grown?

   _____

4. If you found a lamprey with eyes that measured 3 millimeters, how old do you think the fish would be?

   _____

5. For which two periods does eye growth remain the same?

   _____

6. The line in the graph above goes up. Do you think it will ever start going down? Explain.

   _____

Name _____

GPS | PROBLEM 4, STUDENT PAGE 17

How much would it cost to buy a fake leather baseball and a
rubber baseball?

Cost of Baseballs					
Leather					
Fake leather					
Rubber					

= $2

— Understand —

1. What do you need to find out? _____

_____

— Plan —

2. What will you do to find the answer? _____

   A. I'll compare, so I'll subtract.   **B.** I want a total, so I'll add.

— Solve —

3. Which statement solves this problem? _____

   A. 9 + 4 = 13   **B.** 4 + 2 = 6   **C.** 4 − 2 = 2   **D.** 9 + 2 = 11

4. What's your answer to the problem? _____

— Look Back —

5. How can you check your answer? _____

_____

SOLVE ANOTHER PROBLEM

How much more would you have to pay for a real
leather baseball than a fake leather baseball? _____

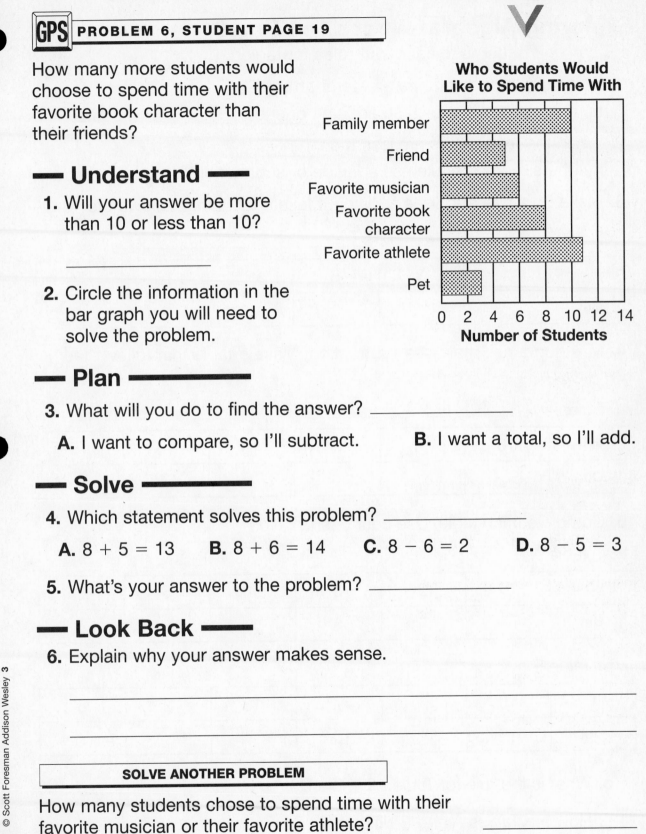

GPS PROBLEM 6, STUDENT PAGE 19

How many more students would choose to spend time with their favorite book character than their friends?

Who Students Would Like to Spend Time With

Family member
Friend
Favorite musician
Favorite book character
Favorite athlete
Pet

0 2 4 6 8 10 12 14
Number of Students

— Understand —

1. Will your answer be more than 10 or less than 10?

_____

2. Circle the information in the bar graph you will need to solve the problem.

— Plan —

3. What will you do to find the answer? _____

A. I want to compare, so I'll subtract.   **B.** I want a total, so I'll add.

— Solve —

4. Which statement solves this problem? _____

A. 8 + 5 = 13   **B.** 8 + 6 = 14   **C.** 8 − 6 = 2   **D.** 8 − 5 = 3

5. What's your answer to the problem? _____

— Look Back —

6. Explain why your answer makes sense.

_____

_____

| SOLVE ANOTHER PROBLEM |

How many students chose to spend time with their favorite musician or their favorite athlete? _____

Exploring Algebra: What's the Rule?

You can find patterns to figure out rules for tables.

1. When the **In** numbers are <u>greater</u> than the Out numbers, does the rule use addition or subtraction? _____

2. When the **In** numbers are <u>less</u> than the Out numbers, does the rule use addition or subtraction? _____

3. Make up a rule that uses addition. Make a table that follows the rule.

Rule: _____

In	1	3	5	6	10	14
Out						

4. Make up a rule that uses subtraction. Make a table that follows the rule.

Rule: _____

In	10	11	12	13	14	15
Out						

5. Complete each table. Use counters to help.

a. Table A

In	1	2	3	4	5	6
Out	4	5	6			

b. Table B

In	10	1	7	13	2	8
Out	13	4	10			

c. What is the rule for Table A? Table B? _____

d. How are Tables A and B different? _____

e. How are Tables A and B the same? _____

Exploring Organizing Data

Use the space below to make a tally table. Use the data you took of your classmates' favorite animals.

Animals						
Tally						

Compare your tally table with the first table you made.

1. Is it easier to make a tally table instead of a table with each students' name? Explain.

_____

_____

2. If you want to count how many students picked a certain animal, which table would be easier to read? Explain.

_____

_____

Take a survey of your classmates' favorite colors. Make a tally table of your data in the table to the right.

Finish this table with other colors that your classmates choose.

Color	Tally
Red	
Blue	
Green	

3. How many of your classmates chose red?

_____

4. Did any 2 colors have the same number

of votes? _____

5. How many students did you survey in all?

_____

Exploring Making Pictographs

You can use pictographs to organize data.

1. How are pictographs and tally tables alike?

_____

2. How are pictographs and tally tables different?

_____

_____

To the right is a tally table of students' favorite fruits.

Banana	ⵜⴰ ⵜⴰ ‖
Apple	ⵜⴰ ‖‖
Orange	‖‖‖‖

Use the tally table to make a pictograph in the space to the right.

Draw the symbol you will use. ☐

Have each symbol = 2 votes.

Banana	
Apple	
Orange	

3. Suppose each symbol in your pictograph were equal to 4 votes.

a. How many symbols would you draw for the number of students who like bananas? _____

b. How many symbols would you draw for the number of students who like apples? _____

c. How many symbols would you draw for the number of students who like oranges? _____

d. Would both pictographs show the same data for each category? Explain.

_____

_____

Name _____

Exploring Making Bar Graphs

This tally table shows students' favorite subjects.

Subject	Tally	Number
Math	卌 卌 卌 卌 卌 IIII	29
Reading	卌 卌 卌 卌 IIII	24
Social Studies	卌 卌 卌 卌 II	22
Science	卌 卌 卌 卌 III	23

You can choose the scale you use for making a bar graph.

Sometimes it's better to use certain scales than others.
Answer each question, then make your bar graph below.

1. What would happen if you used 1 as your scale?

_____

2. What would happen if you used 20 as your scale?

_____

_____

3. Which scale would you use for the data above?

_____

Favorite Subjects

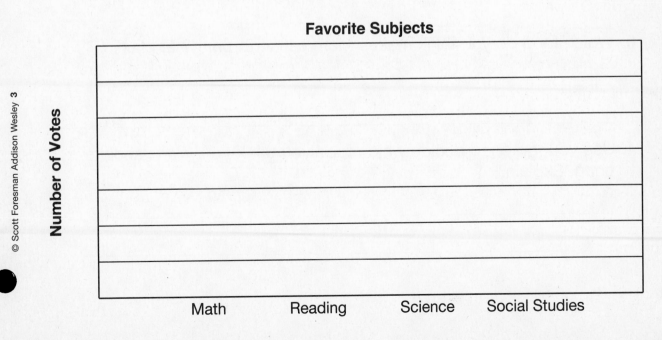

Number of Votes

Math   Reading   Science   Social Studies

Decision Making

Your class is planning a picnic. You have to decide which food to bring.

Below is a tally table of your classmates' votes.

Sandwiches	卌 卌 II
Spaghetti	卌 卌 卌

1. What do you need to decide?

   _____

2. Use the tally table to make a pictograph. Have each symbol = 3 votes.

   a. What symbol will you use in your graph? _____

   b. What title will you give your graph?

   _____

   c. Complete your graph in the space below.

   _____

3. Which food do you think makes more sense to bring? Explain.

   _____

   _____

4. Use your graph to decide which food you think your class should bring. Explain.

   _____

   _____

Name _____

GPS **PROBLEM 8, STUDENT PAGE 40**

What are the next three numbers?

12, 14, 16, 18, ▨ , ▨ , ▨

— Understand —

1. What do you know? _____

2. What do you need to find out? _____
_____

— Plan —

3. a. 14 − 12 = _____

   b. 16 − 14 = _____

   c. 18 − 16 = _____

— Solve —

4. What is the pattern? _____

5. What are the next 3 numbers? _____, _____, _____

— Look Back —

6. How can you check to see if your answer makes sense?
_____
_____

SOLVE ANOTHER PROBLEM

Maurice found 1 penny on Monday, 5 pennies on Tuesday,
and 9 pennies on Wednesday. If the pattern continues,
how many pennies will Maurice find on Friday? _____

Place Value Through Hundreds

Science The table shows how many eggs
different insects and spiders lay.

Insect or Spider	Number of Eggs
Water spider	About 50 – 100
Cabbage butterfly	About 300
Praying mantis	About 10 – 400

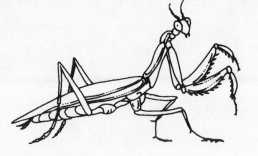

1. Which insects or spiders can lay more than 150 eggs?

_____

2. What is the least number of eggs the water spider lays?
   Use words to write the number. _____

3. Which insects can lay more than 300 eggs?

_____

Solve.

4. The post office has 100 mailboxes for people to rent. If
   each person receives 2 pieces of mail, how many pieces
   of mail are in the boxes? _____

5. A post office has 100 mail boxes. If each box holds 20
   pieces of mail, how many pieces of mail can be held? _____

6. If there were only 10 boxes and 10 pieces of mail in
   each box, how many pieces of mail are there? _____

7. There were 5 magazines, 3 letters, 4 catalogs and
   1 package in Sue's mail box. How many pieces of
   mail did she receive? _____

Exploring Place-Value Relationships

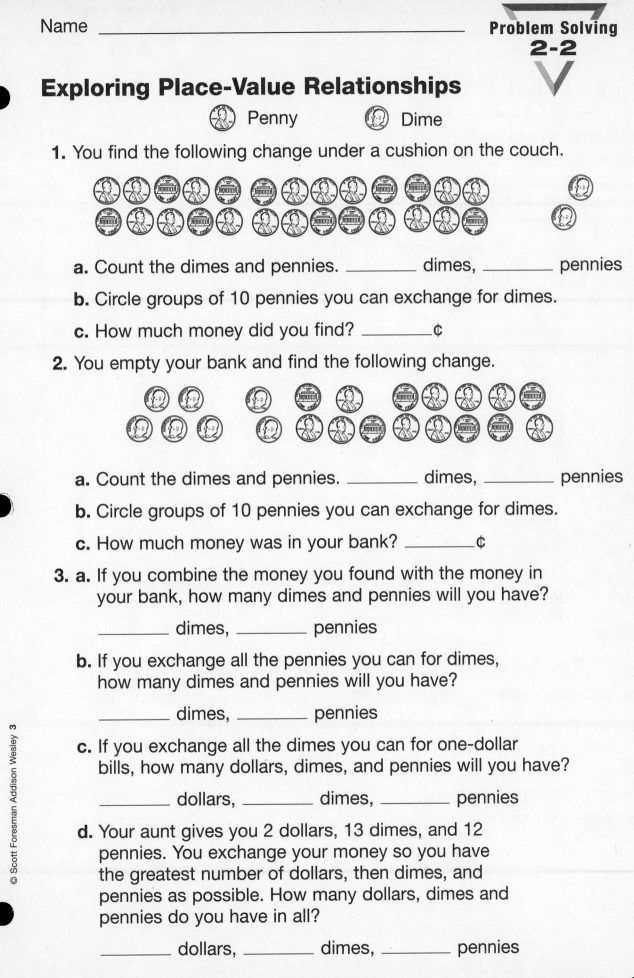

🪙 Penny   🪙 Dime

1. You find the following change under a cushion on the couch.

a. Count the dimes and pennies. _____ dimes, _____ pennies

b. Circle groups of 10 pennies you can exchange for dimes.

c. How much money did you find? _____¢

2. You empty your bank and find the following change.

a. Count the dimes and pennies. _____ dimes, _____ pennies

b. Circle groups of 10 pennies you can exchange for dimes.

c. How much money was in your bank? _____¢

3. a. If you combine the money you found with the money in
your bank, how many dimes and pennies will you have?

_____ dimes, _____ pennies

b. If you exchange all the pennies you can for dimes,
how many dimes and pennies will you have?

_____ dimes, _____ pennies

c. If you exchange all the dimes you can for one-dollar
bills, how many dollars, dimes, and pennies will you have?

_____ dollars, _____ dimes, _____ pennies

d. Your aunt gives you 2 dollars, 13 dimes, and 12
pennies. You exchange your money so you have
the greatest number of dollars, then dimes, and
pennies as possible. How many dollars, dimes and
pennies do you have in all?

_____ dollars, _____ dimes, _____ pennies

Place Value Through Thousands

Geography Population is the number of people who live in an area. Here is the population of some towns in New Mexico.

UNITED STATES

New Mexico

Town	Population
Aztec	5,480
Corrales	5,453
Espanola	8,389
Shiprock	7,687

1. Write the population of Espanola in words.

_____

2. Which two towns have populations that are very close?

_____

3. Which town has the greatest population? _____

Solve.

4. What is the value of the underlined digit in 270? _____

5. Which is greater: 4,302 or 4,203? _____

6. The Declaration of Independence was signed in 1776. Write 1776 in words.

_____

7. Write the current year in words.

_____

Place Value Through Hundred Thousands

Social Studies On June 23, 1995, Merrick Johnston stood on the top of Alaska's Mt. McKinley in Denali National Park. At 12 years old, she was the youngest person ever to climb Mt. McKinley.

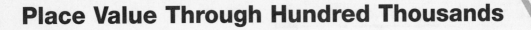

Here are some facts about her climb.

Height of Mt. McKinley: 20,320 feet

Weight of supplies that Merrick towed behind her on a sled: about 50 pounds

Time spent climbing each day: 6 hours

Time spent setting up camp each day: 4 hours

1. Write Mt. McKinley's height in words.

_____

2. How many more hours did Merrick spend climbing each day than setting up camp? _____

3. Merrick's last camp was at 17,000 feet. The next day she reached the top of Mt. McKinley. About how far did she climb the last day?

_____

Use these digits to solve **4–6**.

7   3   9   1   4   5

4. What is the greatest number you can write using the digits? _____

5. What is the least number you can write using the digits? _____

6. What do you notice about your answers for **4** and **5**? _____

_____

_____

Name _____

GPS | PROBLEM 3, STUDENT PAGE 61

Suppose Peter wants to order 45 pounds of soil. He can order the soil in 10-pound bags or 1-pound bags. How many ways could he order the soil?

— Understand —

1. How many pounds of soil will Peter order? _____

2. What kind of bags does the soil come in? Underline them in the problem above.

— Plan —

3. If Peter buys three 10-pound bags, how much soil will he have?

   _____

   How much soil will he still need? _____

   _____ 10-pound bag and _____ 1-pound bags

— Solve —

4. List all possible ways Peter can order the soil.

10-lb bags					
1-lb bag					

— Look Back —

5. How can you check your answer?

   _____

SOLVE ANOTHER PROBLEM

Suppose Peter wants to order 50 pounds of soil. He can buy the soil in 10 pound or 5-pound bags. How many ways can he order the soil? _____

Comparing Numbers

Geography These pictures show some of the tallest mountains in the world. The height of each mountain is written next to its picture.

Mt. Blanc, Europe
4,805 meters

Mt. Kilimanjaro, Africa
5,895 meters

Mt. McKinley, North America
6,190 meters

Mt. Aconcagua, South America
6,960 meters

Mt. Everest, Asia
8,850 meters

1. Which is the tallest mountain?

_____

2. Which are the two shortest mountains?

_____

3. Which mountain would take longer to climb, Mt. McKinley or Mt. Aconcagua? Explain.

_____

4. How much taller is Mt. Aconcagua than Mt. McKinley?

_____

5. The distance between New York City and Boston is about 410 miles; the distance between New York City and Washington D.C. is about 490 miles. Which trip should take longer—New York City to Boston or to Washington D.C.? Explain.

_____

Ordering Numbers

Science The depth at which each of these ocean animals usually lives is next to its picture.

Whale: 500 feet

Jellyfish: 10 feet

Sponge: 300 feet

Shark: 250 feet

Octopus: 5,000 feet

1. If you dove from a boat, which animal would you probably see first?

_____

2. Put the animals in order by depth, from the one that lives at the least depth to the one that lives at the greatest depth.

_____

_____

3. Sandy asked his relatives when they were born and made a list: Mom, 1963; Aunt Julie, 1959; Uncle Willy, 1955; Aunt Mamie, 1965; Dad, 1962; Grandma, 1938.

List Sandy's relatives in order, from oldest to youngest.

_____

_____

4. The following years were important in the history of the United States. Put them in order from most recent to earliest.

1969   1918   1776   1865   1945   1963

_____

Name _____

Rounding to Tens

Social Studies Farmers need to keep track of the number of animals they keep on their farms. Compare the numbers of animals from these two neighboring farms.

	Hopewell Farm	Sunnycrest Farm
Cows	48	147
Horses	54	40
Chickens	217	112
Pigs	112	30
Goats	70	76

1. Which farm has about 220 chickens? _____

2. Which farm has about 110 pigs? _____

3. About how many goats are kept at Sunnycrest Farm? _____

4. Which kind of animal seems to be the most popular on the two farms? How many are there all together?

_____

5. Darrell's mother said he could spend about $10 on a birthday present for his best friend. He found an action figure for $12. Do you think his mother will let him buy it? Explain your reasoning.

_____

6. There are 347 kittens and 125 puppies at the animal shelter. The shelter wants to put a list of animals in the paper.

To the nearest 10 how many kittens are there? _____

To the nearest 10 how many puppies are there? _____

Rounding to Hundreds

History It's been a busy century for inventors! Here is a list of some inventions of the 1900s.

Inventions	Year Invented
Radio	1913
Air Conditioning	1911
Television	1924
VCR	1969
Ballpoint Pen	1943
Photocopy Machine	1937
Compact Disc	1972
Velcro	1948

1. Was the ballpoint pen invented closer to the beginning or the end of the 1900s? Explain.

   _____

   _____

2. Which items were invented closer to 1900 than 2000?

   _____

   _____

3. Which items were invented closer to 2000?

   _____

   _____

4. Tamiko's family wants to buy a new VCR for about $300. Here is a list of the prices they saw at the store. Circle the price that comes closest to what the family plans to spend.

   $219 $319 $399 $279

Name _____

Time to the Nearest Five Minutes

Careers Ana is a tour guide in Washington, D.C. Here is the day's schedule for her tour group.

Time Bus Leaves	Activity
10:10 A.M.	The White House
11:30 A.M.	Lunch
12:20 P.M.	Air and Space Museum
2:30 P.M.	Vietnam War Memorial
3:05 P.M.	Washington Memorial
3:40 P.M.	Snack

Use the schedule to answer the questions.

1. Where will the group be going to at ten minutes after ten?

_____

2. Five minutes after she gets the group onto the bus going to the Washington Memorial, Ana will take a break. At what time will Ana take a break? _____

3. Ana must allow 5 minutes for the group to board the bus. At what time should she have the group meet at the bus to leave for the Air and Space Museum? _____

4. Tony wants to leave for the bookstore before four o'clock. A bus will stop near his home at the times below. Which bus should he take? Circle the correct time.

   4:10   5:40   3:45   4:00

5. Tony planned to be home by six o'clock. He left the store at 6:05 P.M. Was he going to be early or late? Explain.

_____

Exploring Time to the Nearest Minute

1. Circle the activities you think take about one minute.

    a. running twenty miles   **b.** making your bed

    c. counting to 100   **d.** doing your homework

    e. writing 5 sentences   **f.** solving a 500-piece jigsaw puzzle

2. Name two more one-minute activities.

_____

_____

3. How many times do you breathe in a minute? Estimate. Record your estimate in the 1st row of the table. Then use a clock with a second hand. Count your breaths in one minute. Record your actual number in the 1st row of the table.

	Breaths in 1 Minute	
	Estimate	**Actual**
At Rest		
After Running in Place		

4. How do you think your breathing will change after running in place for one minute? Estimate. Record your estimate in the 2nd row of the table. Run in place for one minute. Then complete the 2nd row of the table.

Time to the Half Hour and Quarter Hour

Science The Ecology Club is holding a Playground Cleanup today and everyone's helping out!

TIME	ACTIVITY
2:45 P.M.	School's Out; Teams Get Ready
3:00 P.M.	Welcome Speeches
3:15 P.M.	Cleanup Starts
4:15 P.M.	Cleanup Ends

Use the schedule to answer the questions. Write the times in words.

1. When should cleanup teams get ready?

   _____

2. When will the cleanup end?

   _____

3. If the principal arrives at a quarter past three to give her speech, will she be on time? Explain.

   _____

4. Will the Ecology Club be ready to go home by half past four? Explain.

   _____

   _____

5. Darnelle got up early Saturday morning. List three things she could have done on Saturday. Write a time for each thing you list. Write A.M. or P.M.

   _____

   _____

6. Darnelle's mother planned to have dinner ready at six. Dinner was ready at 5:45. Was she early or late? Explain.

   _____

Elapsed Time

Science You test equal amounts of 5 different liquids to find how much time it takes each to boil. Calculate each elapsed time.

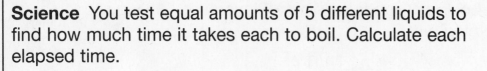

Liquid	Starting time	Began to boil	Time to Boil (Elapsed time)
1. Water	1:12	1:14	_____
2. Milk	1:17	1:22	_____
3. Syrup	1:43	1:51	_____
4. Vinegar	1:48	1:52	_____
5. Oil	2:14	2:19	_____

6. Which liquid took the longest time to boil? _____

7. Which liquid took the shortest time to boil? _____

On your mark, get set, go! Four runners started a marathon at 8:00 A.M. Use each runner's finish time to calculate each running time.

	Finish Time	Elapsed Time
Runner 1	11:14	**8.** _____
Runner 2	10:48	**9.** _____
Runner 3	12:30	**10.** _____
Runner 4	12:27	**11.** _____

12. Which runner was the fastest? _____

13. Which runners took more than 4 hours? _____

Name _____

Ordinal Numbers and the Calendar

Physical Education It's time to make January's after-school schedule for the gym. Use this list to help you fill in the calendar. Use a picture or letter to mark when each event will take place.

Basketball games are planned for the 1st and 3rd Tuesdays and 2nd and 4th Wednesdays.

Indoor Soccer games are planned for the 1st, 2nd, and 4th Saturdays.

Volleyball games are planned for the 1st and 3rd Mondays and the 2nd and 4th Fridays.

The State Gymnastics Tournament is planned for the twenty-seventh of January.

January

Sun.	Mon.	Tues.	Wed.	Thur.	Fri.	Sat.
	1	2	3	4	5	6
7	8	9	10	11	12	13
14	15	16	17	18	19	20
21	22	23	24	25	26	27
28	29	30	31			

1. There's a problem! Which two events are scheduled for the same day?

_____

2. How can you change the schedule to solve this problem?

_____

_____

3. Mike's birthday is on the sixth of the fifth month, and his sister's birthday is on the fifth of the sixth month. Give the date of each birthday.

_____

Decision Making

It's Saturday morning. Time for chores. You begin at
9:00 A.M. and want to be done before 11:00 A.M. to play
basketball. Here's your list of chores:

• Clean a room.   _____

• Do the dishes.   _____

• Sweep the floors.   _____

• Take out the garbage.   _____

1. How much time do you have to get it all done? _____

2. Decide how much time you will need for each chore on
the list. Write the time on the line next to the chore's
name, above.

3. Should you plan extra time in case of problems? Why?

_____

_____

4. How much extra time will you plan?

_____

5. Make a schedule that shows when to start each chore.

Time   Chore

_____   _____

_____   _____

_____   _____

_____   _____

Show your schedule to someone else. Does he or she agree
with your estimates of times? Explain how you planned your
schedule.

_____

_____

Exploring Addition Patterns

Use basic facts and place-value patterns to find each sum.

1. How can you use patterns to add 400 and 900?

_____

2. What basic fact can you use to find 200 + 700? Explain.

_____

3. Can you use the basic fact 5 + 1 to solve $50 + $10?
Explain.

_____

4. Can you use the basic fact 5 + 1 to solve 500 + 10?
Explain.

_____

5. a. Find 3 pairs of numbers to fill in the
boxes so that the sum does not
have a digit in the thousands place.

☐ hundreds + ☐ hundreds _____

    b. What patterns do you notice in your number pairs?

_____

_____

6. a. Find 3 pairs of numbers to fill in the
boxes so that the sum has a digit in
the thousands place.

☐ hundreds + ☐ hundreds _____

    b. What patterns do you notice in your number pairs?

_____

_____

Exploring Adding on a Hundred Chart

1	2	3	4	5	6	7	8	9	10
11	12	13	14	15	16	17	18	19	20
21	22	23	24	25	26	27	28	29	30
31	32	33	34	35	36	37	38	39	40
41	42	43	44	45	46	47	48	49	50
51	52	53	54	55	56	57	58	59	60
61	62	63	64	65	66	67	68	69	70
71	72	73	74	75	76	77	78	79	80
81	82	83	84	85	86	87	88	89	90
91	92	93	94	95	96	97	98	99	100

You can use a hundred chart to help you find sums.

1. Describe one way you could use a hundred chart to find
the sum of 73 and 25.

_____

_____

2. Find the sum of 45 + 31. Find the sum of 31 + 45. What
do you notice about the two sums?

_____

3. How could you use a hundred chart to find $22 + $57?

_____

_____

_____

4. Are there two ways to find 17 + 64 on a hundred chart?
Explain.

_____

_____

© Scott Foresman Addison Wesley 3

Name _____

Exploring Algebra: Missing Numbers

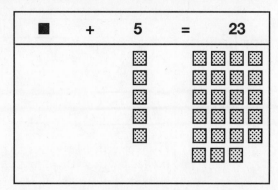

For the equation to be true, each side of the number sentence must be equal.

1. a. How can you use drawings to find the missing number? Explain.

_____

_____

b. Draw squares to find the missing number. How many squares did you draw to make both sides equal?

_____

c. Fill in the missing number. _____ + 5 = 23.

Use drawings to find each missing number.

2. _____ + 8 = 21   **3.** _____ + 13 = 22

4. 6 + _____ = 13   **5.** 7 + _____ = 24

6. Is there another way to use drawings to find the missing numbers? Explain using the example at the top of the page.

_____

_____

7. If you know the missing number in ☐ + 8 = 14, how can you find the missing number in ☐ + 9 = 14? Explain.

_____

_____

Name _____

Estimating Sums

Geography The Finger Lakes of New York state are long and narrow and look a bit like fingers on a hand. Each lake has an Iroquois name. This map shows several of these lakes, including Seneca Lake, Cayuga Lake, Keuka Lake, and Canandaigua Lake.

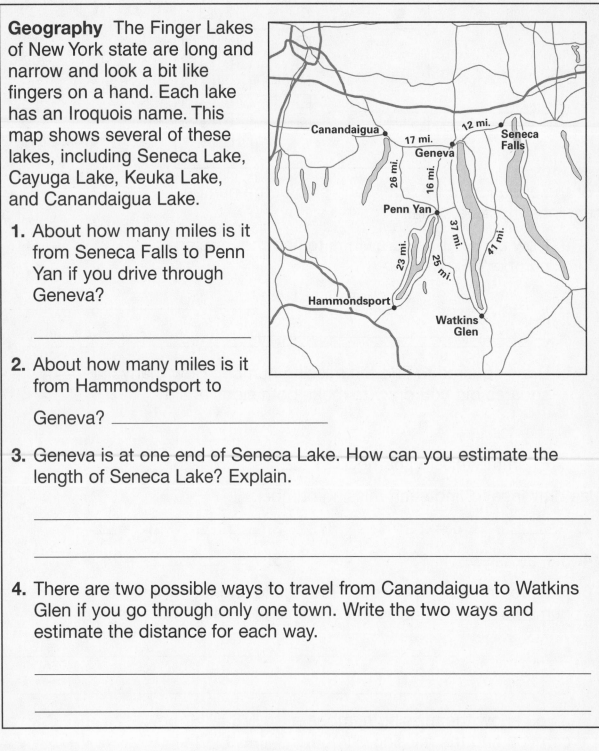

1. About how many miles is it from Seneca Falls to Penn Yan if you drive through Geneva?

   _____

2. About how many miles is it from Hammondsport to

   Geneva? _____

3. Geneva is at one end of Seneca Lake. How can you estimate the length of Seneca Lake? Explain.

   _____

   _____

4. There are two possible ways to travel from Canandaigua to Watkins Glen if you go through only one town. Write the two ways and estimate the distance for each way.

   _____

   _____

5. On Monday, 125 students bought lunch. On Tuesday, 187 bought lunch. About how many students bought lunch on Monday and Tuesday?

   _____

Name _____

Exploring Adding with Regrouping

1. Antonio has 18 markers. Jan has 24 markers. How many markers do they have all together?

    a. Draw place-value blocks in the space below to help you find the answer.

    b. Did you have to regroup ones for tens? Explain.

    _____

    c. What is the sum? Write the number sentence.

    _____

2. a. Do you need to regroup ones for tens when you add 55 + 36? Explain.

    _____

    b. What is the sum of 55 + 36? _____

3. Name two 2-digit numbers that do not need to be regrouped when added.

_____

_____

4. Blane says that the sum of 57 and 34 is 81. Is he correct? Explain.

_____

_____

5. If you add 27 + 66 using place-value blocks, how many tens blocks will you have in the sum? _____

Adding 2-Digit Numbers

Social Studies The President of the United States is elected by members of the electoral college. Each state has a different number of electoral votes. Below is a map showing the number of electoral votes for each state.

1. In the 1996 presidential election, Bill Clinton won all of the electoral votes in California (CA) and Michigan (MI). How many electoral votes is that? _____

2. In the 1996 election, Bob Dole won all of the electoral votes in Texas (TX) and South Carolina (SC). How many electoral votes is that? _____

3. Are there more electoral votes in Georgia (GA) or Washington (WA)? Explain.

_____

4. Write an addition word problem that does not use regrouping. Use two 2-digit numbers. Then solve the problem.

_____

_____

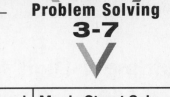

Adding 3-Digit Numbers

The town of Oakdale prepared
a time capsule. Students at
two schools in the town wrote
letters for the capsule. The
table shows how many letters
were written by each grade
in the schools. Use the table
to answer the questions.

Grade	Oakville School	Maple Street School
1	107	96
2	116	212
3	87	123
4	263	107
5	198	254

1. How many letters did
all the students in Grade 4
write for the capsule?   _____

2. How many letters were written by students
in Grades 1 and 2 at Oakville School? At
Maple Tree School?   _____

3. Who wrote more letters, all students in Grade 1
or all students in Grade 3?   _____

4. Which grade wrote the most letters? How many?

_____

5. Choose a Strategy Newspapers and
magazines were also put in Oakdale's time
capsule. A total of 51 pages were put in
the capsule. The number of newspaper
pages was 34. How many magazine pages
were put in the capsule?

| • Use Objects/Act It Out |
| • Draw a Picture |
| • Look for a Pattern |
| • Guess and Check |
| • Use Logical Reasoning |
| • Make an Organized List |
| • Make a Table |
| • Solve a Simpler Problem |
| • Work Backward |

a. What strategy would you
use to solve the problem?

_____

_____

b. Answer the problem. _____

Adding 4-Digit Numbers:
Choose a Calculation Method

Science Jupiter, the largest planet in the solar system, has 16 known satellites or moons. The four largest moons were discovered by Galileo in 1610. Their names and diameters are given in the following table.

Moon	Diameter in miles
Ganymede	3,275
Europa	1,945
Callisto	3,008
Io	2,262

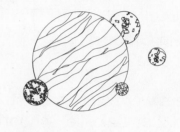

1. Which moon has the greatest diameter? _____

2. Which moon has a diameter closest to 3,000 miles? _____

3. What is the total of the diameters of Io and Europa? _____

4. What is the total of the diameters of the two largest moons? _____

5. Ian traveled 2,136 miles to visit her grandfather. Then she traveled 1,814 miles to visit her aunt. How far did she travel in all? _____

6a. To go from Minneapolis to Phoenix by plane you travel 1,270 miles. To continue your trip to Portland, Oregon you go another 1,009 miles. How far will you travel? _____

b. Is the distance from Minneapolis to Phoenix or from Phoenix to Portland greater?

_____

Name _____

Column Addition

Science The General Sherman tree is a redwood tree in California. It is over 275 feet tall! Not all trees grow to such great heights. The table gives the average height of other trees found in the United States.

Tree	Average Height
American Holly	40 to 50 feet
American Mountain Ash	20 to 30 feet
Pecan	90 to 120 feet
Red Maple	50 to 70 feet
Sugar Pine	175 to 200 feet

1. About how many American holly trees would equal the height of a sugar pine with the tallest average height?

   _____

2. What is the least number of pecan trees you'd need to reach the same height as the General Sherman tree?

   _____

3. Suppose one of each type of tree of the greatest average height listed was cut down. If the trees were laid end to end, what distance would they cover?

   _____

Trees need water just as people do. A large apple tree can take in 95 gallons of water in a single day!

4. At this rate, how much water would 3 apple trees take in?

   _____

5. How much water would 1 apple tree take in during a week?

   _____

GPS **PROBLEM 4, STUDENT PAGE 121**

The sum of two numbers is 80. The numbers are 2 apart. What are they?

— Understand —

1. What do you know about the two numbers that the problem asks you to find?

_____

— Plan —

2. Write 3 pairs of numbers in the table whose sum is 80. Find their differences.

Pairs of Numbers		Sum	Difference	Comments

— Solve —

3. How do your differences compare to the difference you need? Write your comments in the table.

4. Use your previous guesses to help you make more guesses. Continue filling in the table until you find a pair of numbers that work. What are the two numbers?

_____

— Look Back —

5. How can you be sure your answer is correct?

_____

_____

SOLVE ANOTHER PROBLEM

Use guess and check to answer this problem. The sum of two numbers is 96. The numbers are 6 apart. What are they?

_____

Name _____

Mental Math

Recreation The 1994 Winter Olympic Games were held in Lillehammer, Norway. The chart shows the number of medals won by 5 different countries at the games.

Country	Gold	Silver	Bronze
Russia	11	8	14
Germany	9	7	8
South Korea	4	1	1
Norway	10	11	5
United States	6	5	2

Use the table and mental math to answer these questions.

1. What was the total number of medals won by the United States?

_____

2. Which country won the most medals? How many were won?

_____

3. How many gold medals were won by these five countries?

_____

Oak Street School held an art fair. The chart shows the number of ribbons won by each grade. Use the chart to answer the questions.

Grade	Blue	Red	White
1	12	5	9
2	18	7	4
3	15	8	5
4	19	6	3

4. Which two grades won the same number of ribbons?

_____

5. Which grade won the greatest number of ribbons? How many?

_____

6. How many blue ribbons were awarded at the art fair?

_____

Name _____

Counting Coins

Recreation One of Sarah's favorite hobbies is coin collecting. She collects nickels, dimes and quarters. Sarah uses a chart to record the original value of the coins she adds to her collection each week.

Week	Total
1	$1.30
2	$1.65
3	$1.30
4	$1.65

1. What 8 coins did Sarah add to her collection the first and third week?

_____

2. What 8 coins did Sarah add to her collection the second and fourth week?

_____

3. a. What is the greatest number of coins you could use to buy a pencil that costs 36 cents? _____

b. What are the coins?

_____

4. a. Using quarters and lesser coins, what is the least number of coins you could use to buy a notebook that costs 79 cents? _____

b. What are the coins?

_____

5. Lee has 49 cents. She has the following coins plus 5 more coins. What are the other coins Lee has?

_____

Name _____

Using Dollars and Cents

Careers A store clerk must count the money in the cash register at the end of each day. Suppose you are a store clerk. The following change is in your cash register at the end of the day. Find the total value of each set of coins. Then tell the total value of all the coins.

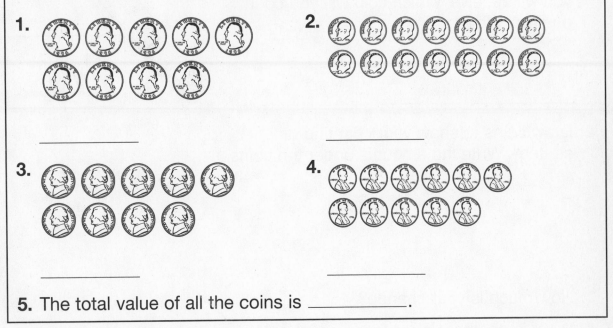

1.

2.

3.

4.

5. The total value of all the coins is _____.

Someone gives you $3.12 using no bills.

6. What is the least number of coins you could get using quarters and lesser coins? Name them.

_____

7. What is the greatest number of coins you could get? Name them.

_____

8. If you get 30 dimes, will you get any quarters? Explain.

_____

_____

9. What is the greatest number of nickels you could get?

_____

Name _____

Exploring Making Change

You are going to the art supply store with $5.00. You can buy one item but you need to return home with some change.

You decide to buy a color marker for $1.17.

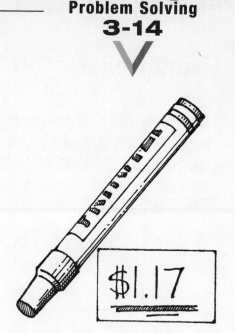

$1.17

1. Count on to find out how much change you will receive. Which coin will you count on first? Why?

   _____

   _____

2. Draw coins to show your counting-on strategy. Write the amounts under the coins.

3. How much is your change? _____

4. What is another way you can count on to find the answer? Explain.

   _____

   _____

5. Name three other ways you can receive your change. Which coins and bills can you use?

   _____

   _____

   _____

Name _____

Adding Money

Fine Arts Your school's band is selling used instruments and musical supplies to raise money for a trip to New York City to march in the Thanksgiving Day Parade.

Price List	
music stand	$6.68
drum sticks	$5.54
saxophone reeds	$1.19
used recorder	$3.93
sheet music	$1.21

1. Joseph bought sheet music and a music stand. How much did both items cost?

   _____

2. You have $6.50. Which three items could you buy?

   _____

3. What is the sum of the cost of your purchases and Joseph's purchases?

   _____

4. What is the greatest amount of money you could spend on 2 items? Which items?

   _____

5. Which amount is greater?

   a. 3 dollars, 2 quarters, 2 dimes, 1 nickel, 1 penny, or $3.86

   _____

   b. 4 dollars, 1 quarter, 2 dimes, 7 pennies, or $4.49

   _____

   _____

6. Will $15.00 be enough to buy a plant that costs $7.95 and a plant stand that costs $11.35? Explain.

   _____

Name _____

Front-End Estimation

Social Studies The table shows the amount of money the average person spends on food items in one year. Use front-end estimation and the table to answer the questions.

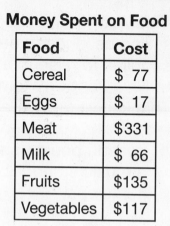

Money Spent on Food

Food	Cost
Cereal	$ 77
Eggs	$ 17
Meat	$331
Milk	$ 66
Fruits	$135
Vegetables	$117

1. Is the amount of money spent on fruits and vegetables greater or less than the amount spent on meat? Explain.

   _____

2. Is $200 enough money to budget for fruit and vegetables? Explain.

   _____

   _____

3. About how much would a family of three spend on cereal in one year?

   _____

4. Tickets to the State Fair cost $6.75 for adults and $3.50 for students. Is $11.00 enough for 1 adult and 2 students? Explain.

   _____

5. Three groups of students go on a class trip to New York City. The groups have 11, 25, and 17 students. One elevator at the Empire State Building holds 40 people. Can all three groups fit in one elevator? Explain.

   _____

   _____

Name _____

GPS PROBLEM 4, STUDENT PAGE 139

Blaine wants to know if $8.00 is enough to buy a guidebook and a compass. Does he need to find the exact total? Explain.

Supplies	
Hammer	$15.80
Guidebook	$ 2.95
Gloves	$ 5.89
Compass	$ 5.49

— Understand —

1. What do you know? What do you need to find out?

_____

_____

— Plan —

2. How will you decide if an exact answer or an estimate will do?

_____

— Solve —

3. Estimate. _____

_____

4. Do you need to find the exact answer to solve the problem? Explain, then answer the problem.

_____

SOLVE ANOTHER PROBLEM

Write if you need an exact answer or an estimate. Can Blaine buy a hammer and a guidebook with $20? Explain.

_____

_____

Reviewing the Meaning of Subtraction

Physical Education To qualify for the President's Physical Fitness Award students must score in the 85th percentile on 5 physical fitness items. Students do curlups, shuttle runs, 1 mile walk/runs, pull-ups and V-sit reaches.

Write a number sentence for each. Then solve.

1. Carrie did six curlups. Timothy did four. How many more curlups did Carrie do than Timothy?

   _____

2. Yvonne did six pull-ups and Helen did five. How many pull-ups did they do all together?

   _____

3. Jon did eight V-sit reaches on Monday and nine on Tuesday. How many V-sit reaches did he do all together?

   _____

4. Ned wants to do eight shuttle runs. He has done five already. How many more shuttle runs does he have to run?

   _____

5. The boys' chorus will sing five songs. The girls' chorus will sing four. How many songs will be sung all together?

   _____

6. The band will play eight songs. Four of these songs will be slow songs. The other songs will be fast songs. How many songs will be fast?

   _____

7. Carlos will sing three songs at the school concert. Tanya will sing five. How many more songs will Tanya sing than Carlos?

   _____

Name _____

Exploring Subtraction Patterns

Answer the following questions.

1. How is subtracting 900 − 200 like subtracting 9 − 2?

_____

2. What basic fact can you use to find $60 − $30? Explain.

_____

3. How could you check your work if you wrote
70 − 40 = 30?

_____

_____

4. How is subtracting $1,200 − $800 like subtracting
$12 − $8?

_____

5. Suppose it takes you 30 minutes to ride your bike to
school and 70 minutes to walk to school. How much
longer does it take you to walk than to ride?

_____

6. Calvin scored 20 points in one basketball game. Susan
scored 40 points. How many more points did Susan
score than Calvin?

_____

7. Vanessa had 40 minutes of homework last night. She
has 90 minutes tonight. How many more minutes of
homework does she have tonight?

_____

8. Alice had 500 sheets of notebook paper. During the
school year she used 200 sheets. How many sheets did
she have at the end of the school year?

_____

Exploring Subtracting on a Hundred Chart

Use a hundred chart to answer each question.

1. Choose a number greater than 35.

    a. What number is 7 less than your number? _____

    b. 17 less than your number? _____

    c. 27 less than your number? _____

    d. Explain the steps you took to solve the problems.

    _____

    _____

    _____

    e. What do you notice about your answers to **a–c**?

    _____

2. Describe two ways to find 64 − 49 on a hundred chart.

    _____

    _____

3. On a hundred chart, start with your finger on 87. Move back 3 rows and 9 spaces.

    a. On what number do you land? _____

    b. What number did you subtract? _____

4. How can you find 74 − 40 by counting by 10's?

    _____

5. Phillip chose a number that is 32 less than 61. What is the number? Explain.

    _____

Estimating Differences

Science The drawing below shows the number of days it takes some of the planets in our solar system to orbit the sun. One full orbit of the sun is one year.

Earth
365 days

Mars
687 days

Mercury
86 days

Venus
243 days

Sun

1. About how many days longer does it take for Mars to circle the sun than Earth? _____

2. About how many days longer does it take Mars to circle the sun than Mercury? _____

3. About how many days shorter is a year on the planet Venus than a year on Earth? _____

4. If a movie lasts 186 minutes and you have been watching for 105 minutes, about how much longer will the movie run?

_____

5. Suppose the school day lasts 6 hours and 25 minutes, or 385 minutes total. By lunch time 172 minutes of the school day is over. About how many minutes are there left until the end of the school day?

_____

Exploring Regrouping

1. Are fourteen tens and six ones the same as one hundred forty-six? Explain.

_____

_____

2. How many tens will you have if you regroup

   1 hundred for 10 tens in the number 651? _____

3. How many ones will you have if you regroup

   1 ten for 10 ones in the number 98? _____

4. Are 15 ones the same as 5 tens and 1 one? Explain.

_____

_____

5. Is 112 the same as 11 tens and 2 ones? Explain.

_____

_____

6. a. How do you regroup 1 ten for 10 ones in the number 896?

_____

_____

   b. How do you regroup 1 hundred to 10 tens in the number 896?

_____

_____

7. How are ones, tens, and hundreds related?

_____

_____

Exploring Subtracting 2-Digit Numbers

The number of cable television channels that you can watch on your television depends on where you live. Here is a list of some towns and the number of channels they have available to watch.

Town	Number of Cable Channels
Acton	63
Springfield	45
Border City	36

1. Suppose you want to find out the difference between the number of channels in Acton and the number of channels in Border City.

   a. Would you need to regroup? Explain.

   _____

   _____

   b. What is the difference? _____

2. Suppose you want to find out the difference between the number of channels in Acton and the number in Springfield.

   a. Would you need to regroup? Explain.

   _____

   _____

   b. What is the difference? _____

3. Suppose you moved from Springfield to Border City. Find out how many channels you would lose.

   a. Do you have to regroup to subtract? Explain.

   _____

   _____

   b. How many channels would you lose?

   _____

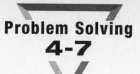

Subtracting 2-Digit Numbers

Geography The month of January can be very cold in some parts of the world. However, it can be very warm in other places. Here are some average temperatures for the month of January from around the world.

City	Average January Temperature °F
Bombay, India	88
Shanghai, China	47
Bogotá, Colombia	67
Sidney, Australia	78
Montreal, Canada	21
Tampa, Florida	60
Des Moines, Iowa	19
Nairobi, Kenya	77
San Francisco, California	49

1. a. What is the warmest city in January in the table?

_____

b. What is the coldest city in January in the table?

_____

c. What is the difference in temperature between the warmest city and the coldest city? _____

2. How much colder is it in San Francisco, California than in Bogotá, Columbia? _____

3. How much warmer is it in Tampa, Florida than in Montreal, Canada? _____

4. Arthur is 53 inches tall. His 3-year-old brother, Andrew, is 25 inches tall. How much taller is Arthur than Andrew? _____

5. Bill made 34 oatmeal cookies for the art club's bake sale. Kathie made 18 gingerbread cookies. How many more cookies did Bill make than Kathie? _____

6. Justin exercised for 42 minutes on Friday and 33 minutes on Saturday. How many more minutes did he exercise on Friday? _____

Exploring Subtracting 3-Digit Numbers

1. Find the difference of 148 and 92.

    a. Draw place-value blocks in the space below to show 148 − 92.

    b. Do you need to regroup? Explain.

    _____

    _____

    c. What is the difference of 148 and 92? _____

2. Would you have to regroup to find 233 − 183? Explain.

_____

_____

3. Would you have to regroup to find the difference of 364 and 136? Explain.

_____

_____

4. Johanna says, "To find 323 − 142, you need to regroup a hundred." Do you agree? Explain.

_____

5. Suppose you had 2 hundreds blocks, 3 tens blocks, and 8 ones blocks. Could you subtract 56 without regrouping? Explain.

_____

© Scott Foresman Addison Wesley 3

Subtracting 3-Digit Numbers

Technology When we hear the word technology, we often think of computers. However, technology can mean many things. Drawbridges are an example of technology. Drawbridges are special bridges that can be raised, lowered, or drawn aside so that boats can pass under them.

1. The Arthur Kill drawbridge connecting New York and New Jersey is 558 feet long and is the longest drawbridge in the United States. The Second Narrows bridge in Vancouver, British Columbia is the longest drawbridge in Canada and is 493 feet long. How much longer is the Arthur Kill drawbridge than the Second Narrows drawbridge? _____

2. Two of the largest drawbridges in the United States are in Florida. They are the Main Street bridge in Jacksonville, at 386 feet and the St. Andrew's Bay bridge in Panama City, at 327 feet. What is the difference in length of the two drawbridges? _____

3. The Marine Parkway drawbridge in New York City is 540 feet long. The Martinez railroad drawbridge in California is 328 feet long. How much shorter is the Martinez bridge than the Marine Parkway bridge? _____

4. There are 219 students in the 4th grade at Tammy's school. There are 188 students in the 3rd grade. How many more students are in the 4th grade than in the 3rd grade? _____

5. The rug in Theresa's living room is 116 inches long and 74 inches wide. What is the difference between the rug's length and width? _____

6. Ryan has read a total of 365 pages in his book. Yesterday he had read to page 229. How many pages did he read today? _____

Name _____

Subtracting with 2 Regroupings

1. How many more students are there in the 3rd grade than in the 4th grade? _____

2. How many fewer students are there in the 1st grade than in the 2nd grade? _____

3. If there are 249 girls in the 3rd grade, how many boys are in the 3rd grade? _____

Students at County Elementary School	
1st grade	347
2nd grade	415
3rd grade	422
4th grade	368

4. What is the total number of students in all four grades? _____

5. Suppose 14 new students will be entering the third grade next year and none of the current students leave. How many students will there be in the third grade?

_____

6. Janine had 213 thumb tacks. She has 176 left. How many did she use?

_____

7. Aaron was in school 176 days last year. How many days was Aaron not in school? (Remember: 1 year = 365 days)

_____

8. **Choose a strategy** Farmer Joe has 551 animals on his farm. He only has cows and pigs. There are 394 cows on the farm. How many pigs are on the farm?

   a. What strategy would you use to solve the problem?

   _____

   b. Answer the problem. _____

| • Use Objects/Act It Out |
| • Draw a Picture |
| • Look for a Pattern |
| • Guess and Check |
| • Use Logical Reasoning |
| • Make an Organized List |
| • Make a Table |
| • Solve a Simpler Problem |
| • Work Backward |

Name _____

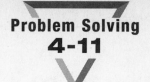
Subtracting Across 0

Health The table shows the amount of calories in certain foods. Use the chart to solve the problems.

Food	Calories	Food	Calories
Apple juice, 1 cup	120	Lentil soup, 1 cup	606
Beef stew, 1 cup	260	Lobster, 1 cup	105
Chocolate malted milk	502	Macaroni and cheese, $\frac{1}{2}$ cup	215
Flounder, baked, 1 serving	204	Wild rice, cooked, $\frac{2}{3}$ cup	103

1. Ted had 1 cup of apple juice. Paula had a chocolate malted milk. How many more calories did Paula have? _____

2. Maleek had baked flounder for dinner. Jerome had lobster. How many more calories did Maleek have? _____

3. What is the difference in calories between 1 cup of beef stew and $\frac{1}{2}$ cup of macaroni and cheese? _____

4. Carly decided to have $\frac{2}{3}$ cup of wild rice with her dinner instead of 1 cup of lentil soup. How many fewer calories did she have? _____

Solve the problems.

5. Dina burned 360 calories playing volleyball for one hour. Pam burned 288 calories bowling. How many more calories did Dina burn than Pam? _____

6. Scrubbing floors burns 360 calories per hour. Walking fast burns 480. How many more calories does walking fast burn? _____

Subtracting 4-Digit Numbers: Choose a Calculation Method

> **Geography** Cities across the United States are different in many ways. For example, the temperature in January can be very cold in New York City while it is very warm in Los Angeles, California. Some cities are surrounded by mountains, like Denver, Colorado and some cities are next to lakes, like Chicago, Illinois. Think about how far these cities are from one another, and what differences you might see between them.
>
> **1.** Between 1962 and 1991, Florida had a total of 1,590 tornadoes. During the same period of time, Nebraska had 1,118 tornadoes. How many fewer tornadoes did Nebraska have than Florida? _____
>
> **2.** Iowa had 1,079 tornadoes from 1962 to 1991, and Texas had 4,174. How many more tornadoes did Texas have than Iowa? _____
>
> **3.** Kansas had 1,198 tornadoes, and Oklahoma had 1,412. How many more did Oklahoma have? _____

4. There are 3,291 ants in the ant colony at the State University. There are 1,583 ants in the ant colony at City College. How many more ants are in the colony at the State University than at City College? _____

5. Ms. Atkins is shopping for a new computer for her business. She has narrowed her choices down to two computers. One costs $3,465 and the other costs $2,870. What is the difference in the two prices? _____

Joy hiked in Bryce Canyon for an hour. She took one 10-minute rest and one 13-minute rest. How many minutes did she walk?

— Understand —

1. How many minutes are in one hour? _____

2. About how long did Joy rest? _____

3. Which of these is a reasonable answer to the question?

   A. about 60 min   **B.** about 20 min   **C.** about 40 min   **D.** about 30 min

— Plan —

4. What steps will you take to solve the problem?

   _____

— Solve —

5. Write number sentences to solve.

   _____

6. Joy walked _____ minutes.

— Look Back —

7. Does your answer make sense? How do you know?

   _____

SOLVE ANOTHER PROBLEM

Maddie has $12. Jim has $3 less than Maddie. How much more money does Jim need to buy a theme park admission ticket that costs $20?

_____

Mental Math

Recreation Ice hockey began in Canada in the mid-1800s. The National Hockey League was formed in 1916 and has been in operation ever since. It is made up of teams from the United States and Canada.

1. There was a disagreement between the players and the owners at the beginning of the 1994–1995 hockey season. The season was only 48 games rather than the usual 84. How many fewer games did they play? _____

2. During the 1994–1995 season, the Boston Bruins won 27 games and lost 18 games. How many more games did they win than lose? _____

3. In the 1994–1995 season, there were 26 teams in the NHL with 19 teams in the United States. The other teams were from Canada. How many teams were from Canada? _____

4. In the year 2,000, how many years old will the National Hockey League be? _____

---

5. Hawaii is the only state made up entirely of islands. There are 122 Hawaiian islands. People live on 7 of the islands. How many islands do not have people living on them? _____

6. In 1788, Maryland became the seventh state to enter into the Union, which later became known as the United States. How many years ago was that? _____

7. In 1997 there were 30 countries in Europe. 15 of them belonged to the European Union. How many did not? _____

8. 9 countries applied to join the European Union. If they all joined, how many countries would be members? _____

Name _____

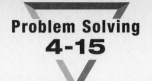

Subtracting Money

Careers This advertisement shows regular and sale prices. Use the advertisement to answer the questions.

Strong's Annual August Sale		
	Regular	**Sale**
Twin sheet (flat or fitted)	$18.50	$12.99
Full sheet (flat or fitted)	$24.49	$15.89
Queen sheet (flat or fitted)	$28.65	$18.98
Standard pillowcases (2)	$14.39	$12.99
King pillowcases (2)	$18.79	$14.99
Down comforter (any size)	$150 – $280	$129.99

1. A salesperson sold a queen sheet in July. How much less would he have charged the customer in August? _____

2. If the regular price of a comforter is $220, how much less is the sale price? _____

3. What is the difference between the regular prices of standard pillowcases and king pillowcases? _____

4. By how much did the store manager reduce 2 king pillowcases for the August sale? _____

5. Which costs more? _____

   a. 2 full sheets at the regular price

   b. 2 queen sheets and 2 king pillowcases at the sale price

6. The sale price of jeans that regularly sell for $42.00 is $28.99. What is the price difference? _____

7. Sunglasses are on sale for $12.49 instead of $15.98. What is the price difference? _____

GPS | PROBLEM 5, STUDENT PAGE 192

Amy, Santiago, and their mother and father are in line for the ferry to the Statue of Liberty. Amy is the only person between her mother and father. Santiago is directly behind his mother. Who is first in line?

▬ Understand ▬

1. What does the problem ask you to find?

_____

2. How many people in the family are waiting in line? _____

▬ Plan ▬

3. Use counters to act out the problem. What will the counters show?

_____

▬ Solve ▬

4. Draw a picture on a separate sheet of paper to show how you can use counters to solve this problem.

5. Who is first in line? _____

▬ Look Back ▬

6. What other strategy could you use to solve this problem?

_____

SOLVE ANOTHER PROBLEM

Amy and her family are talking to a man, woman, and teenager while they are standing in line. The man is in front of Amy's father. The teenager is the only person between Santiago and the woman. Who is last in line?

_____

Exploring Equal Groups

Write the next three numbers in each pattern. Then write the
rule used to make the pattern.

1. 2, 4, 6, 8, _____, _____, _____

Rule: _____

2. 5, 10, 15, 20, _____, _____, _____

Rule: _____

3. 3, 6, 9, 12, _____, _____, _____

Rule: _____

4. 4, 8, 12, 16, _____, _____, _____

Rule: _____

5. 6, 12, 18, 24, _____, _____, _____

Rule: _____

6. 7, 14, 21, 28, _____, _____, _____

Rule: _____

7. 9, 18, 27, 36, _____, _____, _____

Rule: _____

8. 10, 20, 30, 40, _____, _____, _____

Rule: _____

9. Do you see a pattern as you answer each question and
state each rule?

_____

Name _____

Writing Multiplication Sentences

Careers A worker is packing juice boxes.
Juice boxes come 3 to a pack.

1. The worker puts 4 packs in a container.
How many boxes of juice is that?

_____

2. The worker puts 5 packs in a container. How many
boxes of juice is that?   _____

3. Suppose juice boxes cost $1.19 a pack. How
much would 2 packs cost?   _____

4. What operations could you use to solve the problems above?

_____

Use the table for **4–7**.

Apple Cider Sale	
1 Half-Gallon	$2.50
1 Gallon	$4.00
2 half-gallons = 1 gallon	

4. How many gallons of cider can you buy for $8? _____

5. How much would $1\frac{1}{2}$ gallons of cider cost? _____

6. Suppose you have $3. How much cider could you buy?

_____

7. Suppose you want 1 gallon of cider. Which would you
buy: 2 half-gallons or 1 gallon? Explain.

_____

_____

Exploring Multiplication Stories

Look at each picture. Decide if you can write a multiplication story about it. For yes, write a multiplication story that goes with the picture. For no, explain.

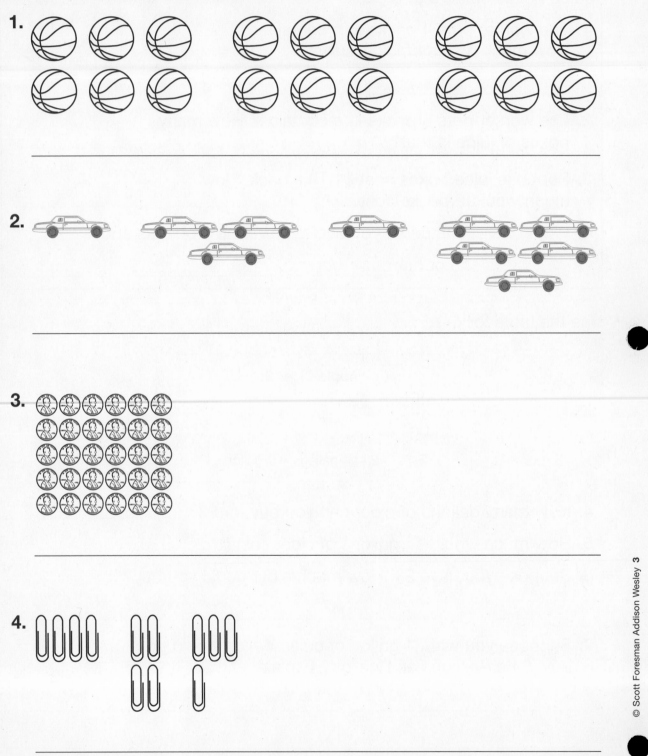

1.

2.

3.

4.

2 as a Factor

Art Use the recipe to answer **1–2**.

Modeling Dough Recipe

1 cup salt
2 cups hot water
4 cups flour

Makes about 5 cups of modeling dough.

1. Lee wants to make twice as much dough. He multiplies each ingredient by 2.

   a. How much salt does he need? _____

   b. How much water does he need? _____

   c. How much flour does he need? _____

   d. How much dough would he make? _____

2. Suppose each person in your class wants 1 cup of dough. How many cups of dough would you need? _____

Marisol makes friendship bracelets. She sells them for $2 each.

3. She sold 3 bracelets. How much money did she make?   _____

4. She made 4 bracelets Friday, 5 bracelets Saturday, and 7 bracelets on Monday. How many did she make in all?   _____

5. Each bracelet costs $0.65 to make. How much does it cost to make 2 bracelets?   _____

5 as a Factor

Careers A gardener is planning a garden. She divides it into 8 squares. Each square will have 5 lettuce plants.

1. How many plants are in the top part of the garden? _____

2. How many plants will she have in all? _____

3. Suppose the garden had only 6 squares. How many plants would the gardener have? _____

Use the table for 4–7.

Seed Pack Sale	
flower seeds	2 for $1
vegetable seeds	3 for $1

4. How many flower seed packs can you buy for $1? _____

5. How many vegetable seed packs can you buy for $5? _____

6. Suppose you have $2. What could you buy?

_____

_____

7. Which costs less: flower seeds or vegetable seeds?

Explain. _____

_____

Name _____

Exploring Patterns on a Hundred Chart: 2s and 5s

Draw a circle around each multiple of 2 and a triangle around each multiple of 5 on this chart. Then answer the questions.

1	2	3	4	5	6	7	8	9	10
11	12	13	14	15	16	17	18	19	20
21	22	23	24	25	26	27	28	29	30
31	32	33	34	35	36	37	38	39	40
41	42	43	44	45	46	47	48	49	50
51	52	53	54	55	56	57	58	59	60
61	62	63	64	65	66	67	68	69	70
71	72	73	74	75	76	77	78	79	80
81	82	83	84	85	86	87	88	89	90
91	92	93	94	95	96	97	98	99	100

1. Which numbers are marked twice on the chart?

_____

2. Why do you think multiples of 10 are also multiples of 2 and of 5?

_____

3. What other multiples are also multiples of 2, 5, and 10?

_____

4. Write a multiplication sentence for the product 15. Use 5 as a factor.

_____

5. Write two multiplication sentences for the product 30. Use 5 as a factor.

_____

6. Lizette has a pocket full of nickels. Could she have 49¢? Explain. What could she have?

_____

Exploring 0 and 1 as Factors

Finish the multiplication sentences on this table. Then answer the questions.

Using 1 as a Factor	Using 0 as a Factor
$1 \times 1 =$	$1 \times 0 =$
$10 \times 1 =$	$10 \times 0 =$
$25 \times 1 =$	$25 \times 0 =$
$1.515 \times 1 =$	$1.515 \times 0 =$
$75.264 \times 1 =$	$75.264 \times 0 =$

1. What pattern do you see when 1 is a factor?

_____

2. What pattern do you see when 0 is a factor?

_____

3. Can you think of anything that will change these patterns?

_____

4. Will any of the patterns you found work for other factors? Explain.

_____

_____

_____

5. If you were to multiply the largest number you could think of by 0, what would the product be? Explain.

_____

9 as a Factor

Health There are 9 people in the James family. Mr. James wrote the following information to help him decide how much to buy when he goes to the store.

Each week, each person eats:

1 loaf of bread	1 pound of rice
1 quart of milk	8 pieces of fruit
7 vegetables	5 packets of oatmeal
3 eggs	1 quart of orange juice

1. How many pounds of rice should Mr. James buy? _____

2. How many eggs? _____

3. How many pieces of fruit? _____

4. If a quart of orange juice and a quart of milk each cost a dollar, how much will Mr. James spend on juice and milk for the week? _____

5. Alexandra will be gone for 9 days on a camping trip and needs to leave food for her fish. One food pellet will feed all 4 of the fish in one tank for a day. How many food pellets should Alexandra leave behind for this fish tank? _____

6. How many food pellets should Alexandra leave if she has 2 fish tanks like the one above, each with 4 similar fish? _____

7. Joan goes to camp for 9 weeks in the summer. She has gone the past three years. How many weeks total has she spent at camp? _____

Name _____

Guided Problem Solving
5-9

GPS PROBLEM 4, STUDENT PAGE 225

An ostrich weighs about 340 pounds and can move up to 15 feet in one stride. How many feet could an ostrich move in 2 strides?

— Understand —

1. What does the problem tell you about ostriches?

_____

2. What does the problem ask you to find?

_____

3. Circle the information needed to solve the problem.

— Plan —

4. Do you have enough information to solve the problem? _____

5. How can you find out how far the ostrich can move in 2 strides? _____

— Solve —

6. Write a number sentence to solve the problem. _____

7. How many feet can an ostrich move in 2 strides? _____

8. Is there too much or too little information? _____

— Look Back —

9. Can you think of another strategy to use to solve the problem?

_____

| SOLVE ANOTHER PROBLEM |

The average human moves about 1 meter per stride. About how many meters will a human move in 3 strides?

_____

© Scott Foresman Addison Wesley 3

Brenda can use either small or large safety pins to make friendship pins. On each pin she can put one color of beads: blue, green, or silver. How many different kinds of pins can Brenda make?

— Understand —

1. How many different sizes of pins can Brenda make? _____

2. How many different colors of beads can Brenda use? _____

3. How many different colors can Brenda put on each pin? _____

— Plan —

4. What does the picture need to show? _____

_____

— Solve —

5. Draw the picture.

6. How many different kinds of pins can Brenda make? _____

— Look Back —

7. How can you check your answer? _____

SOLVE ANOTHER PROBLEM

Brenda has decided to use two colors on each friendship pin. How many different kinds of two-color pins can Brenda make? Explain.

_____

_____

3 as a Factor: Using Known Facts

Music Music is written in measures. Each measure has notes which show how long to hold a pitch. Each measure in a song has notes that show the same number of beats.

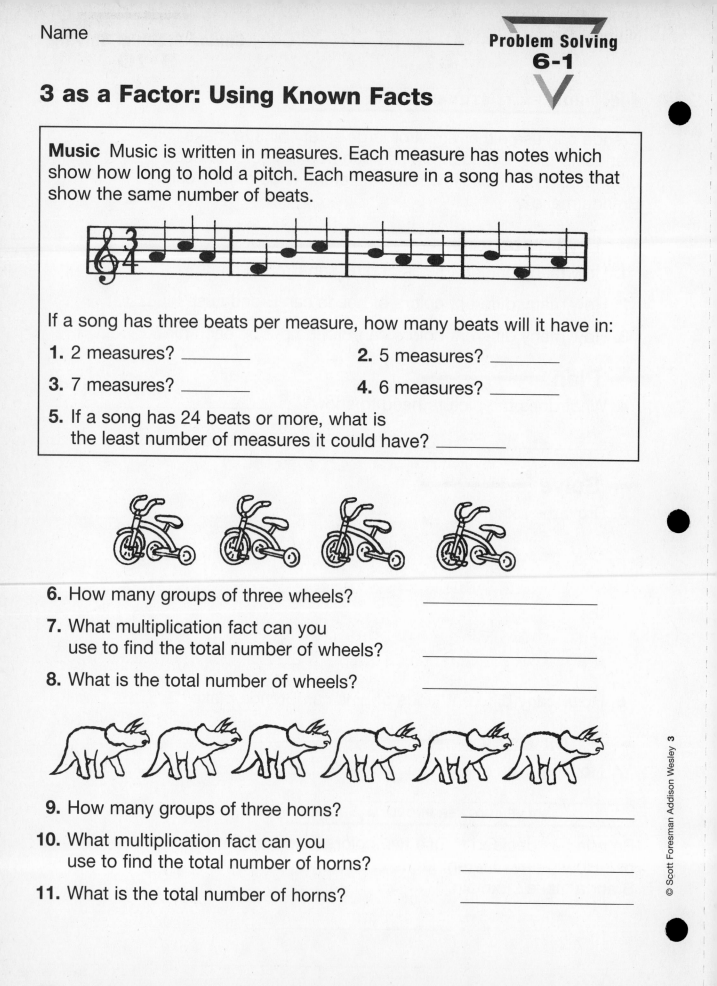

If a song has three beats per measure, how many beats will it have in:

1. 2 measures? _____   **2.** 5 measures? _____

3. 7 measures? _____   **4.** 6 measures? _____

5. If a song has 24 beats or more, what is
the least number of measures it could have? _____

6. How many groups of three wheels? _____

7. What multiplication fact can you
use to find the total number of wheels? _____

8. What is the total number of wheels? _____

9. How many groups of three horns? _____

10. What multiplication fact can you
use to find the total number of horns? _____

11. What is the total number of horns? _____

4 as a Factor: Doubling

Science Most insects have either 2 or 4 wings. Dragonflies have 4 wings (or 2 pairs of wings). The additional wings help them to fly more quickly.

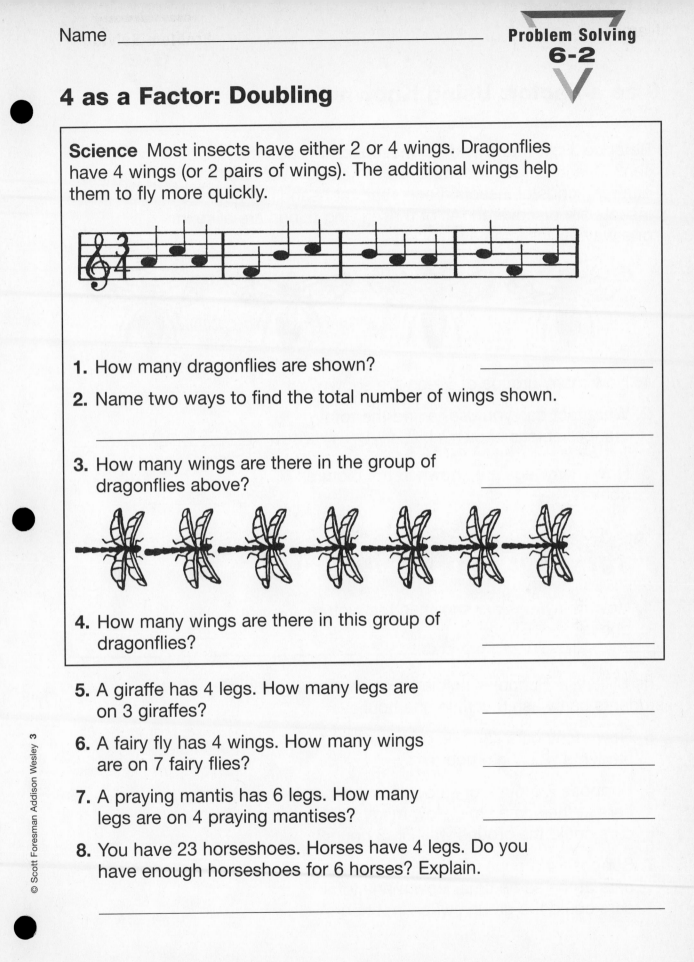

1. How many dragonflies are shown? _____

2. Name two ways to find the total number of wings shown.

_____

3. How many wings are there in the group of
   dragonflies above? _____

4. How many wings are there in this group of
   dragonflies? _____

5. A giraffe has 4 legs. How many legs are
   on 3 giraffes? _____

6. A fairy fly has 4 wings. How many wings
   are on 7 fairy flies? _____

7. A praying mantis has 6 legs. How many
   legs are on 4 praying mantises? _____

8. You have 23 horseshoes. Horses have 4 legs. Do you
   have enough horseshoes for 6 horses? Explain.

_____

6 as a Factor: Using Known Facts

Science How many kinds of insects can you name? Five? Ten? One hundred? Scientists have named over 800,000 different kinds of insects. Each year, thousands of new insects are discovered. All of these living things are alike in one way: all insects have six legs!

1. How many groups of 6 legs are shown? _____

2. What fact can you use to find the total number of legs shown? _____

3. How many legs are shown in the picture above? _____

4. How many legs are shown in the picture above? _____

The Millerville School is holding a car wash. A group of students can wash 6 cars in one hour.

5. How many cars can one group of students wash in 5 hours? _____

6. Suppose 2 groups of students wash cars at the same time. How many total cars could the groups wash in 3 hours? _____

7. Suppose 4 groups of students wash cars at the same time. How many total cars could the groups wash in 2 hours? _____

7 and 8 as Factors

Health Our bodies need calcium for strong teeth and bones. The Recommended Daily Allowance (RDA) tells how much calcium our bodies need in one day. Each of the items below would give a student the RDA of calcium.

Foods that Provide the Recommended Daily Allowance of Calcium

| 4 slices cheese | 3 cups spinach | 6 cups broccoli | 8 pieces tofu |

1. If Patrick ate 4 slices of cheese per day, how many slices would he eat in one week? _____

2. If you ate enough broccoli each day to get the RDA of calcium, how many cups would you eat in eight days? _____

3. If you ate enough tofu each day to get the RDA of calcium, how many pieces would you eat in one week? in 5 days? _____

Mia is decorating sweatshirts for a craft fair. She sews 8 buttons and 7 fabric squares on each sweatshirt.

4. How many buttons and fabric squares will Mia sew on 6 sweatshirts?

_____

5. How many buttons and fabric squares will Mia sew on 9 sweatshirts?

_____

Decision Making

A scout troop is going on an overnight camping trip. Two adults and eight scouts will be on the trip. You have been asked to create a menu for the campers. You need to choose a breakfast, lunch, and dinner that can be cooked over a camp fire. Use the food pyramid on page 250 of your book to help plan the meals.

1. Name three things that you know.

_____

_____

2. What do you need to decide?

_____

3. What kinds of food should the campers have 9 servings of?

_____

4. What kinds of food should the campers have 3 servings of?

_____

5. Write your menu.

Breakfast _____

_____

_____

Lunch _____

_____

_____

Dinner _____

_____

_____

6. Share your menu with the class. Check that you have the appropriate number of servings per food group and that these foods can be cooked over a camp fire.

Name _____

Exploring Patterns on a Hundred Chart: 3s and 6s

1	2	3	4	5	6	7	8	9	10
11	12	13	14	15	16	17	18	19	20
21	22	23	24	25	26	27	28	29	30
31	32	33	34	35	36	37	38	39	40
41	42	43	44	45	46	47	48	49	50

Use basic facts and patterns to find all the multiples of 3 and 6 on the chart above. Shade each multiple of 3 red. Shade each multiple of 6 blue.

1. What are the purple (red and blue) numbers called?

_____

2. What pattern do you see in the shaded squares?

_____

3. Are there any boxes that are only blue? Why or why not?

_____

4. What other patterns do you see in the chart?

_____

_____

_____

_____

5. Describe how one pattern you see will help you remember the basic facts for 3 or 6.

_____

_____

Exploring Patterns on a Fact Table

×	0	1	2	3	4	5	6	7	8	9	10	11	12
0	0	0	0	0	0	0	0	0	0	0	0	0	0
1	0	1	2	3	4	5	6	7	8	9	10	11	12
2	0	2	4	6	8	10	2	14	16	18	20	22	24
3	0	3	6	9	12	15	18	21	24	27	30	33	36
4	0	4	8	12	16	20	24	28	32	36	40	44	48
5	0	5	10	15	20	25	30	35	40	45	50	55	60
6	0	6	12	18	24	30	36	42	48	54	60	66	72
7	0	7	14	21	28	35	42	49	56	63	70	77	84
8	0	8	16	24	32	40	48	56	64	72	80	88	96
9	0	9	18	27	36	45	54	63	72	81	90	99	108
10	0	10	20	30	40	50	60	70	80	90	100	110	120
11	0	11	22	33	44	55	66	77	88	99	110	121	132
12	0	12	24	36	48	60	72	84	96	108	120	132	144

Use the fact table to help you answer the questions.

1. Shade all the multiples of 3 yellow. What pattern do you see?

   _____

   _____

2. Shade all the multiples of 6 red. What patterns do you see?

   _____

3. The multiples of 12 are what color? Why?

   _____

4. 0, 1, 4, 9, 16, 25, 36, 49, 64, 81, 100, 121, 144

   This sequence of numbers appears in the table.

   a. Draw a blue line to connect this sequence of numbers.

   b. Shade in these numbers whenever they appear in the table.

   c. What patterns do you see? _____

   _____

   _____

   d. What do these numbers have in common?

   _____

Multiplying with 3 Factors

Physical Education Your school is building a new gymnasium. Each floor of the gym will have a basketball court. For each new basketball court they build, the school needs to buy 2 hoops. For each new hoop, they need 6 basketballs.

1. Your school decides to build a gym with 2 floors.

    a. How many hoops will they need? _____

    b. How many basketballs? _____

2. If your school builds a gym with 3 floors, how many basketballs will they need? _____

3. How many hoops are needed for a gym with 5 floors? _____

4. If a 4-floor gym is built, how many hoops and balls will be needed?

_____

5. Suppose you make oatmeal raisin cookies for 3 people. Each person gets 3 cookies. Each cookie has 5 raisins. How many raisins will you need? _____

6. You make ham sandwiches for 2 people. Each person gets 2 sandwiches. Each sandwich has 2 slices of ham. How many ham slices will you need? _____

7. You give 4 friends 2 packages of markers. Each package has 6 markers in it. How many markers do you give? _____

8. 3 friends each purchase 3 sheets of stickers. There are 8 stickers on each sheet. How many stickers in all? _____

GPS PROBLEM 2, STUDENT PAGE 263

One package of pita bread makes 6 sandwiches. How many packages do you need to make 45 sandwiches?

— Understand —

1. How many sandwiches can you make with one package of pita bread? _____

2. What do you need to find out? _____
_____

— Plan —

3. How could you use a pattern to solve the problem?
_____

4. What could you draw to help you solve the problem?
_____

— Solve —

5. Choose one of the strategies. Show how you solved the problem.

6. What is the answer? _____

— Look Back —

7. How can you check your answer? _____
_____

SOLVE ANOTHER PROBLEM

One package of English muffins makes 6 egg sandwiches. How many packages do you need to make 20 sandwiches? _____

Exploring Division as Sharing

Draw a picture to show how you can solve these problems.
Then write your answer.

1. A Boys and Girls club is on a special trip to an amusement park. There are 15 children in the club. Everyone wants to ride the giant roller coaster. Each car of the roller coaster has room for 3 people. How many cars will be needed if all 15 children go on the ride?

_____

2. 12 of the children want to ride the log flume. Each log will hold 4 people. How many logs will be needed?

_____

3. The log flume ride was so much fun that 8 of the children want to ride it again. This time, how many logs will be needed?

_____

4. 14 children want to ride the ferris wheel. Each car holds 2 passengers. How many cars will be needed?

_____

Exploring Division as Repeated Subtraction

1. Carlos has 14 envelopes. He has to deliver 2 envelopes to each classroom.

   a. How many classrooms will Carlos visit? _____

   b. Explain how you solved the problem.

   _____

   _____

2. Suppose you had 6 flowers to put into 2 flower pots. How would you solve this problem? How many flowers in each pot?

   _____

   _____

3. Bonnie Lee puts 2 bows on each package. Can she decorate 8 packages with 15 bows? Draw a picture and explain.

   _____

   _____

4. You have 24 sheets of paper to put into folders. Each folder needs to have the same number of sheets of paper in it. How many folders could there be? (Hint: There's more than 1 answer.)

   _____

Exploring Division Stories

Decide whether the following stories are division stories.
Explain your answers and solve each problem.

1. A lobster boat off the coast of New England caught 6
   lobsters. The captain plans to give the same number of
   lobsters to his wife, sister, and a restaurant owner. How
   many lobsters will each be given?

   _____

   _____

2. A drycleaning store cleaned 50 garments on Wednesday.
   On Thursday, 35 of those garments were picked up by
   customers. How many garments were still there on
   Friday morning?

   _____

   _____

Here is a division story that shows 18 ÷ 3 = 6. Mrs. Ramirez
had 18 students in her class. She wanted 3 students to work
on reports together. That meant she needed to divide the
class into 6 groups.

3. Write your own division story for 18 ÷ 3 = 6.

   _____

   _____

   _____

4. How is your division story like Mrs. Ramirez's story?
   How is it different?

   _____

   _____

   _____

Connecting Multiplication and Division

Science Astronauts require a great deal of training before they can travel into space. Not only do they learn to maneuver aircraft, but they also learn a great deal about weightlessness and other subjects related to space and space travel.

1. **a.** Three astronauts are traveling to the moon. The trip takes 4 days. Each astronaut wants 1 freeze-dried pear each day. How many pears do they need to pack? _____

   b. Write a number sentence to show this. _____

2. **a.** Upon landing an astronaut looked out each of the four windows. Out of each one she saw 5 craters. How many craters did she see? _____

   b. Write a number sentence to show this. _____

3. **a.** Suppose she saw a total of 8 craters, the same number from each window. How many did she see out of each window? _____

   b. Write a number sentence to show this. _____

4. Write your own multiplication or division story about 4 friends traveling to another country by boat. It should take 8 days to get there.

   _____

   _____

   _____

5. Mary-Beth had 6 plants which she divided equally among 3 friends. How many plants did each friend get? _____

6. Each plant had 3 flowers.

   a. How many flowers did each friend have? _____

   b. How many flowers were there in all? _____

Dividing by 2

Fine Arts Many art supplies come packaged in 8s, 12s, 16s, and 32s. You can find paints, chalk, and crayons packaged this way.

1. In a paintbox, 12 watercolor paints are in 2 rows. How many paints are in each row? _____

2. Large crayons are packed 8 to a box. If you need 16 crayons how many boxes should you buy? _____

3. A brush pack has four brushes. If you and a friend share, how many do you each get? _____

4. Two students share a 16-stick pack of chalk. How many sticks does each get? _____

5. A block of clay weighs 14 ounces. How many ounces will Niki and Anastasia have if they share the clay equally? _____

6. Ken has 10 toy cars. He wants to share them with Tomas while they play. How many toy cars will each boy have to play with? _____

7. Kelly has 6 pretzels. If she shares them with Pat, how many pretzels will each one get? _____

8. Jeff has 8 kitty treats which he shares amongst his cats. If each cat gets 2 kitty treats, how many cats does Jeff have? _____

9. Lisa made 18 scones. She gave half to Rebecca and half to Darren. How many scones did each receive? _____

Dividing by 5

Recreation Five players from one team are on the court at the same time in a basketball game. There are 2 forwards, 2 guards, and a center.

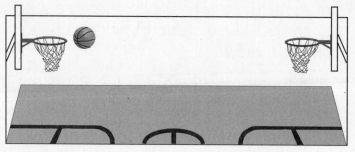

1. If you have 45 people how many teams can you make? _____

2. If 30 players show up, how many teams can you make? _____

3. Twenty-five players go on a road trip. If they split into teams, how many teams can they make? _____

4. Admission to a game costs $5 per person. How much will it cost for 2 people to attend? _____

5. Andrew earns $5 an hour working at a grocery store after school. If he earned $40 dollars in one week, how many hours did he work? _____

6. Erica earned $35 working at a craft fair. If she worked for 5 hours, how much money did she earn per hour? _____

7. Jane is playing tiddlywinks with 5 friends. She divides the 25 counters amongst the players. How many will each get? _____

Name _____

Dividing by 3 and 4

Physical Education Your gym class is having a jump rope-a-thon after school to help raise money for a local charity. Students jump rope for as long as they can. People agree to give them a certain amount of money per minute that they jump. For example, Mrs. Hughes sponsored Jennifer for 1¢ per minute she jumps. Students compete in teams of 3 for prizes for the most money raised.

1. After the jump rope-a-thon, Larry collected 36¢ from Mr. Jackson. If Mr. Jackson pledged 4¢ per minute, how many minutes did Larry jump rope? _____

2. Caitlin jumped rope for 3 minutes. If she collected 21¢ from Mr. Fernandez, how much did he pledge per minute? _____

3. Antonio, Martha, and Ming are all on one team.

   a. If each person on the team earns $5 from their pledges, how much did the entire team earn? _____

   b. If the entire team earned $24, and each team member earned the same amount, how much did each member earn? _____

4. Ana brought 12 apples to the picnic. If 4 people are at the picnic, how many apples can each person eat?

_____

5. Your class is working with computers. There are 18 students in your class and 3 students are working at each computer. How many computers are in the classroom?

_____

Exploring Dividing With 0 and 1

You can find patterns when you divide with 0 and 1.

1. a. What pattern do you see when 0 is divided by a number?

_____

b. How can you find the answer to 0 ÷ 98? Explain.

_____

_____

2. a. What pattern do you see when a number is divided by 1?

_____

b. How can you find the answer to 2,952 ÷ 1? Explain.

_____

_____

3. a. What pattern do you see when a number (except zero) is divided by itself?

_____

b. How can you find the answer to 423 ÷ 423? Explain.

_____

_____

4. Write a word problem showing division by 1.

_____

_____

_____

5. Write a word problem showing a number being divided by itself.

_____

_____

GPS PROBLEM 5, STUDENT PAGE 297

Suppose Bonnie bought a 5-pound bag of cat food for $4.95. She also bought a 3-pound bag of bird seed for $1.50. How much money did she spend?

── Understand ──

1. Draw X's through numbers in the problem you do not need.

2. What do you need to find out?

_____

── Plan ──

3. How much did Bonnie spend on cat food? _____

4. How much did Bonnie spend on bird seed? _____

5. What operation would you choose to solve the problem? _____

   A. Multiplication   **B.** Division   **C.** Addition   **D.** Subtraction

── Solve ──

6. Write the number sentence and solve the problem.

_____

── Look Back ──

7. Explain how you can check to make sure your answer is reasonable.

_____

_____

_____

SOLVE ANOTHER PROBLEM

Alex buys 6 cartons of milk for $12. If all of the cartons cost the same amount, how much does each carton cost? _____

Name _____

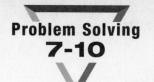

Dividing by 6 and 7

Music A symphony orchestra consists of 4 different sections: the string section, the woodwind section, the percussion section, and the brass section. Each section contains several instruments and can vary in size. The conductor of the orchestra organizes the seating of each group in order to achieve a particular sound.

1. If the string section has 24 violinists and the conductor seats them in 6 rows, how many violinists are in each row?   _____

2. If there are 18 musicians in the brass section and 6 musicians in each row, how many rows are there in the brass section?   _____

3. The entire orchestra has 63 musicians. If the conductor wants to arrange them in 7 rows, how many musicians would be in each row?   _____

---

4. Alice has 24 pencils to share with her friends. If she gives an equal number of pencils to 6 friends, how many pencils will each friend receive?   _____

5. Alice wants to buy bean bag dolls for her collection. Each doll costs $5.00. How much will she spend for 6 dolls?   _____

6. a. Alice wants to line up her doll collection. She wants to put 28 dolls in 7 equal rows. How many dolls will be in each row?   _____

   b. If she places the dolls in 6 equal rows how many will be left over?   _____

7. a. Emma arranges her 56 books in 7 equal rows. How many are in each row?   _____

   b. If she arranges them in rows of 6, how many will be in each row, and how many will be left over?

_____

Name _____

Dividing by 8 and 9

Science The eagle is the national bird of the United States. It is one of the largest birds in the world.

1. An eagle's nest is called an *eyrie*. If 8 eyries had a total measurement of 32 feet across, how wide is each eyrie?

_____

2. 9 eagle eggs are laid end to end. The total length is 27 inches. How long is each egg?

_____

3. 8 eagles have a total weight of 64 pounds. How much does each eagle weigh? _____

4. Golden eagles are about 32 inches long and have a wingspan of about 7 feet. How much greater is their wingspan than their length? _____

5. a. Arthur spends 72¢ on a pack of 8 sports trading cards. How much does each card cost? _____

b. Arthur loses one card. How much are his cards worth now? _____

6. Arthur buys 5 more cards for 40¢. How much does each of these cards cost? _____

7. Arthur keeps 3 cards and divides the remaining 9 cards among 9 friends. How many cards does each friend get? _____

Exploring Even and Odd Numbers

Cut a 10 × 10 grid into five 2 × 10 arrays. From these arrays cut out models of the even numbers 2, 4, 6, 8, and 10. Also cut out models of the odd numbers 3, 5, 7, and 9. Shade or color the even number models.

1. Add two even numbers by joining the models. What do you notice about the sum?

_____

2. Add an even and an odd number by joining the models. What do you notice about the sum?

_____

3. Add two odd numbers using the models. What do you notice about the sum?

_____

4. Conduct experiments finding differences. Write even or odd to describe each difference.

a. Subtract an even number from an even number.

The difference is _____.

b. Subtract an even number from an odd number.

The difference is _____.

c. Subtract an odd number from an even number.

The difference is _____.

d. Subtract an odd number from an odd number.

The difference is _____.

5. Kirsten is packing puzzle cubes into different size boxes. Each box must have an even number of puzzle cubes. She has twelve cubes.

a. Can she pack her twelve cubes? _____

b. She can't pack 3 of them because they are broken. Can she pack all of the rest? _____

c. She finds she must pack another nine cubes. Can she pack all of her non-broken cubes? _____

GPS | **PROBLEM 3, STUDENT PAGE 309**

Kate wants to take a picture of 20 students in the band. She wants the students to stand in equal rows. What are all the ways she can arrange them?

━ Understand ━

1. How many students are in the band? _____

2. How does Kate want the students to stand? _____

━ Plan ━

3. Make a table of all the ways Kate could arrange the rows. What number will always be in the total column?

_____

Rows	Students in Each Row	Total

━ Solve ━

4. Complete the table.

    a. How many different arrangements of rows are in the list? _____

    b. List the different ways Kate can arrange the students.

_____

_____

━ Look Back ━

5. How do you know your answer is reasonable? _____

_____

| **SOLVE ANOTHER PROBLEM** |

Kate is also taking a picture of the nature club which has 28 members. What are all the ways she can arrange the students in equal rows?

_____

_____

Name _____

Exploring Algebra: Balancing Scales

Here is an addition chart for the digits 0–9. Some of the sums have been filled in for you.

1. Complete the chart by filling in the missing sums.

2. How many times does the sum of 3 appear on the chart?

_____

3. Is there a pattern to these 3s?

_____

_____

4. Find all the different ways numbers can be added to total 3. Make an organized list to show all the ways.

_____

+	0	1	2	3	4	5	6	7	8	9
0	0	1	2	3	4	5	6	7	8	9
1	1	2	3	4	5	6				
2	2	3	4	5						
3	3	4	5							
4	4									
5	5									
6										
7										16
8										17
9									17	18

5. How does the addition chart help in finding the ways to total 3? Explain.

_____

6. How many different ways are there to total 5? _____

7. Box A has 3 cubes inside. Use the addition chart to list how many cubes can be in boxes B and C.

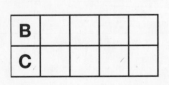 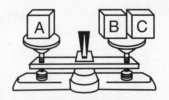

8. Each box A has 4 cubes inside. Use the addition chart to list how many cubes can be in boxes B and C.

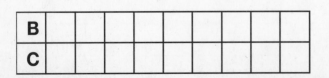 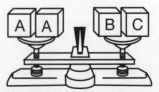

© Scott Foresman Addison Wesley 3

Exploring Solids

1. Look at the solids below.

 a. Cross out any figures that cannot be stacked on top
 of each other.

 b. What figures did you cross out? Why can't they be stacked?

 _____

 _____

 c. What are the figures that can be stacked? Why?

 _____

 _____

2. Which solid figure has only one flat face? _____

3. How is a cone like a cylinder? How is it different?

 _____

 _____

4. A solid figure has six faces and all of its
 sides are equal in length. What is the figure? _____

5. Why is a pyramid a good shape for a roof?

 _____

Exploring Solids and Shapes

1. Draw the shape of a face of each solid figure.

    a. rectangular prism   **b.** pyramid

    c. cylinder   **d.** cube

2. What 2 kinds of shapes have 4 sides and 4 corners?

    _____

3. What shape has no sides and no corners? _____

4. What solid figure could have
these shapes as faces?

    _____

    A. cube   **B.** cone

    C. pyramid   **D.** rectangular prism

5. What shape could be used to continue this pattern? _____

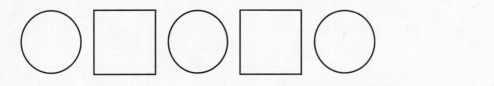

6. What shape could be used to continue this pattern? _____

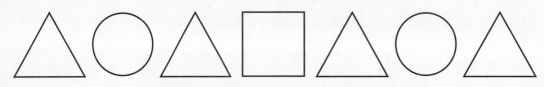

Name _____

Lines and Line Segments

Fine Arts Many modern artists use simple lines and line segments in their work. The Dutch artist Modrian is one famous example. The art on this page is based on his work. But the shaded areas should have bright colors. Color them in if you like. Then answer the questions.

1. a. How many lines run up and down? (Do not include the border.)

_____

   b. How many run from left to right? _____

2. The parallel lines and intersecting lines form 2 kinds of shapes. What are they? _____

Write parallel or intersecting for each.

3.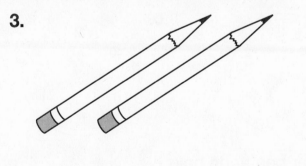

4.

_____   _____

5. A grandfather clock strikes 3:00. Are the hands parallel or intersecting? _____

Name ______________________________

Problem Solving
8-4

Exploring Angles

1. Angles are all around us.

a. Find 5 angles in your classroom. Write where you found each angle and whether the angle is a right angle, less than a right angle, or greater than a right angle.

Angle 1: ______________________________

Angle 2: ______________________________

Angle 3: ______________________________

Angle 4: ______________________________

Angle 5: ______________________________

b. What type of angle did you find most often in your classroom? Why do you think this is?

____

____

____

2. Jean says, "An octagon has 8 sides, but it only has 6 angles." Do you agree? Explain.

____

3. Which clock has hands that form a right angle? __________

a.

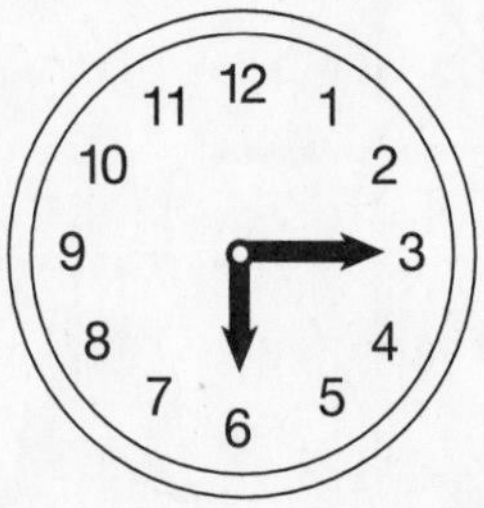

b.

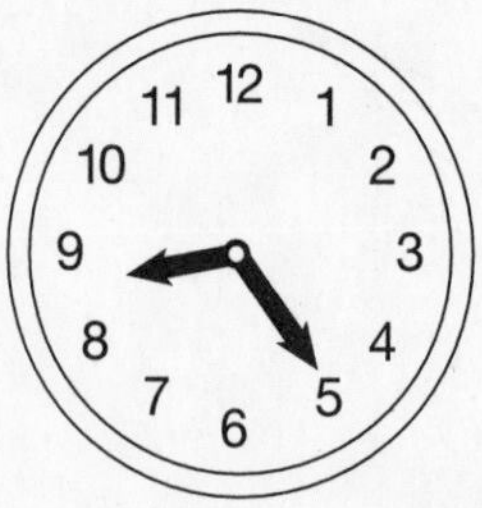

c.

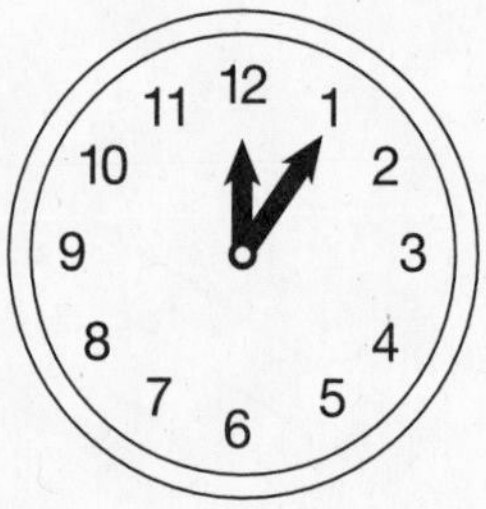

4. What sort of angles does a regular pentagon have?

____

Exploring Slides, Flips, and Turns

Trace the mitten shapes below.

Color the mittens that are congruent.

Now cut out the congruent shapes. Paste one of the mittens on a piece of grid paper. This is the first mitten.

1. Use a second mitten to show a slide of the first mitten on the grid paper. Paste the second mitten on the paper and write "slide."

2. Use a third mitten to show a flip of the first mitten on the grid paper. Paste the third mitten on the paper and write "flip."

3. Use a fourth mitten to show a turn of the first mitten on the grid paper. Paste the fourth mitten on the paper and write "turn."

4. Can you turn the remaining mitten to make it lie directly on top of the flipped mitten? _____

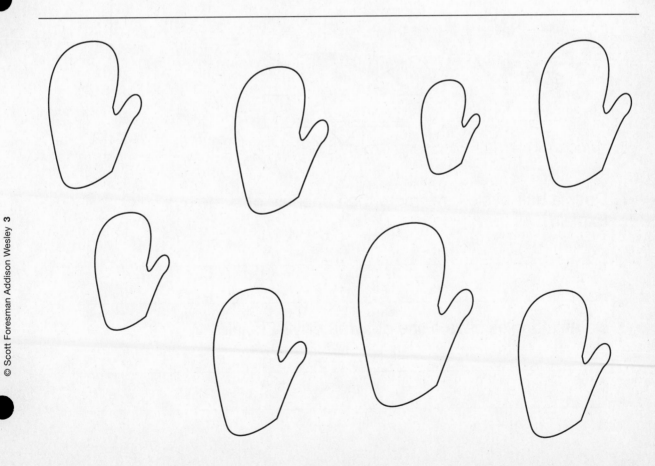

Exploring Symmetry

None of the shapes below has a line of symmetry. Change each shape to make it symmetrical (so if you fold it, it will be the same on both sides). Then draw the line of symmetry.

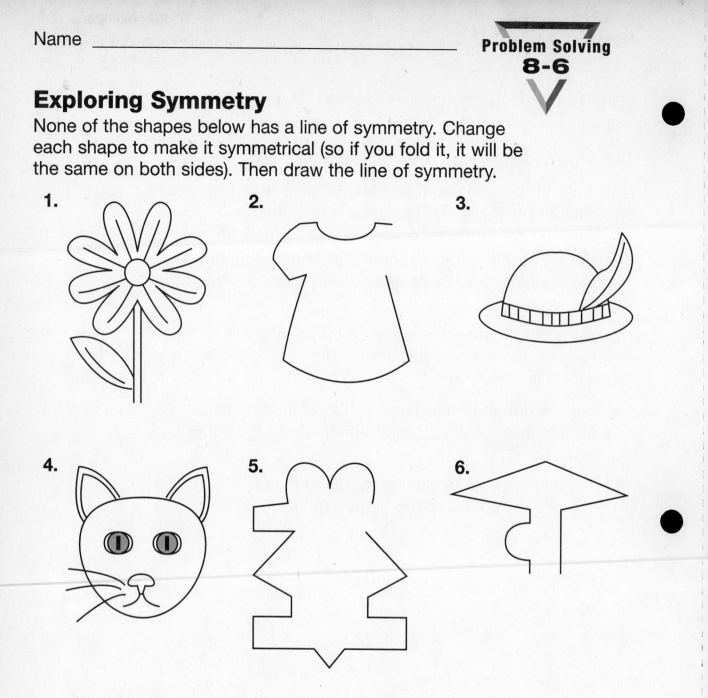

1.

2.

3.

4.

5.

6.

7. Does a half-circle have more than one line of symmetry? Explain.

_____

_____

8. Do all triangles have a line of symmetry? Explain.

_____

_____

GPS | PROBLEM 3, STUDENT PAGE 337

Elise packs boxes that hold 1 or 5 flowers each. If she has 25 flowers, how many ways can she pack the boxes?

━ Understand ━

1. How many different kinds of boxes can Elise use

   to pack her flowers? _____ Describe the boxes.

   _____

2. How many flowers does she have? _____

━ Plan ━

3. If Elise uses only large boxes, can she pack all the flowers? Explain.

   _____

4. If Elise uses four large boxes, how many small boxes should she use?

   _____

5. What other simpler problems can you solve to help you solve this problem?

   _____

   _____

━ Solve ━

6. How many ways can Elise pack her flowers? _____

━ Look Back ━

7. Name another strategy you could use to solve the problem.

   _____

| SOLVE ANOTHER PROBLEM |

Eric has three baseball caps: the Tigers, the Orioles, and the Blue Jays. He wants to line them up on his bookcase. How many different ways can he arrange the caps?

_____

Exploring Perimeter

A   B   C   D

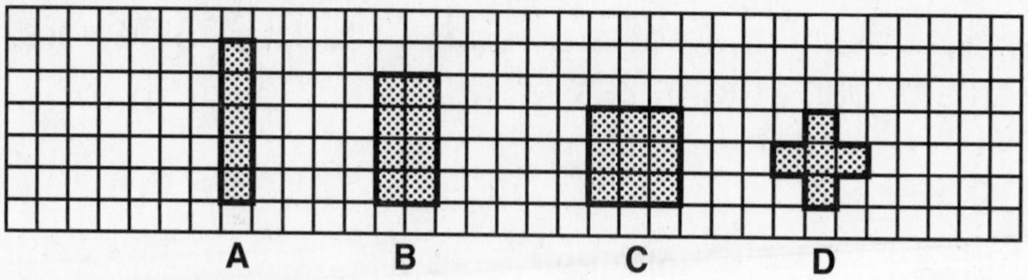

1. What are the perimeters of each shape?

a. _____   b. _____   c. _____   d. _____

2. Write an addition number sentence that would help you find the perimeter for each figure above.

a. _____

b. _____

c. _____

d. _____

3. Write a multiplication number sentence to help find the perimeter of:

a. Figure **C**   b. Figure **D**

_____   _____

4. What shapes make it possible to use a multiplication number sentence to find the perimeter? Explain.

_____

_____

5. a. What is the perimeter of this shape? _____

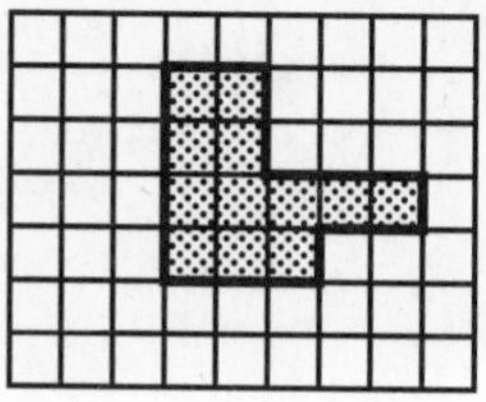

b. Add to the shape to make a new perimeter of 25 units.

c. Draw a square that has the same perimeter as your new shape.

Exploring Area

Each drawing shows a floor that is only partially tiled. Each tile is a square that measures 1 foot on each side. Find the area of each floor. Then tell the number of tiles needed to finish tiling the floor.

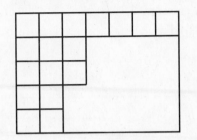
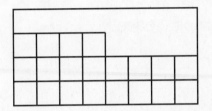

1. **a.** Area: _____ square feet

    b. Tiles needed: _____

2. **a.** Area: _____ square feet

    b. Tiles needed: _____

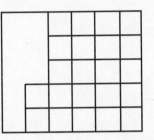
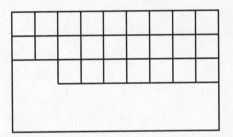

3. **a.** Area: _____ square feet

    b. Tiles needed: _____

4. **a.** Area: _____ square feet

    b. Tiles needed: _____

5. In **1**, if you knew that 17 tiles had been put on the floor, how could you find the number of tiles still needed?

_____

6. How could you find the area of the floor already covered with tile in **1–4**?

_____

_____

© Scott Foresman Addison Wesley 3

Decision Making

The art club is putting on an art show for the school. Most of the artwork will be shown in the classroom. The club will also have use of a display case in the main hallway. The case measures 10 feet by 3 feet. The students must decide which artwork will be displayed in the case.

1. What information is important to know about the display case?

   _____

   _____

2. Many of the club members' artwork is on poster board that is 2 feet wide and 3 feet tall. How many of these can be displayed in the case?

   _____

3. Much of the rest of the club's artwork is on smaller-sized paper, 1 foot wide by 2 feet high. How many of these works of art can be displayed in the case?

   _____

4. The art club has 18 members with artwork in the show. How shall the club decide whose art is displayed in the case? List some things the members must consider in making their choices.

   _____

   _____

5. Would it be better to show the most works of art in the case, or only a few of the best creations? Give some reasons for your answers.

   _____

   _____

   _____

Exploring Volume

Ryan wants to build a model castle. He is using cardboard cubes for the basic frame. Build a model of Ryan's castle frame.

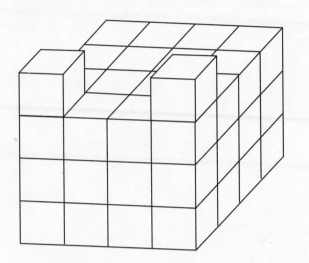

1. How many cubes did you use?

   _____

2. What is the volume of Ryan's castle in cubic units?

   _____

3. Ryan removed 4 cubes to make room for the windows and doors. What is the volume of his castle now?

   _____

4. He wants 2 more towers. If each tower is twice as big as each existing tower, how many more cubes does Ryan need?

   _____

5. Ryan uses 8 more cubes to add the new towers and extend the walls. What is the volume of his castle now?

   _____

Name _____

Coordinate Grids

Careers Taxicab drivers must know the streets of an area well. They must also be able to read a map.

1. Suppose you are a taxicab driver.

   a. How many blocks forward would you drive from the taxi stand on your way to the post office?

   _____

   b. After turning left, how many more blocks would you drive to get to the post office?

   _____

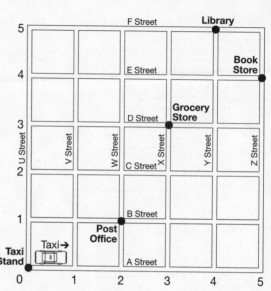

2. You are sitting at the taxi stand waiting for a call. Give the coordinate of each place on the map.

   a. library _____   **b.** book store _____   **c.** post office _____

3. Suppose you were at the post office and received a call to pick up someone at the book store. Describe the shortest way to get there.

   _____

   _____

Use the map above to answer each question.

4. How many different ways are there to ride your bike from (2, 3) to (3, 4) if you do not backtrack? _____

5. How many different ways are there to ride your bike from (2, 3) to (4, 5) if you do not backtrack? _____

6. What strategy did you use to solve **5**? _____

   _____

Exploring Multiplying Tens

Basic facts and patterns help you multiply tens. You can use place-value blocks to help.

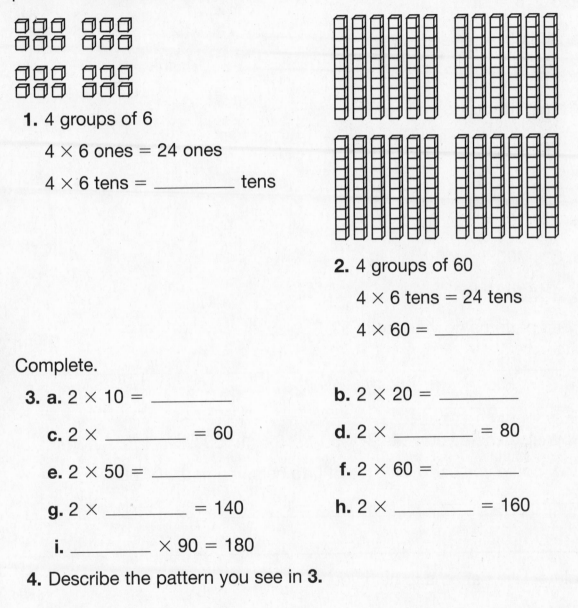

1. 4 groups of 6

4×6 ones = 24 ones

4×6 tens = _____ tens

2. 4 groups of 60

4×6 tens = 24 tens

$4 \times 60 =$ _____

Complete.

3. a. $2 \times 10 =$ _____   **b.** $2 \times 20 =$ _____

c. $2 \times$ _____ $= 60$ **d.** $2 \times$ _____ $= 80$

e. $2 \times 50 =$ _____   **f.** $2 \times 60 =$ _____

g. $2 \times$ _____ $= 140$ **h.** $2 \times$ _____ $= 160$

i. _____ $\times 90 = 180$

4. Describe the pattern you see in **3.**

_____

_____

5. Describe how you could use place value to find the missing number in **3g.**

_____

Exploring Multiplication Patterns

You may use a calculator to help answer the following.

1. **a.** $5 \times 6 =$ _____

   b. $5 \times 60 =$ _____

   c. $5 \times 6 \times 10 =$ _____

2. What patterns do you see in **1**?

   _____

   _____

3. **a.** $3 \times 70 =$ _____

   b. $3 \times 700 =$ _____

   c. $3 \times 70 \times 10 =$ _____

4. What patterns do you see in **3**?

   _____

   _____

5. How else could you write $3 \times 50 \times 10 = 1,500$? _____

6. How could you use $7 \times 80 = 560$ to help you find 7×800?

   _____

   _____

Complete. Use patterns to help you.

7. $90 \times 40 =$

   $9 \times \boxed{} \times 4 \times \boxed{} =$

   $9 \times 4 \times \boxed{} \times \boxed{} =$

   $9 \times 4 \times \boxed{} =$ _____

8. $300 \times 20 =$

   $3 \times \boxed{} \times 2 \times \boxed{} =$

   $3 \times 2 \times \boxed{} \times \boxed{} =$

   $3 \times 2 \times \boxed{} =$ _____

Estimating Products

Careers A carpenter uses estimation to order supplies. Nails come in boxes of 100, 500, or 1,000.

Estimate to solve.

1. The carpenter is building a deck with 32 boards. She plans to use 10 nails for each board. Which box of nails should she buy?

_____

2. The carpenter is building a picnic table with 6 boards. She plans to use 12 nails for each board. Which box of nails should she buy?

_____

3. The carpenter is building a barn with 116 boards. She plans to use 8 nails in each board. Which box of nails should she buy?

_____

4. The carpenter is building a house with 251 boards. She plans to use 9 nails in each board. Which boxes of nails should she buy?

_____

Follow the rule to find each missing number.

5. Rule: Multiply by 4.

Input	Output
3	_____
40	_____
60	_____
700	_____

6. Rule: Multiply by 700.

Input	Output
5	_____
7	_____
9	_____
2	_____

7. Robert has 42 inches of wood to make 1 picture frame. About how much wood will he need to make 7 frames? _____

Exploring Multiplication with Arrays

You can use grid paper to help you multiply.

1. Multiply 3 × 24. Use grid paper to show an array.

   a. Show 20 and 4 ones. Make the ones a different color so you can tell them from the tens. This shows 1 × 24.

   b. Put 2 more rows of 24 on your array. This shows 3 × 24.

   c. How many rows of 20 does the array show? _____

   d. How many rows of 4 does the array show? _____

   e. Find the sum of the number of boxes in each section

   of the array. _____ + _____ = _____

   f. 3 × 24 = _____

2. Multiply 4 × 17.

   a. Make an array on grid paper.

   b. _____ + _____ = _____

   c. 4 × 17 = _____

3. Multiply 6 × 14.

   a. Make an array on grid paper.

   b. _____ + _____ = _____

   c. 6 × 14 = _____

4. Tell how you would use a grid paper array to solve 3 × 31.

   _____

   _____

   _____

5. Explain how you would solve 2 × 47 by breaking apart the numbers.

   _____

   _____

Multiplying: Partial Products

Recreation The height of a
pony or horse is measured from
the ground to the top of its
back. Instead of being measured
in centimeters or inches, the
animal is measured in *hands*.
Each hand equals about 4 inches.

14 hands

1. Juwan's pony is 13 hands high.

   How tall is it in inches? _____

2. Sadie's horse is 16 hands high.

   How tall is it in inches? _____

3. Matt's pony is 48 inches high. How tall is it in hands? _____

4. Lynn's pony is 80 inches high. How tall is it in hands? _____

5. Keri is training for a race that takes place in 7 weeks. If
   she runs 24 miles a week, how many miles will she run

   before the race? _____

6. Mr. Duff needs 150 apples to sell the day of the race.
   A case contains 36 apples. If he buys

   4 cases, will he have enough apples? _____

7. Mr. Duff also needs 150 oranges for the runners to eat.
   The oranges come in boxes of 24. If he buys 7 boxes,

   will he have enough oranges? _____

8. There are 8 groups of runners. Each group has 34

   people. How many runners in all? _____

Multiplying 2-Digit Numbers

New York, New York! It's a great place for a vacation.

1. The ferry tickets to visit the Statue of Liberty cost 12 dollars each. How much money will we need to buy tickets for 6 people? _____

2. How about a show? If there are 4 shows every day, including weekends, at Radio City Music Hall, how many shows are there in March? (Hint: March has 31 days.) _____

3. New York City has 5 *boroughs* (or parts). If each borough has 25 libraries, about how many libraries are in New York City? _____

4. New York City is known for its skyscrapers. If 4 new skyscrapers are built this year and each one has 98 floors, how many new floors are there in all? _____

5. You will be spending 12 days in New York. If you plan 3 activities each day, how many activities will you have planned for the entire trip? _____

6. **Choose a strategy**   A family of 4 want to ride 17 rides at Coney Island Amusement Park. If each ride costs 2 tickets, how many tickets will they need to buy?

   ┌─────────────────────────────┐
   │ • Use Objects/Act It Out   │
   │ • Draw a Picture   │
   │ • Look for a Pattern   │
   │ • Guess and Check   │
   │ • Use Logical Reasoning   │
   │ • Make an Organized List   │
   │ • Make a Table   │
   │ • Solve a Simpler Problem   │
   │ • Work Backward   │
   └─────────────────────────────┘

   a. What strategy would you use to solve the problem?

   _____

   _____

   b. Answer the problem. _____

© Scott Foresman Addison Wesley 3

Name _____

Multiplying 3-Digit Numbers

Science Human beings are *primates*. So are gorillas, chimps, orangutans, baboons, and lemurs!

The World's Largest Primates	
Primate	**Average weight**
Gorilla	485 pounds
Human	170 pounds
Orangutan	165 pounds
Chimpanzee	110 pounds

Use the chart to help you solve each problem.

1. How much would 4 gorillas weigh? _____

2. How much would half a dozen chimpanzees weigh? _____

3. The elevator sign says "Limit 1,000 pounds." Which group could not ride together: 8 chimpanzees, 7 orangutans, or 5 humans? Explain.

_____

_____

4. The Statue of Liberty is 151 feet high. If another statue were 3 times higher, how tall would it be? _____

5. The drama club presented a play on Thursday, Friday, Saturday, and Sunday. Each night the play was sold out. If there are 128 seats in the auditorium, how many people saw the play all together? _____

6. If 122 people can travel in 1 train car, how many people could travel on a train with 7 cars? _____

Multiplying Money

Literature In the 19th century, Charles Dickens wrote a famous book called *A Tale of Two Cities*. The book is still very popular and the library is purchasing several new copies. They can buy a hardcover edition of the book for $9.95, or a paperback edition for $3.95.

1. How much would 3 hardcover editions cost?

   _____

2. How much would 5 paperback editions cost?

   _____

3. How much would 2 hardcover editions and 2 paperback editions cost?

   _____

4. A soccer ball costs $14.95. Your school needs to buy 9 new ones. How much will they cost? _____

5. A package of D-batteries costs $3.99. How much would 3 packages of D-batteries cost? _____

6. A single floppy disk costs $1.29. A box of 9 floppy disks costs $10.95. Which is less expensive: 9 single disks or a box? Explain.

   _____

   _____

7. A package of 3 t-shirts costs $6.95. A package of 4 t-shirts costs $7.95. How much would it cost to purchase 10 t-shirts? Explain.

   _____

Name _____

Mental Math

Science Swans are large, beautiful birds which sometimes live in city parks. Male swans weigh about 41 pounds. Female swans weigh about 37 pounds.

Use mental math to solve these problems.

1. How much would 4 male swans weigh? _____

2. How much would 2 female swans weigh? _____

3. How much would two pairs of swans weigh, 2 males and 2 females? _____

Snack	Calories
1 fresh apple	61 calories
1 graham cracker	58 calories
1 cup of popcorn	41 calories

4. The table shows the number of calories in each of the following snacks. Find the total number of calories in:

a. 2 fresh apples _____

b. 4 cups of popcorn _____

c. 3 graham crackers _____

d. 1 apple, 2 cups of popcorn, and 5 graham crackers _____

5. There are 27 books on each shelf of a 9-shelf bookcase. How many books are in the entire bookcase? _____

© Scott Foresman Addison Wesley 3

Name _____

GPS PROBLEM 5, STUDENT PAGE 387

There are 63 apartments in a building. After 1 month, 7 apartments were rented. After 2 months, 14 were rented. After 3 months, 21 were rented. If the pattern continues, how long will it take for all of the apartments to be rented?

▬ Understand ▬

1. What do you know?

_____

2. What do you need to find out?

_____

▬ Plan ▬

3. Complete the table. Fill in what you know.

Month	1	2	3	4	5	6	7	8	9
Apartments Rented									

▬ Solve ▬

4. Find a pattern and complete the table. What is your answer?

_____

▬ Look Back ▬

5. How could you have solved the problem in another way?

_____

SOLVE ANOTHER PROBLEM

The fire alarms in all the apartments must be inspected. After one week, the fire marshal has inspected 9 alarms. After 2 weeks, she has inspected 18 alarms. How long will it take her to inspect all 63 alarms? _____

Exploring Division Patterns

Write the basic fact that you can use to solve these
problems. Then, solve each problem.

	Basic Fact	Quotient
1. $140 \div 2$	_____	_____
2. $30 \div 3$	_____	_____
3. $40 \div 2$	_____	_____
4. $600 \div 3$	_____	_____
5. $80 \div 2$	_____	_____
6. $800 \div 4$	_____	_____
7. $900 \div 3$	_____	_____
8. $120 \div 6$	_____	_____
9. $500 \div 5$	_____	_____
10. $70 \div 7$	_____	_____

11. Sam picks out a videotape that is 90 minutes long. His
mother says he may watch it in 3 parts.

a. If Sam wants each part to be equal, how long will each part be?

_____

b. How could you use a basic fact to find the answer?

_____

12. An insect is 120 centimeters long. It has three body
parts of nearly equal length.

a. About how long is each body part? _____

b. How could you use a basic fact to find the answer?

_____

_____

Estimating Quotients

Physical Education Every day at baseball camp, a different number of players show up! Estimate how many teams can be made each day. (Hint: there are 9 players on a baseball team.) Complete the table.

	Day	Number of Players	Number of Teams
1.	Monday	73	
2.	Tuesday	37	
3.	Wednesday	82	
4.	Thursday	55	
5.	Friday	46	

6. How many baseball games can be played at the same time on Monday? _____

7. You have $9 and need to buy presents for 4 people. You want to spend the money equally. About how much can you spend on each person? _____

8. Your class is studying the solar system. You must divide the 26 students into groups. Each group will research one of the nine planets. About how many students will be in each group? _____

9. Your web browser lists 57 web sites about paper recycling in your area. You want to visit them all in 7 days. About how many web sites should you visit each day? _____

10. There are 65 students visiting a museum. If they are divided into 8 tour groups, about how many students are in each group? _____

Name _____

Exploring Division with Remainders

Mari bought 22 bananas at the fruit market. She wants to make some banana bread for the school party.

The recipe for Old Time Banana Bread uses 4 bananas per loaf. The recipe for Fab–Fab Banana Bread uses 3 bananas per loaf. Mari needs to decide which recipe to use.

Answer each question. You may use the bananas to help you.

1. Suppose Mari makes as much Old Time Banana Bread as possible.

   a. How many bananas for each loaf? _____

   b. How many loaves all together? _____

   c. How many bananas left over? _____

2. What if Mari makes as much Fab–Fab Banana Bread as possible.

   a. How many bananas for each loaf? _____

   b. How many loaves all together? _____

   c. How many bananas left over? _____

3. How did you find out how many bananas were left over?

   _____

   _____

4. How will dividing and finding leftovers help Mari decide what kind of banana bread to make?

   _____

   _____

Name _____

Dividing

> **Geography** The United States of America has 50 states.
> Did you know that Mexico has 29 states?
>
> Your class wants to study Mexico. The class will work in
> groups. Each group will study the same number of Mexican
> states and give a report to the class. How many states
> would each group study if the class was divided into:
>
> **1.** 3 groups? _____ states with _____ left over
>
> **2.** 4 groups? _____ states with _____ left over
>
> **3.** 5 groups? _____ states with _____ left over
>
> **4.** 6 groups? _____ states with _____ left over
>
> **5.** 7 groups? _____ states with _____ left over
>
> **6.** 8 groups? _____ states with _____ left over
>
> **7.** 9 groups? _____ states with _____ left over
>
> **8.** Into how many groups would you divide the class? How
> many states would each group study? Explain your
> reasoning.
>
> _____
>
> _____
>
> _____

9. If a 25-foot rope is used to make 3 jump ropes of equal
length, how long will each jump rope be? How much
rope will be left over?

_____

10. A cross-country race is 12 miles long and has 4 equal
"legs" (or parts). How long is each leg? _____

Decision Making

Your community is planning a Walk Against Hunger and they have asked you to help. First, you must plan a route. It must be 12 miles long, finish at the town hall, and go through the park.

Draw your route on the grid paper below. Let each square represent 1 mile.

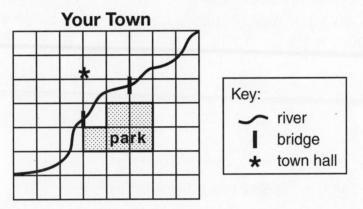

Your Town

Key:
~ river
| bridge
* town hall

1. You want to put a snack table every three miles on the route. How many will you need?   _____

Mark your snack tables on the map.

2. There should be 1 snack per walker at each table. You are expecting 30 walkers this year. How many snacks will you need?   _____

3. You want to put some juice stands on the route as well. At what intervals do you think they should be? Remember, the walkers will be thirsty!

_____

4. How many juice stands will you have?
Mark them on the map.   _____

5. If every walker needs 1 glass of juice at each stand, how many glasses of juice will you need in total?

_____

6. 1 juice bottle serves 5 people. How many bottles will you need for the walk?

_____

Exploring Equal Parts

Use the clock to answer each question.

1. You can divide the clock into 2 equal parts by drawing a line from 12 to 6. You can also draw a line from 1 to 7 that divides the clock into 2 equal parts.

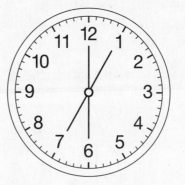

   a. In what other ways can you divide the clock into 2 equal parts? Show them on the clock.

   _____

   _____

   _____

   b. What pattern do you notice in the pairs of numbers?

   _____

   _____

2. You can divide the clock into 3 equal parts. You can draw lines from the center to 1, 5 and 9.

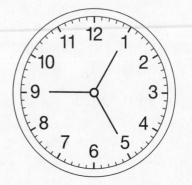

   a. What other lines can you draw to divide the clock into 3 equal parts? Show them on the clock.

   _____

   _____

   b. What pattern do you notice in the sets of 3 numbers?

   _____

   _____

Naming and Writing Fractions

Social Studies Indonesia, a country made up of many islands in southeast Asia, made its flag official in 1945. Italy, a country in southern Europe, made its flag official when all its provinces united in 1870.

Indonesia   Italy

1. a. What fraction of Italy's flag is white? _____

b. What fraction of Italy's flag is not white? _____

2. a. What fraction of Indonesia's flag is white? _____

b. What fraction of Indonesia's flag is not white? _____

3. Draw your own flag. Make $\frac{2}{5}$ of the flag white.

Write the fraction for the part that is left.

4.   **5.**   **6.**

_____   _____   _____

7. Kara poured a cup of milk. She drank $\frac{2}{3}$ of a cup. How much milk is left?   _____

Exploring Equivalent Fractions

You may use fraction strips to help answer the following.

1. a. Write as many fractions as you can that are equivalent to $\frac{1}{2}$.

_____

b. What relationship do you see between the numerators and denominators?

_____

_____

c. Use this pattern to complete the fraction. $\frac{1}{2} = \dfrac{\boxed{}}{20}$

2. a. Write as many fractions as you can that are equivalent to $\frac{1}{3}$.

_____

b. What relationship do you see between the numerators and denominators?

_____

_____

c. Use this pattern to complete the fraction. $\frac{1}{3} = \dfrac{\boxed{}}{24}$

3. How could you prove that $\frac{1}{4}$ is equivalent to $\frac{2}{8}$?

_____

_____

4. How could you prove that $\frac{1}{4}$ is *not* equivalent to $\frac{1}{5}$?

_____

_____

Name _____

Exploring Comparing and Ordering Fractions

Use fraction strips. Order the fractions from greatest to least.

1. $\frac{1}{2}, \frac{1}{4}, \frac{1}{3}, \frac{1}{6}, \frac{1}{5}$

_____

2. $\frac{1}{3}, \frac{2}{3}, \frac{5}{6}, \frac{1}{2}, \frac{1}{6}$

_____

Use fraction strips. Order the fractions from least to greatest.

3. $\frac{1}{12}, \frac{1}{4}, \frac{1}{10}, \frac{1}{2}, \frac{1}{3}$

_____

4. $\frac{2}{5}, \frac{1}{10}, \frac{1}{3}, \frac{2}{3}, \frac{5}{6}$

_____

5. a. What do you notice about the denominators of the fractions in your answers to **1** and **3?**

_____

_____

b. Do you think this is true of all unit fractions? Explain.

_____

_____

6. Is $\frac{3}{10}$ greater than $\frac{1}{5}$? Explain.

_____

Estimating Fractional Amounts

Physical Education Baseball is a popular American sport. When the player hits the ball, he or she must run all the way around the baseball diamond, shown in the picture, to get a home run.

Estimate the fractional amount.

1. About how far has the runner gone?

_____

2. About how far does the runner have to go before she reaches home plate?

_____

3. Suppose another runner is between 1st and 2nd base. About how far has the runner gone?   _____

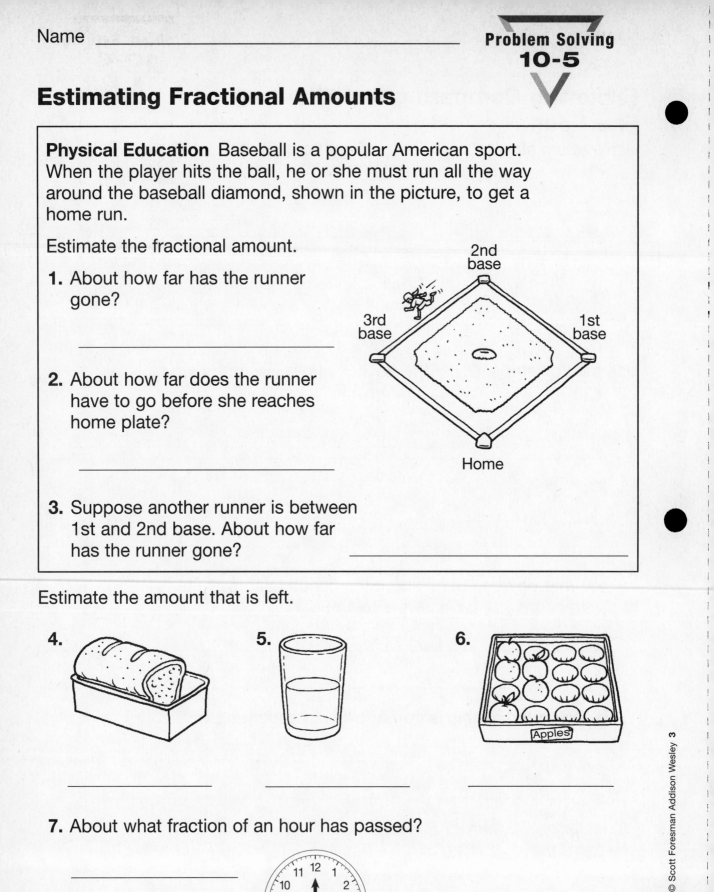

Estimate the amount that is left.

4.

5.

6.

_____   _____   _____

7. About what fraction of an hour has passed?

_____

Name _____

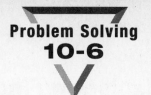

Fractions and Sets

Careers Mrs. Gomez is a school cafeteria manager. She plans lunch for hundreds of students every day!

Look at this week's lunch menu to answer each question.

Lunch Menu					
	Monday	**Tuesday**	**Wednesday**	**Thursday**	**Friday**
Hot dish	Pizza	Turkey Stew	Pizza	Veggie Burger	Fish Sticks
Side dish	Fruit Salad	Fruit Salad	Garden Salad	Spinach Salad	Cole Slaw
Sandwich	Tuna Fish	Veggie Roll	Egg Salad	Veggie Roll	Cheese

1. On what fraction of the days this week will the cafeteria serve

   a. fruit salad? _____   **b.** cole slaw? _____

   c. tuna sandwiches? _____   **d.** veggie rolls? _____

2. The cafeteria will serve pizza on Monday and Wednesday. On what fraction of these "pizza days" will they also serve a garden salad?   _____

3. What fraction of the 15 menu items are fish dishes?   _____

Answer each question.

4. What fraction of a year is one month?   _____

5. Alyssa has 5 sisters. 2 of them are younger. What fraction of her sisters are older than her?   _____

6. Randall has $\frac{1}{5}$ of his garden planted. Terry has $\frac{1}{6}$ of his garden planted. Who has planted more of his garden?   _____

Exploring Finding a Fraction of a Number

Use counters to solve each problem.

1. Alex had 20 crackers. He ate $\frac{1}{4}$ of them. How many crackers did he eat? _____

   How many counters did you use to solve the problem? _____

   How many groups did you make? _____

2. The soccer team sold 12 t-shirts at the fair. Kenny sold $\frac{1}{3}$ of them. How many t-shirts did he sell? _____

   How many counters did you use to solve the problem? _____

   How many groups did you make? _____

3. The math team scored 25 points at the championship. Linda scored $\frac{1}{5}$ of them herself. How many points did she score? _____

   How many counters did you use to solve the problem? _____

   How many groups did you make? _____

4. This is a picture of a garden. Complete the picture to show the following.

   a. $\frac{1}{4}$ of the plants are sunflowers.

   b. $\frac{1}{2}$ of the plants have flowers.

   c. $\frac{1}{8}$ of the plants are trees.

Mixed Numbers

Health Eating well is an important part of staying healthy. We need to eat different kinds of foods every day to give our bodies what they need.

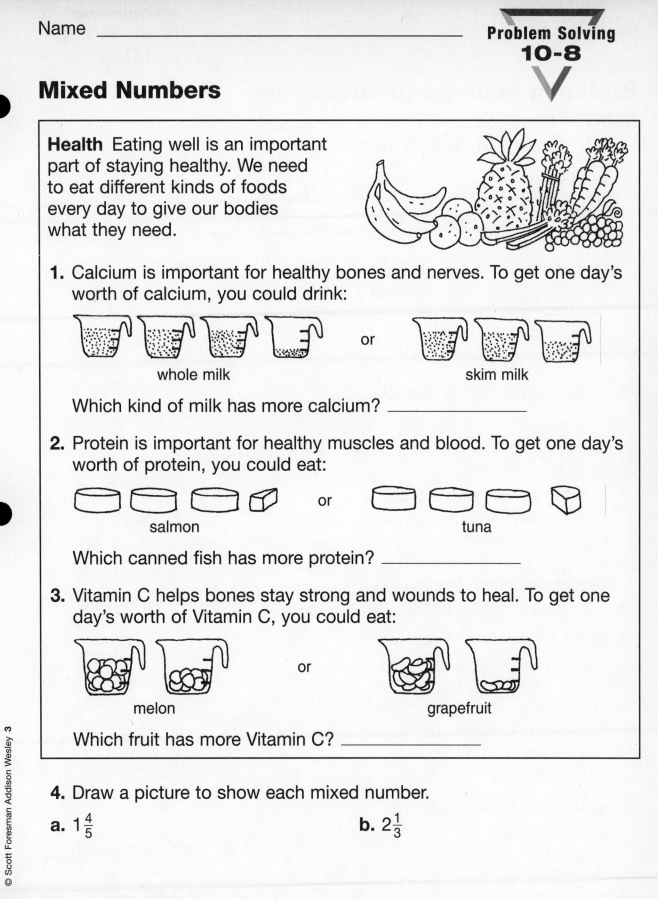

1. Calcium is important for healthy bones and nerves. To get one day's worth of calcium, you could drink:

   whole milk   or   skim milk

   Which kind of milk has more calcium? _____

2. Protein is important for healthy muscles and blood. To get one day's worth of protein, you could eat:

   salmon   or   tuna

   Which canned fish has more protein? _____

3. Vitamin C helps bones stay strong and wounds to heal. To get one day's worth of Vitamin C, you could eat:

   melon   or   grapefruit

   Which fruit has more Vitamin C? _____

4. Draw a picture to show each mixed number.

   a. $1\frac{4}{5}$ **b.** $2\frac{1}{3}$

5. If you cut pies into 6 slices each and gave away $1\frac{1}{6}$ pies, how many slices is that? _____

Name _____

Exploring Adding and Subtracting Numbers

1. Add fractions by drawing pictures.

   a. Draw $\frac{1}{4}$.

   b. Add $\frac{2}{4}$ to your drawing.

   c. $\frac{1}{4} + \frac{2}{4} =$ _____

2. Subtract fractions by drawing pictures.

   a. Draw $\frac{5}{6}$.

   b. Take away $\frac{2}{6}$ from your drawing.

   c. $\frac{5}{6} - \frac{2}{6} =$ _____

3. a. What portion of the pizza will remain after 4 more slices are eaten? _____

   b. Write a number sentence to show the problem you solved. _____

4. a. What portion of a cup will there be if $\frac{1}{3}$ of a cup of water is added? _____

   b. Write a number sentence to show the problem you solved. _____

5. a. How much will $\frac{3}{4}$ yard of fabric cost? _____

   b. Describe how you solved the problem.

_____

_____

Name _____

Decision Making

You're in charge of the holiday party for the 10-member gymnastics team and must decide what to serve. Here is a list of the foods you can offer:

Pizza:	Fruit salad:	Granola bars:	Apple juice:	Milk:
8 slices per pizza	6 servings per jar	9 granola bars per box	8 glasses per bottle	4 glasses per carton

1. What do you know?

_____

_____

2. What do you need to decide?

_____

3. How many people will you serve? _____

4. Which foods will you choose?

_____

5. How many servings will each team member get?

_____

Fill in this chart to show your plan.

Food	Amount Needed for 1 Gymnast	Amount Needed for 10 Gymnasts	Amount to Order
Pizza			**Pizzas**
Fruit Salad			**Jars**
Granola Bars			**Boxes**
Apple Juice			**Bottles**
Milk			**Cartons**

Exploring Length

1. Draw a line to show 5 inches.

2. Look at your line. Then look around your classroom. Name five items that you think have a length of about 5 inches. List the items in the table. Then use a ruler to check your predictions. Record the actual length of each item in the table.

Item	Length in Inches
a.	
b.	
c.	
d.	
e.	

3. Is the length of your nose greater or less than 5 inches?

_____

4. Is the width of your desk greater or less than 5 inches?

_____

5. Write the following list of items in the table in order from longest to shortest. Then measure to the nearest inch. Write the actual measurements in the table.

pencil   width of paper   eraser

Item	Actual Measure
a.	
b.	
c.	

Measuring to the Nearest $\frac{1}{2}$ Inch and $\frac{1}{4}$ Inch

Social Studies People who lived in ancient Rome and Greece had their own systems of measurement. Both systems had a unit called the cubit. The Greek cubit was a little more than $18\frac{1}{4}$ inches. The Roman cubit measured $17\frac{1}{2}$ inches. This difference caused problems for merchants!

1. Suppose you lived in ancient Greece. You want to buy 2 cubits of cloth. How many inches of cloth do you want? _____

2. Suppose the cloth seller used Roman cubits to measure his cloth. Would he give you more or less than 2 Greek cubits? Explain.

_____

3. If a cubit was based on the length of a body part, such as the distance from the elbow to the tip of the finger, do you think an average Greek or Roman was larger? Explain.

_____

Ricki is making bracelets. She uses the following beads.

4. Ricki made a bracelet with beads arranged from smallest to largest. Draw the beads in order.

5. Ricki put one white bead on a bracelet. Next, she wants to add grey beads that have the same total length as one white bead. How many grey beads should she use? _____

Exploring Length in Feet and Inches

1. Work with a partner to measure height.

   a. Estimate your height in feet and inches. Then estimate your partner's height. Record your estimates in the table.

   b. Stand against a wall. Have your partner put a piece of tape on the wall even with the top of your head. Switch places and mark your partner's height.

   c. Use a ruler to measure from the tape to the floor.

Complete the table.

Name	Estimated Height	Actual Height (in feet and inches)	Actual Height (in inches)

2. Why do you think height is usually given in feet and inches rather than just feet?

_____

_____

Write whether each object should be measured in feet or inches.

3. a dog's tail   4. the height of a tree   5. the length of your arm

_____   _____   _____

6. Which object in **3–5** would be better to measure in feet *and* inches?

_____

_____

Feet, Yards, and Miles

Careers A gardener is building a fence around the garden shown below. She plans to put one post every 3 feet.

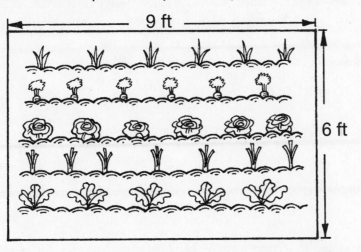

9 ft

6 ft

1. How many yards will there be between posts? _____

2. How many inches will there be between posts? _____

3. What is the perimeter of the garden in feet? _____

4. What is the perimeter of the garden in yards? _____

5. How many posts will the gardener need? _____

A group of students measured the length of their dogs from nose to tail. Amy discovered that Sheeba is 38 inches long. Ryan found that Otis is 1 yard long. Sam learned that Sebastian is 2 feet 10 inches long.

6. List the dogs in order from longest to shortest.

_____

7. How could you make it easier to compare the dog's lengths? Explain.

_____

_____

8. If these dogs stood in a line head to tail, how much would the line measure in inches? Feet? Yards?

_____

GPS PROBLEM 2, STUDENT PAGE 445

Dolores, Mira, Chris, and Isaac are brothers and sisters. Mira is the youngest. Chris is 11 years old. Isaac is younger than Dolores. If each person is either 9, 10, 11, or 12 years old, how old is each person?

── Understand ──

1. What do you need to find out? _____

2. How old is Chris? _____

3. Who is the youngest? _____

4. What are the possible ages of
   the people? _____

── Plan ──

5. Fill in the table with the
   information given in the
   problem.

	9	10	11	12
Dolores				
Mira				
Chris				
Isaac				

── Solve ──

Use the clues to help complete the table.

6. How old is each person? _____

_____

── Look Back ──

7. How can you check your answer? _____

_____

SOLVE ANOTHER PROBLEM

Jim, Anne, Lin and Tanika are friends. Jim is younger than Lin and Tanika. Anne is younger than Jim. Tanika is older than Lin. Give the order of the friends from oldest to youngest.

_____

Exploring Tenths

You can show tenths using grids. You can write tenths as a fraction or as a decimal.

1. Write the word name for $\frac{7}{10}$. _____

2. Write $\frac{7}{10}$ as a decimal. _____

3. a. Draw tenths grids to show one and six tenths in the space below.

b. Write one and six tenths as a fraction. _____

c. Write one and six tenths as a decimal. _____

d. What does the number after the decimal point represent?

_____

4. a. Arrange these tenths from least to greatest: $\frac{7}{10}, \frac{4}{10}, \frac{1}{10}, 1\frac{1}{10}$.
You may use tenths grids to help you.

_____

b. How did you show $1\frac{1}{10}$ on a tenths grid?

_____

5. a. Think of a number greater than 1 in tenths. Draw a picture to show the number.

b. Write the number as a decimal. _____

c. Write the word name of your number.

_____

Name _____

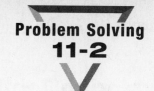

Hundredths

Science Different land animals can run at different speeds. The table below shows how fast some animals can run. Use the table to answer **1–4**.

Animals	Speed in miles per hour (mph)
Cheetah	70
Horse	47.5
Whippet	35.50
Human	27.89
Spider	1.17
Giant Tortoise	0.17
Garden Snail	0.03

1. Which animals are faster, giant tortoises or spiders? Explain how you know.

   _____

   _____

2. Which animal in the table is the slowest? _____

3. Write the word name that tells how fast a human can run.

   _____

4. Which animal is faster, the garden snail or the giant tortoise? Explain how you know.

   _____

5. Phyllis finished the 100-meter race in 14.08 seconds. Trina finished the race in 14.88 seconds, and Andrew finished it in 14.80 seconds.

   a. Write the finishing times from fastest to slowest.

   _____

   b. Write the word name for Trina's finishing time.

   _____

   c. Write the finishing times in fractions.

   _____

Name _____

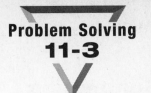

Exploring Adding and Subtracting Decimals

1. Add 0.8 and 0.5.

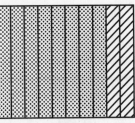 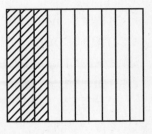

    a. What number does the light shaded area represent? Write the number in three different ways.

_____

    b. What decimal does the striped area represent?

    _____

    c. Write the sum as a decimal. _____

2. Write a number sentence for **1.** _____

3. Subtract 0.4 from 1.1.

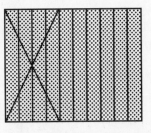 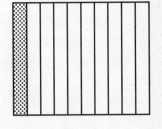

    a. What decimal does the shaded area represent? _____

    b. What decimal does the crossed-out area represent? _____

    c. Write the difference as a decimal. _____

4. Describe how you can solve **1** and **3** without using tenths grids.

_____

_____

_____

5. Is the difference between 1.5 and 0.3 greater than or less than 1? You may use tenths grids to explain.

_____

_____

Connecting Decimals and Money

Careers Mr. Hooper owns a small corner grocery store. He is in charge of ordering groceries and supplies, keeping the store clean, and handling the money. He has few employees and often works the cash register himself.

1. Arnelle buys a loaf of bread that costs $1.19. She gives Mr. Hooper $2.00. How much change should he give her? _____

2. Mr. Hooper is putting price tags on a new shipment of cereal before he puts the boxes on the shelves. Each box of cereal costs two dollars and sixty-seven cents. Write the money amount as it would be shown on each price tag. _____

3. In the picture above, Mr. Hooper just rung up an item on the cash register. What coin is worth the amount shown on the cash register? _____

4. Ms. Martinez is writing a check to pay for some baked goods. Help her complete the check by writing the money amount in the blank box.

Ms. Martinez
12 Willow St.
Bayville, IL

518

July 5, 19 99

BONNIE'S BAKERY $ _____

SEVEN AND 32/100 ~~~ Dollars

MEMO _____   Ms. Martinez

5. What coin is worth $\frac{5}{100}$ of a dollar? _____

6. Allison bought a bagel and juice for $2.64. If she pays with a $10.00 bill, how much change will she receive?

_____

Name _____

Decision Making

You are helping your parents plan a big family dinner. You need to decide when to prepare and cook each item on the menu. Below is the menu and the amount of time needed to prepare each dish from start to finish. Serving time will be 4:00 P.M.

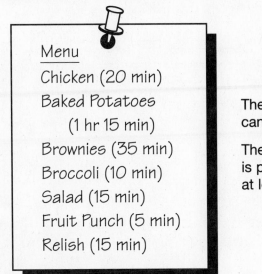

Menu
Chicken (20 min)
Baked Potatoes
    (1 hr 15 min)
Brownies (35 min)
Broccoli (10 min)
Salad (15 min)
Fruit Punch (5 min)
Relish (15 min)

The fruit punch, salad, and brownies can be made ahead of time.

The cranberry-orange relish, once it is prepared, has to be refrigerated for at least 3 hours.

1. What information does the menu give you?

_____

2. What do you already know about some of the foods?

_____

3. It is 11:00 A.M. What foods could be prepared now?

_____

4. When would be a good time to start the potatoes? _____

5. The chicken needs to be served as soon as it is cooked. When would be the best time to start preparing the chicken?

_____

6. While the potatoes are baking in the oven, what other foods need to be prepared? _____

7. Use a separate sheet to make a schedule for the time you will begin preparing each item on the menu.

Exploring Centimeters and Decimeters

Measure each object to the nearest centimeter. Then measure again to the nearest decimeter.

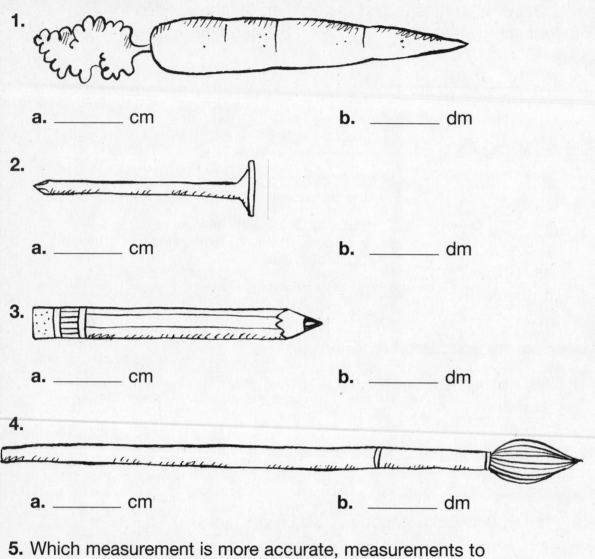

1.

   a. _____ cm   **b.** _____ dm

2.

   a. _____ cm   **b.** _____ dm

3.

   a. _____ cm   **b.** _____ dm

4.

   a. _____ cm   **b.** _____ dm

5. Which measurement is more accurate, measurements to the nearest centimeter or to the nearest decimeter? Explain.

_____

_____

6. If an object measured 14 cm long, what would its measure be to the nearest decimeter? Explain.

10 11 12 13 14 15 16 17 18 19 20 cm
1   2 dm

_____

Name _____

Meters and Kilometers

Geography Geysers are natural hot springs that erupt from time to time, shooting hot water and steam into the air, often to great heights. Here are a few of the world's most famous geysers:

Name and Location	Height of Steam Column
Old Faithful (USA)	50 m
Great Geysir (Iceland)	70 m
Grand Geyser (USA)	70 m
Steamboat (USA)	90 m
Waimangu (New Zealand)	450 m

1. Do any of these geysers reach the height of a kilometer? Explain.

   _____

2. How many times higher does Waimangu shoot its steam than Steamboat?

   _____

3. Imagine that a family traveled 3,200 km in order to visit Yellowstone National Park. It took them three days to make the trip. At the end of the first day, they had covered 1,400 km. How many more kilometers would they need to go in order to reach their destination? _____

4. Suppose that they decide to travel an equal distance on the second and third days of the journey. How many kilometers would they need to travel on each day? Explain your answer.

   _____

GPS PROBLEM 5, STUDENT PAGE 475

Suppose an elevator can hold 23 people. There are 6 people on the elevator on the first floor. On the second floor, 1 person gets off and 13 people get on. On the fifth floor 5 people get off and 9 people get on. Can more people fit? Explain.

— Understand —

1. How many people can the elevator hold? _____

— Plan —

2. How can you use objects to solve the problem?

_____

— Solve —

3. How many people are on the elevator after 5 people get off and 9 people get on at the 5th floor? _____

4. Can any more people get on the elevator? Explain.

_____

— Look Back —

5. Is your answer reasonable? Explain.

_____

_____

SOLVE ANOTHER PROBLEM

After leaving the 5th floor, the elevator goes to the 6th floor. Six people get off and 7 people get on. On the 10th floor, 8 people get off and 3 people get on. The elevator goes to the first floor and lets everyone off. How many people got off? _____

Exploring Capacity: Customary Units

1. Complete the table to show how cups, pints, quarts, and gallons are related.

	1 cup			
a.	2 cups	pint		
b.	4 cups	pints	1 quart	
c.	16 cups	pints	quarts	1 gallon

2. Suppose you had two containers of different sizes. How could you find which container holds more water?

_____

_____

_____

_____

3. Would 1 gallon of water fit in both containers? Why or why not?

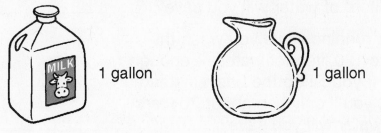

1 gallon   1 gallon

_____

_____

4. Four quarts are in 1 gallon. Suppose your family drank 3 quarts of milk from a gallon container of milk. How many quarts would be left?   _____

5. One pint is $\frac{1}{8}$ of a gallon. Suppose you bought 3 pints of juice. What fraction of a gallon would that be?   _____

Measuring Capacity: Metric Units

Science Your heart is a muscle that pumps blood through your body. Blood carries oxygen to other organs through arteries, and back to the heart through veins.

1. The heart pumps about 5 liters of blood a minute. How many liters is that per hour? _____

2. Mild exercise speeds up the heart so that it pumps about 7 liters of blood a minute. How many liters is that per hour? _____

3. How many more liters of blood does your heart pump in 60 minutes of exercise than in 60 minutes of rest? _____

---

4. Janet filled a 3-liter container with 2040 mL of water. How much more water could she have put in? _____

5. If you leave the water running while you brush your teeth, you can waste 20 liters of water. If you only run the water when you need it, you'll use about 3 liters of water. How many liters of water will you save? _____

6. If you leave the water running while you wash the dishes, you can waste 120 liters of water — enough to wash a whole car! If you fill up the basin instead and rinse dishes in it, you'll only use about 20 liters of water. How much water will you save? _____

7. We need to drink about 2 liters of water a day. How much water is that a week? _____

8. Which unit of measurement would you use for

   a. a spoon? _____

   b. a bucket? _____

Exploring Weight: Customary Units

Work with a partner. Choose 5 items in the classroom that you think weigh about an ounce.

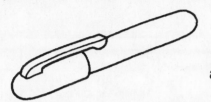 about 1 ounce

Place an ounce weight on one side of the scale. Place one of the items that you chose on the other side of the scale. Record whether the weight of the item is greater than, less than, or equal to an ounce.

	Item	More than 1 oz	1 oz	Less than 1 oz
1.				
2.				
3.				
4.				
5.				

6. Name an item besides a key or a pen that is about 1 ounce.

_____

7. Name an item that is less than 1 ounce.

_____

8. Name an item that is greater than 1 ounce.

_____

9. Suppose you put a pound weight on the balance scale. How many 1-ounce items would you need to balance the pound weight? Explain.

_____

Grams and Kilograms

Recreation These athletes need information filled in on their sports cards. Use the clues to complete.

2.

Chen Lu

figure skater

Height 5' 4"

_____

1.

Tiger Woods

golfer

Height 6' 2"

_____

3.

Martina Hingis

tennis player

Height 5' 6"

_____

4.

Michael Finley

basketball player

Height 6' 7"

_____

a. Michael Finley is just 2 kg less than twice as much as Chen Lu.

b. Chen Lu is 2 kg less than Martina Hingis.

c. Martina Hingis is between 51 and 53 kg.

d. Tiger Woods is 18 kg more than Chen Lu.

5. A catering firm is cooking with apples. They have about 400 g of apples in stock.

a. How many more grams of apples do they need for a recipe which requires 2 kg of apples? _____

b. They receive a shipment of 3,500 g of apples. After preparing the recipe, how many grams of apples do they have left over? _____

c. Do they have enough left over to make a recipe which requires 1 kg of apples? _____

Temperature

Health The average human body temperature is 98.6°F or 37°C. It's normal to have a temperature 1 degree higher or lower. If your temperature is more than 1 degree higher, though, you may have a fever.

1. Color 37°C on the thermometer.

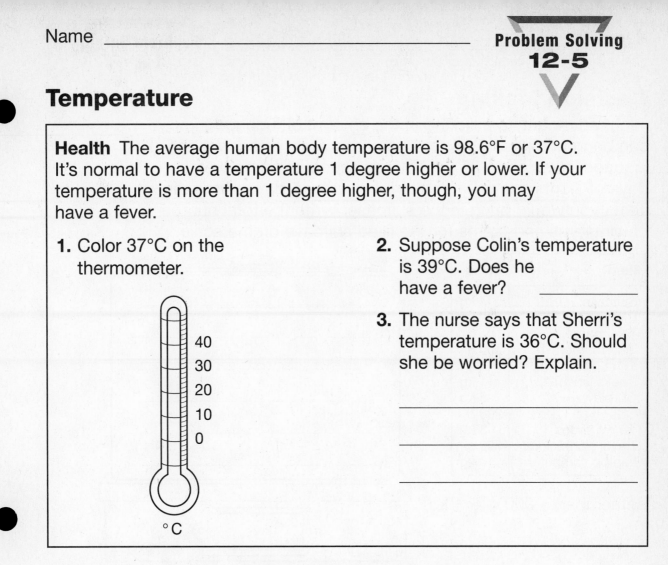

°C

2. Suppose Colin's temperature is 39°C. Does he have a fever? _____

3. The nurse says that Sherri's temperature is 36°C. Should she be worried? Explain.

_____

_____

_____

4. Using °F, estimate the temperature in this room.

_____

5. Using °C, estimate the temperature outside today.

_____

6. You can think of the average human body temperature as about 99°F. How many degrees hotter is this than room temperature?

_____

7. Water boils at 212°F and freezes at 32°F. How many degrees difference is this? _____

Decision Making

Flight attendants are limited in the amount of luggage they can bring on flights. Suppose you are a flight attendant and luggage is limited to 25 kg. You are scheduled for several days of flights and will not return home for 5 days. Write the items you would bring in the suitcase. Write the total number of kilograms and grams for the filled suitcase on the scale.

Item	Mass
Suitcase	4 kg
Clothing for 5 days	12 kg
Toothpaste and toothbrush	600 g
Extra pillow	1 kg
Books (each)	1 kg
CD player	8 kg
CDs	200 g
Tennis shoes	3 kg
Travel alarm clock	750 g
Laptop computer	10 kg

Remember: 1,000 g = 1 kg

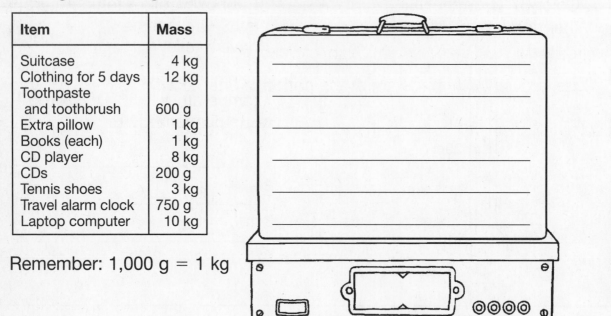

1. Which items do you think are most important?

_____

_____

2. Describe how you decided what items to bring with you.

_____

_____

_____

_____

3. If the limit was 40 kg, could you take everything on the list?

_____

Exploring Likely and Unlikely

Each sentence is about something that is possible. For each one, write a related sentence that is likely and a related sentence that is unlikely.

Example

Some students will be absent tomorrow.

Likely: More than one student will be absent tomorrow.

Unlikely: All students will be absent tomorrow.

1. Several kinds of birds are at the park this afternoon.

a. Likely: _____   **b.** Unlikely: _____

_____   _____

_____

2. Our class will go on a field trip this year.

a. Likely: _____   **b.** Unlikely: _____

_____   _____

_____   _____

3. Some students in our school have their birthdays in March.

a. Likely: _____   **b.** Unlikely: _____

_____   _____

_____   _____

4. Our basketball team will win tomorrow's game.

a. Likely: _____   **b.** Unlikely: _____

_____   _____

_____   _____

Exploring Predictions

Duane has a lot of T-shirts. He stores them in a drawer in
random order. The table shows how many shirts of each
color Duane has.

Shirt color	Number
Blue	15
White	10
Green	9
Red	6
Yellow	3

1. All of Duane's shirts are in his drawer. He reaches in to
   get a shirt. What are the possible outcomes?

   _____

2. Each morning, Duane takes the first shirt he comes to,
   without choosing any special one. On the first day, what
   color is he most likely to wear? Why do you think so?

   _____

   _____

3. After wearing a shirt once, Duane throws it in the wash.
   Three days in a row, Duane wears a yellow shirt. Do you
   think he will wear a yellow shirt again on the fourth day?
   Why?

   _____

4. In the past 10 days, Duane has worn 6 blue shirts, 2 red
   ones, and 2 green ones. What color is he most likely to
   wear on the eleventh day? Explain.

   _____

   _____

Exploring Probability

Circle the spinner that matches the description.

1. On this spinner, the probability of spinning dots is $\frac{2}{5}$.

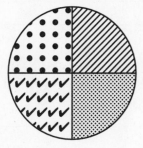 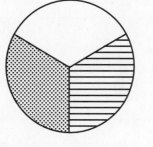 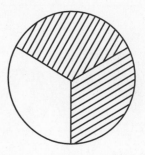

2. On this spinner, the probability of spinning stripes is $\frac{1}{3}$.

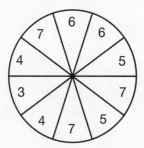 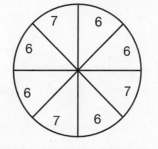 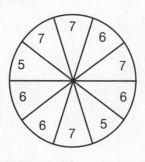

3. On this spinner, the probability of spinning a 7 is $\frac{3}{10}$.

4. On this spinner, the probability of spinning fish is $\frac{1}{6}$.

Exploring Fair and Unfair

Look at each box. Imagine that you are blindfolded, reaching into the box to get a prize. Answer the questions and explain your reasoning.

1. Are the chances of getting a baseball likely, unlikely, or equally likely?

_____

_____

2. Are the chances of getting a butterfly toy likely, unlikely, or equally likely?

_____

3. Are the chances of getting a book likely, unlikely, or equally likely?

_____

4. You have a spinner divided into 4 equal parts. Tell how you would design:

a. a fair game for two players _____

_____

a. an unfair game _____

_____

Name _____

GPS | PROBLEM 3, STUDENT PAGE 511

Sandy likes number riddles. She picked a number to start with. Then she added 16, subtracted 4, and added 5. If Sandy ended up with 45, what number did she start with?

— Understand —

1. What do you need to find out? _____

2. List the things that Sandy did to the number. _____

— Plan —

3. When you work backwards, you undo steps. How do you undo adding 5?

_____

— Solve —

4. Begin with 45. Work backward to find the number that Sandy started with.

_____

— Look Back —

5. a. Could you use the Guess and Check strategy to solve this problem?

_____

b. Would it be as easy as the Work Backward strategy? Explain.

_____

_____

SOLVE ANOTHER PROBLEM

Polly runs 10 miles every week. On Monday, she runs half of the total distance. On Wednesday, she ran 2 miles. If Polly runs the remaining distance on Friday, how far will she run?

_____

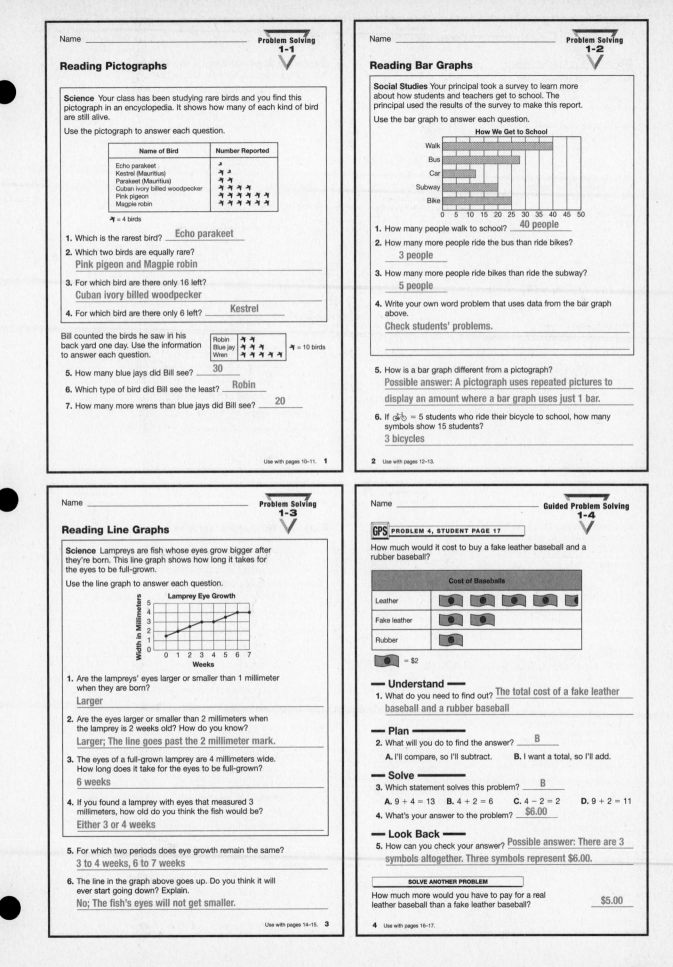

Reading Pictographs

Science Your class has been studying rare birds and you find this pictograph in an encyclopedia. It shows how many of each kind of bird are still alive.

Use the pictograph to answer each question.

Name of Bird	Number Reported
Echo parakeet	✈
Kestrel (Mauritius)	✈ ✈
Parakeet (Mauritius)	✈ ✈
Cuban ivory billed woodpecker	✈ ✈ ✈ ✈
Pink pigeon	✈ ✈ ✈ ✈ ✈
Magpie robin	✈ ✈ ✈ ✈ ✈

✈ = 4 birds

1. Which is the rarest bird? ___Echo parakeet___

2. Which two birds are equally rare?
   Pink pigeon and Magpie robin

3. For which bird are there only 16 left?
   Cuban ivory billed woodpecker

4. For which bird are there only 6 left? ___Kestrel___

Bill counted the birds he saw in his back yard one day. Use the information to answer each question.

Robin	✈ ✈
Blue jay	✈ ✈ ✈
Wren	✈ ✈ ✈ ✈ ✈

✈ = 10 birds

5. How many blue jays did Bill see? ___30___

6. Which type of bird did Bill see the least? ___Robin___

7. How many more wrens than blue jays did Bill see? ___20___

Reading Bar Graphs

Social Studies Your principal took a survey to learn more about how students and teachers get to school. The principal used the results of the survey to make this report.

Use the bar graph to answer each question.

How We Get to School

1. How many people walk to school? ___40 people___

2. How many more people ride the bus than ride bikes?
   3 people

3. How many more people ride bikes than ride the subway?
   5 people

4. Write your own word problem that uses data from the bar graph above.
   Check students' problems.

5. How is a bar graph different from a pictograph?
   Possible answer: A pictograph uses repeated pictures to
   display an amount where a bar graph uses just 1 bar.

6. If 🚲 = 5 students who ride their bicycle to school, how many symbols show 15 students?
   3 bicycles

Reading Line Graphs

Science Lampreys are fish whose eyes grow bigger after they're born. This line graph shows how long it takes for the eyes to be full-grown.

Use the line graph to answer each question.

Lamprey Eye Growth

1. Are the lampreys' eyes larger or smaller than 1 millimeter when they are born?
   Larger

2. Are the eyes larger or smaller than 2 millimeters when the lamprey is 2 weeks old? How do you know?
   Larger; The line goes past the 2 millimeter mark.

3. The eyes of a full-grown lamprey are 4 millimeters wide. How long does it take for the eyes to be full-grown?
   6 weeks

4. If you found a lamprey with eyes that measured 3 millimeters, how old do you think the fish would be?
   Either 3 or 4 weeks

5. For which two periods does eye growth remain the same?
   3 to 4 weeks, 6 to 7 weeks

6. The line in the graph above goes up. Do you think it will ever start going down? Explain.
   No; The fish's eyes will not get smaller.

GPS **PROBLEM 4, STUDENT PAGE 17**

How much would it cost to buy a fake leather baseball and a rubber baseball?

Cost of Baseballs					
Leather	⚾	⚾	⚾	⚾	⚾
Fake leather	⚾	⚾			
Rubber	⚾				

⚾ = $2

── Understand ──
1. What do you need to find out? The total cost of a fake leather
   baseball and a rubber baseball

── Plan ──
2. What will you do to find the answer? ___B___
   A. I'll compare, so I'll subtract.   B. I want a total, so I'll add.

── Solve ──
3. Which statement solves this problem? ___B___
   A. 9 + 4 = 13   B. 4 + 2 = 6   C. 4 − 2 = 2   D. 9 + 2 = 11
4. What's your answer to the problem? ___$6.00___

── Look Back ──
5. How can you check your answer? Possible answer: There are 3
   symbols altogether. Three symbols represent $6.00.

SOLVE ANOTHER PROBLEM

How much more would you have to pay for a real leather baseball than a fake leather baseball?   ___$5.00___

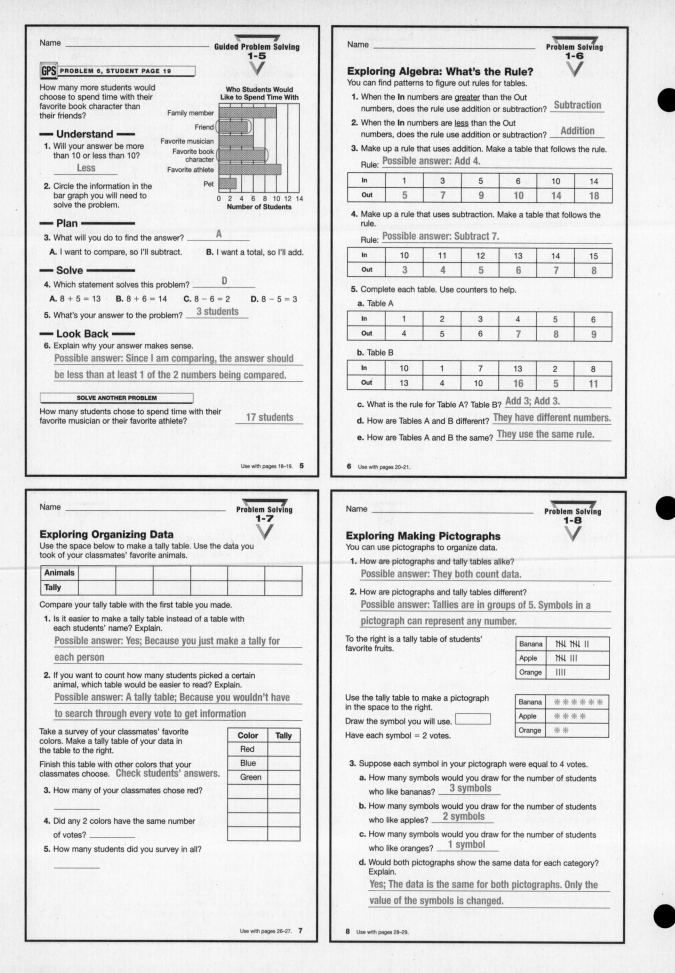

Panel 1-5 (top left)

GPS PROBLEM 6, STUDENT PAGE 19

How many more students would choose to spend time with their favorite book character than their friends?

Who Students Would Like to Spend Time With

Family member
Friend
Favorite musician
Favorite book character
Favorite athlete
Pet

0 2 4 6 8 10 12 14
Number of Students

— Understand —

1. Will your answer be more than 10 or less than 10?
Less

2. Circle the information in the bar graph you will need to solve the problem.

— Plan —

3. What will you do to find the answer? **A**

A. I want to compare, so I'll subtract.   B. I want a total, so I'll add.

— Solve —

4. Which statement solves this problem? **D**

A. 8 + 5 = 13   B. 8 + 6 = 14   C. 8 − 6 = 2   D. 8 − 5 = 3

5. What's your answer to the problem? **3 students**

— Look Back —

6. Explain why your answer makes sense.

Possible answer: Since I am comparing, the answer should be less than at least 1 of the 2 numbers being compared.

SOLVE ANOTHER PROBLEM

How many students chose to spend time with their favorite musician or their favorite athlete?
17 students

Use with pages 18–19.   **5**

Panel 1-6 (top right)

Exploring Algebra: What's the Rule?

You can find patterns to figure out rules for tables.

1. When the **In** numbers are greater than the Out numbers, does the rule use addition or subtraction? **Subtraction**

2. When the **In** numbers are less than the Out numbers, does the rule use addition or subtraction? **Addition**

3. Make up a rule that uses addition. Make a table that follows the rule.
Rule: **Possible answer: Add 4.**

In	1	3	5	6	10	14
Out	5	7	9	10	14	18

4. Make up a rule that uses subtraction. Make a table that follows the rule.
Rule: **Possible answer: Subtract 7.**

In	10	11	12	13	14	15
Out	3	4	5	6	7	8

5. Complete each table. Use counters to help.

a. Table A

In	1	2	3	4	5	6
Out	4	5	6	7	8	9

b. Table B

In	10	1	7	13	2	8
Out	13	4	10	16	5	11

c. What is the rule for Table A? Table B? **Add 3; Add 3.**

d. How are Tables A and B different? **They have different numbers.**

e. How are Tables A and B the same? **They use the same rule.**

6   Use with pages 20–21.

Panel 1-7 (bottom left)

Exploring Organizing Data

Use the space below to make a tally table. Use the data you took of your classmates' favorite animals.

Animals					
Tally					

Compare your tally table with the first table you made.

1. Is it easier to make a tally table instead of a table with each students' name? Explain.
Possible answer: Yes; Because you just make a tally for each person

2. If you want to count how many students picked a certain animal, which table would be easier to read? Explain.
Possible answer: A tally table; Because you wouldn't have to search through every vote to get information

Take a survey of your classmates' favorite colors. Make a tally table of your data in the table to the right.

Finish this table with other colors that your classmates choose. **Check students' answers.**

Color	Tally
Red	
Blue	
Green	

3. How many of your classmates chose red?

_____

4. Did any 2 colors have the same number of votes? _____

5. How many students did you survey in all?

_____

Use with pages 26–27.   **7**

Panel 1-8 (bottom right)

Exploring Making Pictographs

You can use pictographs to organize data.

1. How are pictographs and tally tables alike?
Possible answer: They both count data.

2. How are pictographs and tally tables different?
Possible answer: Tallies are in groups of 5. Symbols in a pictograph can represent any number.

To the right is a tally table of students' favorite fruits.

Banana	𝍒𝍒 II
Apple	𝍒 III
Orange	IIII

Use the tally table to make a pictograph in the space to the right.

Draw the symbol you will use. [   ]

Have each symbol = 2 votes.

Banana	✳ ✳ ✳ ✳ ✳
Apple	✳ ✳ ✳ ✳
Orange	✳ ✳

3. Suppose each symbol in your pictograph were equal to 4 votes.

a. How many symbols would you draw for the number of students who like bananas? **3 symbols**

b. How many symbols would you draw for the number of students who like apples? **2 symbols**

c. How many symbols would you draw for the number of students who like oranges? **1 symbol**

d. Would both pictographs show the same data for each category? Explain.
Yes; The data is the same for both pictographs. Only the value of the symbols is changed.

8   Use with pages 28–29.

Exploring Making Bar Graphs

This tally table shows students' favorite subjects.

Subject	Tally	Number
Math	ⅢⅢ ⅢⅢ ⅢⅢ ⅢⅢ ⅢⅢ IIII	29
Reading	ⅢⅢ ⅢⅢ ⅢⅢ ⅢⅢ IIII	24
Social Studies	ⅢⅢ ⅢⅢ ⅢⅢ ⅢⅢ II	22
Science	ⅢⅢ ⅢⅢ ⅢⅢ ⅢⅢ III	23

You can choose the scale you use for making a bar graph.

Sometimes it's better to use certain scales than others. Answer each question, then make your bar graph below.

1. What would happen if you used 1 as your scale?
   Possible answer: The graph wouldn't fit on the page.

2. What would happen if you used 20 as your scale?
   Possible answer: The graph would be too small and hard to read.

3. Which scale would you use for the data above?
   Possible answer: Between 3 and 10

Favorite Subjects

(Bar graph: Number of Votes, scale 0–35. Math ≈29, Reading ≈24, Science ≈23, Social Studies ≈22)

Decision Making

Your class is planning a picnic. You have to decide which food to bring.

Below is a tally table of your classmates' votes.

Sandwiches	ⅢⅢ ⅢⅢ II
Spaghetti	ⅢⅢ ⅢⅢ ⅢⅢ

1. What do you need to decide?
   Which food to bring to the picnic

2. Use the tally table to make a pictograph. Have each symbol = 3 votes.
   a. What symbol will you use in your graph? **Answers will vary.**
   b. What title will you give your graph?
      Possible answer: Suggestions for Our Picnic
   c. Complete your graph in the space below.

   Suggestions for Our Picnic

Sandwiches	■ ■ ■
Spaghetti	■ ■ ■ ■ ■

   ■ = 3 votes

3. Which food do you think makes more sense to bring? Explain.
   Possible answer: Sandwiches; Because they're easy to pack and they're not as messy

4. Use your graph to decide which food you think your class should bring. Explain.
   Possible answer: Sandwiches; Because they're better for a picnic and only a few more people wanted spaghetti

---

GPS PROBLEM 8, STUDENT PAGE 40

What are the next three numbers?

12, 14, 16, 18, ▨ , ▨ , ▨

— **Understand** —

1. What do you know? **The numbers so far are 12, 14, 16, and 18.**

2. What do you need to find out? **Which 3 numbers should come next**

— **Plan** —

3. a. 14 − 12 = **2**
   b. 16 − 14 = **2**
   c. 18 − 16 = **2**

— **Solve** —

4. What is the pattern? **Add 2.**

5. What are the next 3 numbers? **20** , **22** , **24**

— **Look Back** —

6. How can you check to see if your answer makes sense?
   Possible answer: Look at all 7 numbers and make sure that each one is 2 more than the one before.

SOLVE ANOTHER PROBLEM

Maurice found 1 penny on Monday, 5 pennies on Tuesday, and 9 pennies on Wednesday. If the pattern continues, how many pennies will Maurice find on Friday? **17 pennies**

Place Value Through Hundreds

Science The table shows how many eggs different insects and spiders lay.

Insect or Spider	Number of Eggs
Water spider	About 50 – 100
Cabbage butterfly	About 300
Praying mantis	About 10 – 400

1. Which insects or spiders can lay more than 150 eggs?
   Cabbage butterfly and praying mantis

2. What is the least number of eggs the water spider lays? Use words to write the number. **Fifty**

3. Which insects can lay more than 300 eggs?
   Cabbage butterfly, praying mantis

Solve.

4. The post office has 100 mailboxes for people to rent. If each person receives 2 pieces of mail, how many pieces of mail are in the boxes? **200**

5. A post office has 100 mail boxes. If each box holds 20 pieces of mail, how many pieces of mail can be held? **2,000**

6. If there were only 10 boxes and 10 pieces of mail in each box, how many pieces of mail are there? **100**

7. There were 5 magazines, 3 letters, 4 catalogs and 1 package in Sue's mail box. How many pieces of mail did she receive? **13**

Exploring Place-Value Relationships

🪙 Penny   🪙 Dime

1. You find the following change under a cushion on the couch.

   a. Count the dimes and pennies. __2__ dimes, __26__ pennies

   b. Circle groups of 10 pennies you can exchange for dimes.

   c. How much money did you find? __46__ ¢

2. You empty your bank and find the following change.

   a. Count the dimes and pennies. __7__ dimes, __15__ pennies

   b. Circle groups of 10 pennies you can exchange for dimes.

   c. How much money was in your bank? __85__ ¢

3. a. If you combine the money you found with the money in your bank, how many dimes and pennies will you have?

   __9__ dimes, __41__ pennies

   b. If you exchange all the pennies you can for dimes, how many dimes and pennies will you have?

   __13__ dimes, __1__ pennies

   c. If you exchange all the dimes you can for one-dollar bills, how many dollars, dimes, and pennies will you have?

   __1__ dollars, __3__ dimes, __1__ pennies

   d. Your aunt gives you 2 dollars, 13 dimes, and 12 pennies. You exchange your money so you have the greatest number of dollars, then dimes, and pennies as possible. How many dollars, dimes and pennies do you have in all?

   __4__ dollars, __7__ dimes, __3__ pennies

Place Value Through Thousands

Geography Population is the number of people who live in an area. Here is the population of some towns in New Mexico.

UNITED STATES

New Mexico

Town	Population
Aztec	5,480
Corrales	5,453
Espanola	8,389
Shiprock	7,687

1. Write the population of Espanola in words.
   Eight thousand, three hundred eighty-nine

2. Which two towns have populations that are very close?
   Aztec and Corrales

3. Which town has the greatest population? __Espanola__

Solve.

4. What is the value of the underlined digit in 270? __200__

5. Which is greater: 4,302 or 4,203? __4,302__

6. The Declaration of Independence was signed in 1776. Write 1776 in words.
   One thousand, seven hundred seventy-six

7. Write the current year in words.
   Possible answer: Two thousand, one

Place Value Through Hundred Thousands

Social Studies On June 23, 1995, Merrick Johnston stood on the top of Alaska's Mt. McKinley in Denali National Park. At 12 years old, she was the youngest person ever to climb Mt. McKinley.

Here are some facts about her climb.

Height of Mt. McKinley: 20,320 feet

Weight of supplies that Merrick towed behind her on a sled: about 50 pounds

Time spent climbing each day: 6 hours

Time spent setting up camp each day: 4 hours

1. Write Mt. McKinley's height in words.
   Twenty thousand, three hundred twenty feet

2. How many more hours did Merrick spend climbing each day than setting up camp? __2 hours__

3. Merrick's last camp was at 17,000 feet. The next day she reached the top of Mt. McKinley. About how far did she climb the last day?
   About 3 thousand feet

Use these digits to solve 4–6.

7 3 9 1 4 5

4. What is the greatest number you can write using the digits? __975,431__

5. What is the least number you can write using the digits? __134,579__

6. What do you notice about your answers for 4 and 5? __Possible__
   answer: The least number you can write uses the same
   digits as the greatest number but in reverse order.

GPS PROBLEM 3, STUDENT PAGE 61

Suppose Peter wants to order 45 pounds of soil. He can order the soil in 10-pound bags or 1-pound bags. How many ways could he order the soil?

Understand

1. How many pounds of soil will Peter order? __45 pounds__

2. What kind of bags does the soil come in? Underline them in the problem above.

Plan

3. If Peter buys three 10-pound bags, how much soil will he have?
   __30 pounds__

   How much soil will he still need? __15 pounds__
   __1__ 10-pound bag and __5__ 1-pound bags

Solve

4. List all possible ways Peter can order the soil.

10-lb bags	4	3	2	1	0
1-lb bag	5	15	25	35	45

Look Back

5. How can you check your answer?
   Possible answer: Make sure each way totals 45 pounds.

SOLVE ANOTHER PROBLEM

Suppose Peter wants to order 50 pounds of soil. He can buy the soil in 10 pound or 5-pound bags. How many ways can he order the soil? __6 ways__

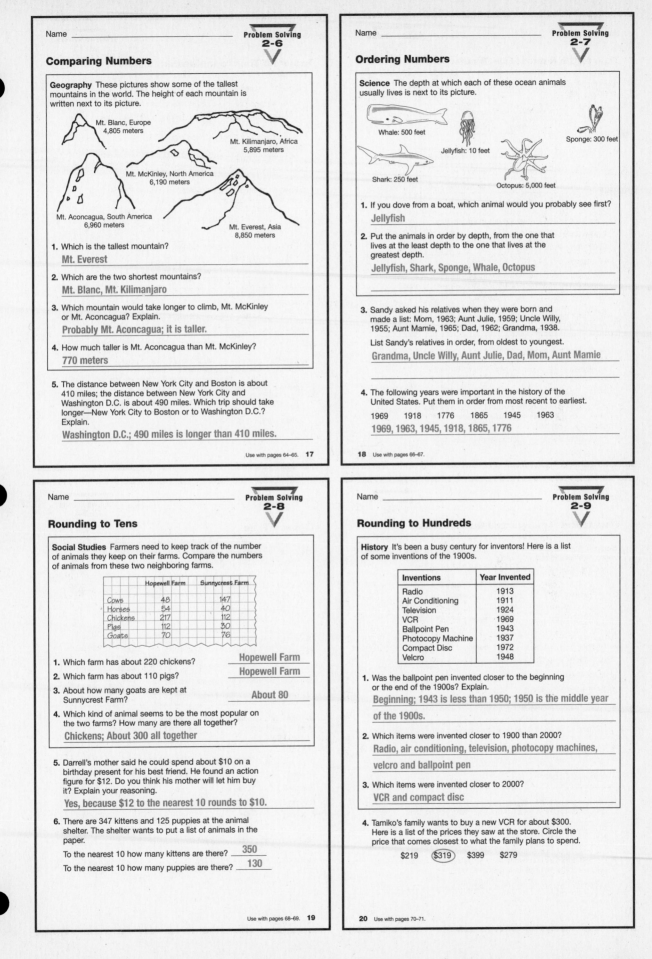

Comparing Numbers

Geography These pictures show some of the tallest mountains in the world. The height of each mountain is written next to its picture.

Mt. Blanc, Europe
4,805 meters

Mt. Kilimanjaro, Africa
5,895 meters

Mt. McKinley, North America
6,190 meters

Mt. Aconcagua, South America
6,960 meters

Mt. Everest, Asia
8,850 meters

1. Which is the tallest mountain?
Mt. Everest

2. Which are the two shortest mountains?
Mt. Blanc, Mt. Kilimanjaro

3. Which mountain would take longer to climb, Mt. McKinley or Mt. Aconcagua? Explain.
Probably Mt. Aconcagua; it is taller.

4. How much taller is Mt. Aconcagua than Mt. McKinley?
770 meters

5. The distance between New York City and Boston is about 410 miles; the distance between New York City and Washington D.C. is about 490 miles. Which trip should take longer—New York City to Boston or to Washington D.C.? Explain.
Washington D.C.; 490 miles is longer than 410 miles.

Ordering Numbers

Science The depth at which each of these ocean animals usually lives is next to its picture.

Whale: 500 feet

Jellyfish: 10 feet

Sponge: 300 feet

Shark: 250 feet

Octopus: 5,000 feet

1. If you dove from a boat, which animal would you probably see first?
Jellyfish

2. Put the animals in order by depth, from the one that lives at the least depth to the one that lives at the greatest depth.
Jellyfish, Shark, Sponge, Whale, Octopus

3. Sandy asked his relatives when they were born and made a list: Mom, 1963; Aunt Julie, 1959; Uncle Willy, 1955; Aunt Mamie, 1965; Dad, 1962; Grandma, 1938.
List Sandy's relatives in order, from oldest to youngest.
Grandma, Uncle Willy, Aunt Julie, Dad, Mom, Aunt Mamie

4. The following years were important in the history of the United States. Put them in order from most recent to earliest.
1969   1918   1776   1865   1945   1963
1969, 1963, 1945, 1918, 1865, 1776

Rounding to Tens

Social Studies Farmers need to keep track of the number of animals they keep on their farms. Compare the numbers of animals from these two neighboring farms.

	Hopewell Farm	Sunnycrest Farm
Cows	48	147
Horses	54	40
Chickens	217	112
Pigs	112	30
Goats	70	76

1. Which farm has about 220 chickens?   Hopewell Farm

2. Which farm has about 110 pigs?   Hopewell Farm

3. About how many goats are kept at Sunnycrest Farm?   About 80

4. Which kind of animal seems to be the most popular on the two farms? How many are there all together?
Chickens; About 300 all together

5. Darrell's mother said he could spend about $10 on a birthday present for his best friend. He found an action figure for $12. Do you think his mother will let him buy it? Explain your reasoning.
Yes, because $12 to the nearest 10 rounds to $10.

6. There are 347 kittens and 125 puppies at the animal shelter. The shelter wants to put a list of animals in the paper.
To the nearest 10 how many kittens are there?   350
To the nearest 10 how many puppies are there?   130

Rounding to Hundreds

History It's been a busy century for inventors! Here is a list of some inventions of the 1900s.

Inventions	Year Invented
Radio	1913
Air Conditioning	1911
Television	1924
VCR	1969
Ballpoint Pen	1943
Photocopy Machine	1937
Compact Disc	1972
Velcro	1948

1. Was the ballpoint pen invented closer to the beginning or the end of the 1900s? Explain.
Beginning; 1943 is less than 1950; 1950 is the middle year of the 1900s.

2. Which items were invented closer to 1900 than 2000?
Radio, air conditioning, television, photocopy machines, velcro and ballpoint pen

3. Which items were invented closer to 2000?
VCR and compact disc

4. Tamiko's family wants to buy a new VCR for about $300. Here is a list of the prices they saw at the store. Circle the price that comes closest to what the family plans to spend.
$219   ($319) $399 $279

Time to the Nearest Five Minutes

Careers Ana is a tour guide in Washington, D.C. Here is the day's schedule for her tour group.

Time Bus Leaves	Activity
10:10 A.M.	The White House
11:30 A.M.	Lunch
12:20 P.M.	Air and Space Museum
2:30 P.M.	Vietnam War Memorial
3:05 P.M.	Washington Memorial
3:40 P.M.	Snack

Use the schedule to answer the questions.

1. Where will the group be going to at ten minutes after ten?

   The White House

2. Five minutes after she gets the group onto the bus going to the Washington Memorial, Ana will take a break. At what time will Ana take a break?

   3:10 P.M.

3. Ana must allow 5 minutes for the group to board the bus. At what time should she have the group meet at the bus to leave for the Air and Space Museum?

   12:15 P.M.

4. Tony wants to leave for the bookstore before four o'clock. A bus will stop near his home at the times below. Which bus should he take? Circle the correct time.

   4:10   5:40   (3:45)   4:00

5. Tony planned to be home by six o'clock. He left the store at 6:05 P.M. Was he going to be early or late? Explain.

   Late; Because 6:05 is five minutes after six

Exploring Time to the Nearest Minute

1. Circle the activities you think take about one minute.

   a. running twenty miles   (b.) making your bed

   c. counting to 100   d. doing your homework

   (e.) writing 5 sentences   f. solving a 500-piece jigsaw puzzle

2. Name two more one-minute activities.

   Possible answers: Doing 20 sit ups, playing a game of

   tic-tac-toe

3. How many times do you breathe in a minute? Estimate. Record your estimate in the 1st row of the table. Then use a clock with a second hand. Count your breaths in one minute. Record your actual number in the 1st row of the table.

	Breaths in 1 Minute		Students' data will vary.
	Estimate	Actual	
At Rest			
After Running in Place			

4. How do you think your breathing will change after running in place for one minute? Estimate. Record your estimate in the 2nd row of the table. Run in place for one minute. Then complete the 2nd row of the table.

   Students' data will vary. Breathing rates should increase after running in place.

Time to the Half Hour and Quarter Hour

Science The Ecology Club is holding a Playground Cleanup today and everyone's helping out!

TIME	ACTIVITY
2:45 P.M.	School's Out; Teams Get Ready
3:00 P.M.	Welcome Speeches
3:15 P.M.	Cleanup Starts
4:15 P.M.	Cleanup Ends

Use the schedule to answer the questions. Write the times in words.

1. When should cleanup teams get ready?

   At a quarter to three

2. When will the cleanup end?

   At a quarter past four

3. If the principal arrives at a quarter past three to give her speech, will she be on time? Explain.

   No, she'll be late because the speeches start at three.

4. Will the Ecology Club be ready to go home by half past four? Explain.

   Yes, because they are scheduled to end the cleanup by 4:15, or quarter after 4

5. Darnelle got up early Saturday morning. List three things she could have done on Saturday. Write a time for each thing you list. Write A.M. or P.M.

   Possible answers: 7:00 A.M., eat breakfast; 11:30 A.M., play a game; 2:15 P.M., read stories

6. Darnelle's mother planned to have dinner ready at six. Dinner was ready at 5:45. Was she early or late? Explain.

   Early, because 5:45 is a quarter to six

Elapsed Time

Science You test equal amounts of 5 different liquids to find how much time it takes each to boil. Calculate each elapsed time.

Liquid	Starting time	Began to boil	Time to Boil (Elapsed time)
1. Water	1:12	1:14	2 minutes
2. Milk	1:17	1:22	5 minutes
3. Syrup	1:43	1:51	8 minutes
4. Vinegar	1:48	1:52	4 minutes
5. Oil	2:14	2:19	5 minutes

6. Which liquid took the longest time to boil? ___ Syrup

7. Which liquid took the shortest time to boil? ___ Water

On your mark, get set, go! Four runners started a marathon at 8:00 A.M. Use each runner's finish time to calculate each running time.

	Finish Time		Elapsed Time
Runner 1	11:14	8.	3 hours, 14 minutes
Runner 2	10:48	9.	2 hours, 48 minutes
Runner 3	12:30	10.	4 hours, 30 minutes
Runner 4	12:27	11.	4 hours, 27 minutes

12. Which runner was the fastest? ___ Runner 2

13. Which runners took more than 4 hours? ___ Runners 3 and 4

Ordinal Numbers and the Calendar

Physical Education It's time to make January's after-school schedule for the gym. Use this list to help you fill in the calendar. Use a picture or letter to mark when each event will take place.

Basketball games are planned for the 1st and 3rd Tuesdays and 2nd and 4th Wednesdays.

Indoor Soccer games are planned for the 1st, 2nd, and 4th Saturdays.

Volleyball games are planned for the 1st and 3rd Mondays and the 2nd and 4th Fridays.

The State Gymnastics Tournament is planned for the twenty-seventh of January.

January

Sun.	Mon.	Tues.	Wed.	Thur.	Fri.	Sat.
	V 1	B 2	3	4	5	S 6
7	8	9	B 10	11	V 12	S 13
14	V 15	B 16	17	18	19	20
21	22	23	B 24	25	V 26	SG 27
28	29	30	31			

1. There's a problem! Which two events are scheduled for the same day?
   An indoor soccer game and the gymnastics tournament

2. How can you change the schedule to solve this problem?
   Possible answer: Move the gymnastics tournament to the 20th of January, or the third Saturday.

3. Mike's birthday is on the sixth of the fifth month, and his sister's birthday is on the fifth of the sixth month. Give the date of each birthday.
   Mike: 6th of May; Mike's sister: 5th of June

Decision Making

It's Saturday morning. Time for chores. You begin at 9:00 A.M. and want to be done before 11:00 A.M. to play basketball. Here's your list of chores: **Possible answers:**

- Clean a room.   15 minutes
- Do the dishes.   20 minutes
- Sweep the floors.   5 minutes
- Take out the garbage.   5 minutes

1. How much time do you have to get it all done? ___ 2 hours

2. Decide how much time you will need for each chore on the list. Write the time on the line next to the chore's name, above.

3. Should you plan extra time in case of problems? Why?
   Possible answers: Yes, in case it takes longer than you think; No, this should be enough time.

4. How much extra time will you plan?
   Possible answer: 5 extra minutes per chore

5. Make a schedule that shows when to start each chore.

   Time   Chore

   _____   _____

   _____   _____

   _____   _____

Show your schedule to someone else. Does he or she agree with your estimates of times? Explain how you planned your schedule.
Answers will vary; Chores should be completed between 9:00 A.M. and 11:00 A.M.

Exploring Addition Patterns

Use basic facts and place-value patterns to find each sum.

1. How can you use patterns to add 400 and 900?
   $4 + 9 = 13$; $40 + 90 = 130$; $400 + 900 = 1,300$

2. What basic fact can you use to find $200 + 700$? Explain.
   $2 + 7 = 9$; 2 hundreds + 7 hundreds = 9 hundreds

3. Can you use the basic fact $5 + 1$ to solve $\$50 + \$10$? Explain.
   Yes; $5 + 1 = 6$, $\$50 + \$10 = \$60$

4. Can you use the basic fact $5 + 1$ to solve $500 + 10$? Explain.
   No; $500 + 10 = 510$

5. a. Find 3 pairs of numbers to fill in the boxes so that the sum does not have a digit in the thousands place.
   Possible answer: 3 and 2, 6 and 1, 4 and 4
   ☐ hundreds + ☐ hundreds _____

   b. What patterns do you notice in your number pairs?
   Possible answer: There is no digit in the thousands place if the basic fact sum is less than 10.

6. a. Find 3 pairs of numbers to fill in the boxes so that the sum has a digit in the thousands place.
   Possible answer: 7 and 6, 9 and 3, 5 and 8
   ☐ hundreds + ☐ hundreds _____

   b. What patterns do you notice in your number pairs?
   Possible answer: There is a digit in the thousands place if the basic fact sum is 10 or greater.

Exploring Adding on a Hundred Chart

1	2	3	4	5	6	7	8	9	10
11	12	13	14	15	16	17	18	19	20
21	22	23	24	25	26	27	28	29	30
31	32	33	34	35	36	37	38	39	40
41	42	43	44	45	46	47	48	49	50
51	52	53	54	55	56	57	58	59	60
61	62	63	64	65	66	67	68	69	70
71	72	73	74	75	76	77	78	79	80
81	82	83	84	85	86	87	88	89	90
91	92	93	94	95	96	97	98	99	100

You can use a hundred chart to help you find sums.

1. Describe one way you could use a hundred chart to find the sum of 73 and 25.
   Possible answer: Start at 73 and move forward 2 tens and 5 ones.

2. Find the sum of $45 + 31$. Find the sum of $31 + 45$. What do you notice about the two sums?
   76; 76; The sums are the same.

3. How could you use a hundred chart to find $\$22 + \$57$?
   Possible answer: Think of $\$22 + \$57$ as $22 + 57$. Start at 22 and move forward 5 tens and 7 ones. $22 + 57 = 79$, so $\$22 + \$57 = \$79$

4. Are there two ways to find $17 + 64$ on a hundred chart? Explain.
   Yes; you could start at 17 and move forward 6 tens and 4 ones or start at 64 and move forward 1 ten and 7 ones.

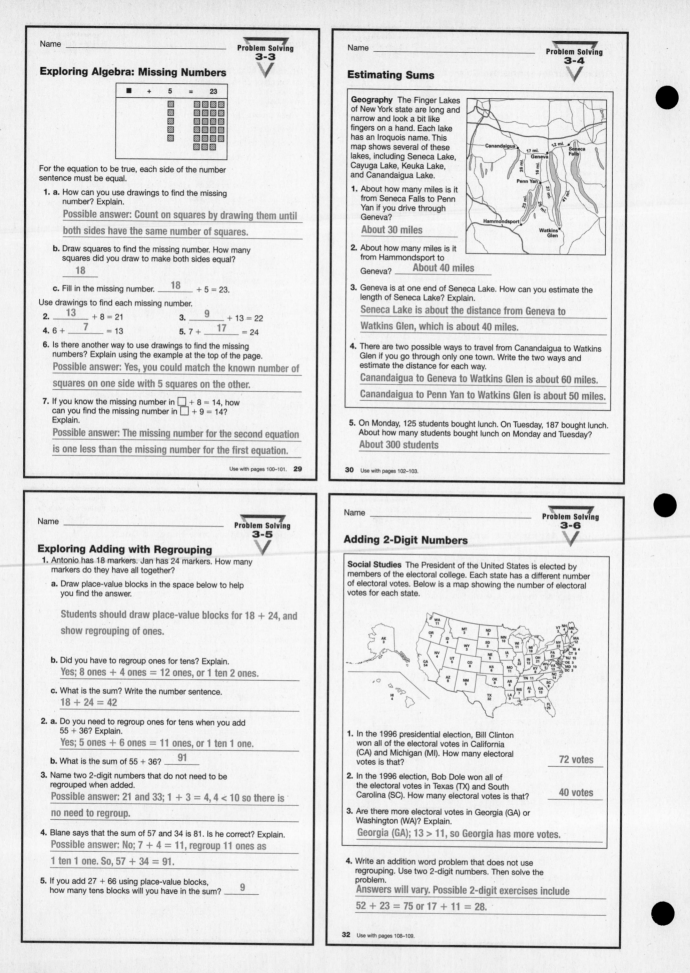

Exploring Algebra: Missing Numbers

| ■ | + | 5 | = | 23 |

For the equation to be true, each side of the number sentence must be equal.

1. a. How can you use drawings to find the missing number? Explain.

Possible answer: Count on squares by drawing them until both sides have the same number of squares.

b. Draw squares to find the missing number. How many squares did you draw to make both sides equal?

18

c. Fill in the missing number. 18 + 5 = 23.

Use drawings to find each missing number.

2. 13 + 8 = 21   **3.** 9 + 13 = 22

4. 6 + 7 = 13   **5.** 7 + 17 = 24

6. Is there another way to use drawings to find the missing numbers? Explain using the example at the top of the page.

Possible answer: Yes, you could match the known number of squares on one side with 5 squares on the other.

7. If you know the missing number in ☐ + 8 = 14, how can you find the missing number in ☐ + 9 = 14? Explain.

Possible answer: The missing number for the second equation is one less than the missing number for the first equation.

Use with pages 100–101. **29**

Estimating Sums

Geography The Finger Lakes of New York state are long and narrow and look a bit like fingers on a hand. Each lake has an Iroquois name. This map shows several of these lakes, including Seneca Lake, Cayuga Lake, Keuka Lake, and Canandaigua Lake.

1. About how many miles is it from Seneca Falls to Penn Yan if you drive through Geneva?

About 30 miles

2. About how many miles is it from Hammondsport to Geneva? About 40 miles

3. Geneva is at one end of Seneca Lake. How can you estimate the length of Seneca Lake? Explain.

Seneca Lake is about the distance from Geneva to Watkins Glen, which is about 40 miles.

4. There are two possible ways to travel from Canandaigua to Watkins Glen if you go through only one town. Write the two ways and estimate the distance for each way.

Canandaigua to Geneva to Watkins Glen is about 60 miles.

Canandaigua to Penn Yan to Watkins Glen is about 50 miles.

5. On Monday, 125 students bought lunch. On Tuesday, 187 bought lunch. About how many students bought lunch on Monday and Tuesday?

About 300 students

30 Use with pages 102–103.

Exploring Adding with Regrouping

1. Antonio has 18 markers. Jan has 24 markers. How many markers do they have all together?

a. Draw place-value blocks in the space below to help you find the answer.

Students should draw place-value blocks for 18 + 24, and show regrouping of ones.

b. Did you have to regroup ones for tens? Explain.
Yes; 8 ones + 4 ones = 12 ones, or 1 ten 2 ones.

c. What is the sum? Write the number sentence.
18 + 24 = 42

2. a. Do you need to regroup ones for tens when you add 55 + 36? Explain.
Yes; 5 ones + 6 ones = 11 ones, or 1 ten 1 one.

b. What is the sum of 55 + 36? 91

3. Name two 2-digit numbers that do not need to be regrouped when added.
Possible answer: 21 and 33; 1 + 3 = 4, 4 < 10 so there is no need to regroup.

4. Blane says that the sum of 57 and 34 is 81. Is he correct? Explain.
Possible answer: No; 7 + 4 = 11, regroup 11 ones as 1 ten 1 one. So, 57 + 34 = 91.

5. If you add 27 + 66 using place-value blocks, how many tens blocks will you have in the sum? 9

Adding 2-Digit Numbers

Social Studies The President of the United States is elected by members of the electoral college. Each state has a different number of electoral votes. Below is a map showing the number of electoral votes for each state.

1. In the 1996 presidential election, Bill Clinton won all of the electoral votes in California (CA) and Michigan (MI). How many electoral votes is that?

72 votes

2. In the 1996 election, Bob Dole won all of the electoral votes in Texas (TX) and South Carolina (SC). How many electoral votes is that?

40 votes

3. Are there more electoral votes in Georgia (GA) or Washington (WA)? Explain.

Georgia (GA); 13 > 11, so Georgia has more votes.

4. Write an addition word problem that does not use regrouping. Use two 2-digit numbers. Then solve the problem.

Answers will vary. Possible 2-digit exercises include 52 + 23 = 75 or 17 + 11 = 28.

32 Use with pages 108–109.

Adding 3-Digit Numbers

The town of Oakdale prepared a time capsule. Students at two schools in the town wrote letters for the capsule. The table shows how many letters were written by each grade in the schools. Use the table to answer the questions.

Grade	Oakville School	Maple Street School
1	107	96
2	116	212
3	87	123
4	263	107
5	198	254

1. How many letters did all the students in Grade 4 write for the capsule? _____ 370

2. How many letters were written by students in Grades 1 and 2 at Oakville School? At Maple Tree School? _____ 223; 308

3. Who wrote more letters, all students in Grade 1 or all students in Grade 3? _____ Grade 3

4. Which grade wrote the most letters? How many?
Grade 5; 452

5. **Choose a Strategy** Newspapers and magazines were also put in Oakdale's time capsule. A total of 51 pages were put in the capsule. The number of newspaper pages was 34. How many magazine pages were put in the capsule?

- Use Objects/Act It Out
- Draw a Picture
- Look for a Pattern
- Guess and Check
- Use Logical Reasoning
- Make an Organized List
- Make a Table
- Solve a Simpler Problem
- Work Backward

a. What strategy would you use to solve the problem?

Possible answer: Draw a Picture or Guess and Check.

b. Answer the problem. _____ 17 pages

Adding 4-Digit Numbers: Choose a Calculation Method

Science Jupiter, the largest planet in the solar system, has 16 known satellites or moons. The four largest moons were discovered by Galileo in 1610. Their names and diameters are given in the following table.

Moon	Diameter in miles
Ganymede	3,275
Europa	1,945
Callisto	3,008
Io	2,262

1. Which moon has the greatest diameter? _____ Ganymede
2. Which moon has a diameter closest to 3,000 miles? _____ Callisto
3. What is the total of the diameters of Io and Europa? _____ 4,207 mi
4. What is the total of the diameters of the two largest moons? _____ 6,283 mi

5. Ian traveled 2,136 miles to visit her grandfather. Then she traveled 1,814 miles to visit her aunt. How far did she travel in all? _____ 3,950 mi

6a. To go from Minneapolis to Phoenix by plane you travel 1,270 miles. To continue your trip to Portland, Oregon you go another 1,009 miles. How far will you travel? _____ 2,279 mi

b. Is the distance from Minneapolis to Phoenix or from Phoenix to Portland greater?
Minneapolis to Phoenix

Column Addition

Science The General Sherman tree is a redwood tree in California. It is over 275 feet tall! Not all trees grow to such great heights. The table gives the average height of other trees found in the United States.

Tree	Average Height
American Holly	40 to 50 feet
American Mountain Ash	20 to 30 feet
Pecan	90 to 120 feet
Red Maple	50 to 70 feet
Sugar Pine	175 to 200 feet

1. About how many American holly trees would equal the height of a sugar pine with the tallest average height?

4 trees to 5 trees

2. What is the least number of pecan trees you'd need to reach the same height as the General Sherman tree?

3 pecan trees

3. Suppose one of each type of tree of the greatest average height listed was cut down. If the trees were laid end to end, what distance would they cover?

470 feet

Trees need water just as people do. A large apple tree can take in 95 gallons of water in a single day!

4. At this rate, how much water would 3 apple trees take in?

285 gallons

5. How much water would 1 apple tree take in during a week?

665 gallons

GPS PROBLEM 4, STUDENT PAGE 121

The sum of two numbers is 80. The numbers are 2 apart. What are they?

— **Understand** —

1. What do you know about the two numbers that the problem asks you to find?
Their sum is 80. The numbers are 2 apart.

— **Plan** —

2. Write 3 pairs of numbers in the table whose sum is 80. Find their differences.

— **Solve** —

3. How do your differences compare to the difference you need? Write your comments in the table.

4. Use your previous guesses to help you make more guesses. Continue filling in the table until you find a pair of numbers that work. What are the two numbers?
39 and 41

Possible answers:

Pairs of Numbers		Sum	Difference	Comments
30	50	80	20	Too high
60	20	80	40	Too high
40	40	80	0	Too low
35	45	80	10	Too high
38	42	80	4	Almost!
39	41	80	2	That's it!

— **Look Back** —

5. How can you be sure your answer is correct?
Double check to make sure the sum of the pair is 80 and their difference is 2.

SOLVE ANOTHER PROBLEM

Use guess and check to answer this problem. The sum of two numbers is 96. The numbers are 6 apart. What are they?
45 and 51

Mental Math

Recreation The 1994 Winter Olympic Games were held in Lillehammer, Norway. The chart shows the number of medals won by 5 different countries at the games.

Country	Gold	Silver	Bronze
Russia	11	8	14
Germany	9	7	8
South Korea	4	1	1
Norway	10	11	5
United States	6	5	2

Use the table and mental math to answer these questions.

1. What was the total number of medals won by the United States?

   13 medals

2. Which country won the most medals? How many were won?

   Russia, 33 medals

3. How many gold medals were won by these five countries?

   40 gold medals

Oak Street School held an art fair. The chart shows the number of ribbons won by each grade. Use the chart to answer the questions.

Grade	Blue	Red	White
1	12	5	9
2	18	7	4
3	15	8	5
4	19	6	3

4. Which two grades won the same number of ribbons?

   Grades 3 and 4

5. Which grade won the greatest number of ribbons? How many?

   Grade 2; 29 ribbons

6. How many blue ribbons were awarded at the art fair?

   64 blue ribbons

Counting Coins

Recreation One of Sarah's favorite hobbies is coin collecting. She collects nickels, dimes and quarters. Sarah uses a chart to record the original value of the coins she adds to her collection each week.

Week	Total
1	$1.30
2	$1.65
3	$1.30
4	$1.65

1. What 8 coins did Sarah add to her collection the first and third week?

   4 quarters, 2 dimes, 2 nickels

2. What 8 coins did Sarah add to her collection the second and fourth week?

   6 quarters, 1 dime, 1 nickel

3. a. What is the greatest number of coins you could use to buy a pencil that costs 36 cents? ___36___

   b. What are the coins?

   36 pennies

4. a. Using quarters and lesser coins, what is the least number of coins you could use to buy a notebook that costs 79 cents? ___7___

   b. What are the coins?

   3 quarters, 4 pennies

5. Lee has 49 cents. She has the following coins plus 5 more coins. What are the other coins Lee has?

   2 nickels, 3 pennies

Using Dollars and Cents

Careers A store clerk must count the money in the cash register at the end of each day. Suppose you are a store clerk. The following change is in your cash register at the end of the day. Find the total value of each set of coins. Then tell the total value of all the coins.

1. $2.25

2. $1.40

3. $0.45

4. $0.11

5. The total value of all the coins is ___$4.21___.

Someone gives you $3.12 using no bills.

6. What is the least number of coins you could get using quarters and lesser coins? Name them.

   15 coins; 12 quarters, 1 dime, 2 pennies

7. What is the greatest number of coins you could get? Name them.

   312; 312 pennies

8. If you get 30 dimes, will you get any quarters? Explain.

   No; 30 dimes = $3.00. The remainder is $0.12 which is not enough for a quarter.

9. What is the greatest number of nickels you could get?

   62

Exploring Making Change

You are going to the art supply store with $5.00. You can buy one item but you need to return home with some change.

You decide to buy a color marker for $1.17.

$1.17

1. Count on to find out how much change you will receive. Which coin will you count on first? Why?

   Pennies; it is easier to count on from $1.20.

2. Draw coins to show your counting-on strategy. Write the amounts under the coins.

   Possible answer: 3 pennies, 3 dimes, 2 quarters, 3 dollar bills; $1.18, $1.19, $1.20, $1.30, $1.40, $1.50, $1.75, $2.00, $3.00, $4.00, $5.00

3. How much is your change? ___$3.83___

4. What is another way you can count on to find the answer? Explain.

   Possible answer: You can use nickels and count on with 3 pennies, 2 nickels, 2 dimes, 2 quarters, and 3 dollar bills.

5. Name three other ways you can receive your change. Which coins and bills can you use?

   Possible answers: 3 pennies, 5 nickels, 3 dimes, 5 quarters, 2 dollar bills; 3 pennies, 10 nickels, 13 dimes, 2 dollar bills; 3 pennies, 8 dimes, 12 quarters; 33 pennies, 14 quarters

Adding Money

Fine Arts Your school's band is selling used instruments and musical supplies to raise money for a trip to New York City to march in the Thanksgiving Day Parade.

Price List	
music stand	$6.68
drum sticks	$5.54
saxophone reeds	$1.19
used recorder	$3.93
sheet music	$1.21

1. Joseph bought sheet music and a music stand. How much did both items cost?

   $7.89

2. You have $6.50. Which three items could you buy?

   The saxophone reeds, sheet music and the used recorder

3. What is the sum of the cost of your purchases and Joseph's purchases?

   $14.22

4. What is the greatest amount of money you could spend on 2 items? Which items?

   $12.22; Music stand and drum sticks

5. Which amount is greater?

   a. 3 dollars, 2 quarters, 2 dimes, 1 nickel, 1 penny, or $3.86

   $3.86; $3.86 is more than $3.76.

   b. 4 dollars, 1 quarter, 2 dimes, 7 pennies, or $4.49

   4 dollars, 1 quarter, 2 dimes, 7 pennies; $4.52 is more than $4.49.

6. Will $15.00 be enough to buy a plant that costs $7.95 and a plant stand that costs $11.35? Explain.

   No; $7.95 + $11.35 = $19.30, $19.30 > $15.00

Front-End Estimation

Social Studies The table shows the amount of money the average person spends on food items in one year. Use front-end estimation and the table to answer the questions.

Money Spent on Food	
Food	Cost
Cereal	$ 77
Eggs	$ 17
Meat	$331
Milk	$ 66
Fruits	$135
Vegetables	$117

1. Is the amount of money spent on fruits and vegetables greater or less than the amount spent on meat? Explain.

   Less than; $200 < $300

2. Is $200 enough money to budget for fruit and vegetables? Explain.

   No; The front-end estimate is $200, but both items are greater than $100.

3. About how much would a family of three spend on cereal in one year?

   About $210

4. Tickets to the State Fair cost $6.75 for adults and $3.50 for students. Is $11.00 enough for 1 adult and 2 students? Explain.

   No; $6.00 + $3.00 + $3.00 is more than $11.00.

5. Three groups of students go on a class trip to New York City. The groups have 11, 25, and 17 students. One elevator at the Empire State Building holds 40 people. Can all three groups fit in one elevator? Explain.

   No; 10 + 20 + 10 = 40, but each group has more students than shown by front-end estimation.

GPS PROBLEM 4, STUDENT PAGE 139

Blaine wants to know if $8.00 is enough to buy a guidebook and a compass. Does he need to find the exact total? Explain.

Supplies	
Hammer	$15.80
Guidebook	$ 2.95
Gloves	$ 5.89
Compass	$ 5.49

— Understand —

1. What do you know? What do you need to find out?

   Blaine has $8.00. Guidebook costs $2.95. Compass costs $5.49. Is the total cost of the 2 items greater than $8.00?

— Plan —

2. How will you decide if an exact answer or an estimate will do?

   Estimating may not work, numbers look close to $8.00.

— Solve —

3. Estimate. $2.95 is close to $3.00, $5.49 is close to $5.00, $3.00 + $5.00 = $8.00.

4. Do you need to find the exact answer to solve the problem? Explain, then answer the problem.

   Yes, the exact answer is $8.44. $8.00 is not enough.

SOLVE ANOTHER PROBLEM

Write if you need an exact answer or an estimate. Can Blaine buy a hammer and a guidebook with $20? Explain.

Estimate. Both prices round to greater numbers whose total is less than $20 so you know $20 is enough.

Reviewing the Meaning of Subtraction

Physical Education To qualify for the President's Physical Fitness Award students must score in the 85th percentile on 5 physical fitness items. Students do curlups, shuttle runs, 1 mile walk/runs, pull-ups and V-sit reaches.

Write a number sentence for each. Then solve.

1. Carrie did six curlups. Timothy did four. How many more curlups did Carrie do than Timothy?

   6 − 4 = 2; 2 curlups

2. Yvonne did six pull-ups and Helen did five. How many pull-ups did they do all together?

   6 + 5 = 11; 11 pull-ups

3. Jon did eight V-sit reaches on Monday and nine on Tuesday. How many V-sit reaches did he do all together?

   8 + 9 = 17; 17 V-sit reaches

4. Ned wants to do eight shuttle runs. He has done five already. How many more shuttle runs does he have to run?

   8 − 5 = 3; 3 shuttle runs

5. The boys' chorus will sing five songs. The girls' chorus will sing four. How many songs will be sung all together?

   5 + 4 = 9; 9 songs

6. The band will play eight songs. Four of these songs will be slow songs. The other songs will be fast songs. How many songs will be fast?

   8 − 4 = 4; 4 songs

7. Carlos will sing three songs at the school concert. Tanya will sing five. How many more songs will Tanya sing than Carlos?

   5 − 3 = 2; 2 songs

Name _____

Exploring Subtraction Patterns
Answer the following questions.

1. How is subtracting 900 − 200 like subtracting 9 − 2?

9 − 2 = 7; 9 hundreds − 2 hundreds = 7 hundreds

2. What basic fact can you use to find $60 − $30? Explain.

6 − 3 = 3; 6 tens − 3 tens = 3 tens

3. How could you check your work if you wrote
70 − 40 = 30?
Possible answers: 30 + 40 = 70; 7 − 4 = 3;

7 tens − 4 tens = 3 tens

4. How is subtracting $1,200 − $800 like subtracting
$12 − $8?

12 − 8 = 4; 12 hundreds − 8 hundreds = 4 hundreds

5. Suppose it takes you 30 minutes to ride your bike to
school and 70 minutes to walk to school. How much
longer does it take you to walk than to ride?

40 minutes

6. Calvin scored 20 points in one basketball game. Susan
scored 40 points. How many more points did Susan
score than Calvin?

20 points

7. Vanessa had 40 minutes of homework last night. She
has 90 minutes tonight. How many more minutes of
homework does she have tonight?

50 minutes

8. Alice had 500 sheets of notebook paper. During the
school year she used 200 sheets. How many sheets did
she have at the end of the school year?

300 sheets

Name _____

Exploring Subtracting on a Hundred Chart
Use a hundred chart to answer each question.

1. Choose a number greater than 35. **Check students' answers.**

a. What number is 7 less than your number? _____

b. 17 less than your number? _____

c. 27 less than your number? _____

d. Explain the steps you took to solve the problems.

Possible answer: Started at 46, moved back 7 ones

to 39; moved back 1 ten and 7 ones to 29; moved back

2 tens and 7 ones to 19.

e. What do you notice about your answers to **a–c**?
They all have the same ones digit.

2. Describe two ways to find 64 − 49 on a hundred chart.

Possible answers: Move back 5 rows and forward 1 space;

Move back 4 rows and back 9 spaces.

3. On a hundred chart, start with your finger on 87. Move
back 3 rows and 9 spaces.

a. On what number do you land? _48_

b. What number did you subtract? _39_

4. How can you find 74 − 40 by counting by 10's?
Possible answer: 74, 64, 54, 44, 34; 74 − 40 = 34

5. Phillip chose a number that is 32 less than 61. What is
the number? Explain.

29; 61 − 32 = 29

Name _____

Estimating Differences

Science The drawing below shows the number of days it
takes some of the planets in our solar system to orbit the
sun. One full orbit of the sun is one year.

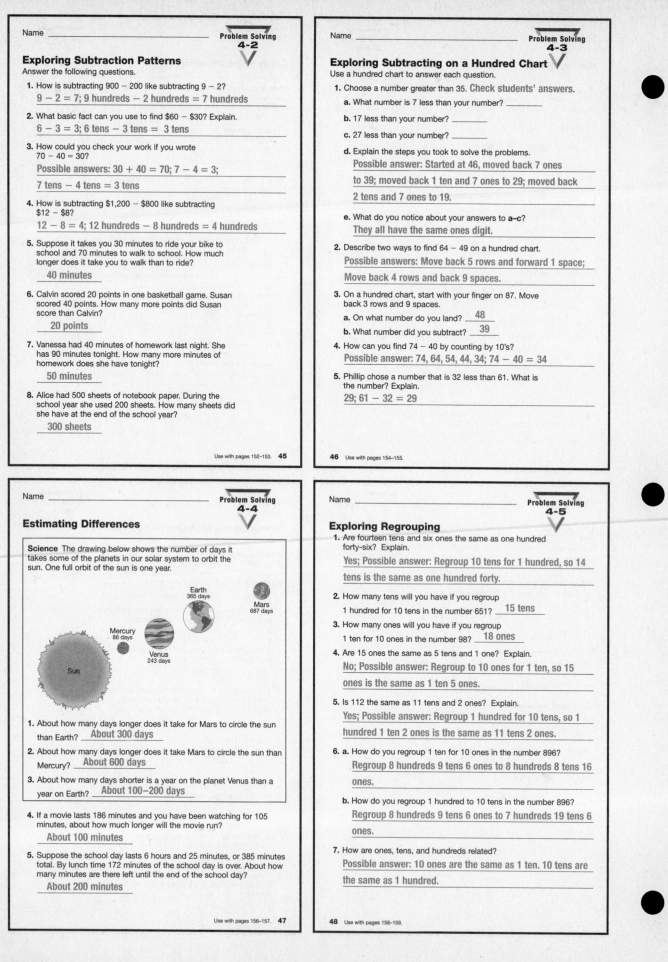

Earth
365 days

Mars
687 days

Mercury
86 days

Venus
243 days

Sun

1. About how many days longer does it take for Mars to circle the sun
than Earth? _About 300 days_

2. About how many days longer does it take Mars to circle the sun than
Mercury? _About 600 days_

3. About how many days shorter is a year on the planet Venus than a
year on Earth? _About 100–200 days_

4. If a movie lasts 186 minutes and you have been watching for 105
minutes, about how much longer will the movie run?

About 100 minutes

5. Suppose the school day lasts 6 hours and 25 minutes, or 385 minutes
total. By lunch time 172 minutes of the school day is over. About how
many minutes are there left until the end of the school day?

About 200 minutes

Name _____

Exploring Regrouping

1. Are fourteen tens and six ones the same as one hundred
forty-six? Explain.

Yes; Possible answer: Regroup 10 tens for 1 hundred, so 14

tens is the same as one hundred forty.

2. How many tens will you have if you regroup
1 hundred for 10 tens in the number 651? _15 tens_

3. How many ones will you have if you regroup
1 ten for 10 ones in the number 98? _18 ones_

4. Are 15 ones the same as 5 tens and 1 one? Explain.

No; Possible answer: Regroup to 10 ones for 1 ten, so 15

ones is the same as 1 ten 5 ones.

5. Is 112 the same as 11 tens and 2 ones? Explain.

Yes; Possible answer: Regroup 1 hundred for 10 tens, so 1

hundred 1 ten 2 ones is the same as 11 tens 2 ones.

6. a. How do you regroup 1 ten for 10 ones in the number 896?

Regroup 8 hundreds 9 tens 6 ones to 8 hundreds 8 tens 16

ones.

b. How do you regroup 1 hundred to 10 tens in the number 896?

Regroup 8 hundreds 9 tens 6 ones to 7 hundreds 19 tens 6

ones.

7. How are ones, tens, and hundreds related?

Possible answer: 10 ones are the same as 1 ten. 10 tens are

the same as 1 hundred.

Exploring Subtracting 2-Digit Numbers

The number of cable television channels that you can watch on your television depends on where you live. Here is a list of some towns and the number of channels they have available to watch.

Town	Number of Cable Channels
Acton	63
Springfield	45
Border City	36

1. Suppose you want to find out the difference between the number of channels in Acton and the number of channels in Border City.

a. Would you need to regroup? Explain.

Yes; You cannot subtract 6 ones from 3 ones; regroup 1 ten for 10 ones for a total of 13 ones.

b. What is the difference? ___27 channels___

2. Suppose you want to find out the difference between the number of channels in Acton and the number in Springfield.

a. Would you need to regroup? Explain.

Yes; You cannot subtract 5 ones from 3 ones; Regroup 1 ten for 10 ones for a total of 13 ones.

b. What is the difference? ___18 channels___

3. Suppose you moved from Springfield to Border City. Find out how many channels you would lose.

a. Do you have to regroup to subtract? Explain.

Yes; You cannot subtract 6 ones from 5 ones; regroup 1 ten for 10 ones for a total of 15 ones.

b. How many channels would you lose?

You would lose 9 channels.

Subtracting 2-Digit Numbers

Geography The month of January can be very cold in some parts of the world. However, it can be very warm in other places. Here are some average temperatures for the month of January from around the world.

City	Average January Temperature °F
Bombay, India	88
Shanghai, China	47
Bogotá, Colombia	67
Sidney, Australia	78
Montreal, Canada	21
Tampa, Florida	60
Des Moines, Iowa	19
Nairobi, Kenya	77
San Francisco, California	49

1. a. What is the warmest city in January in the table?

___Bombay, India___

b. What is the coldest city in January in the table?

___Des Moines, Iowa___

c. What is the difference in temperature between the warmest city and the coldest city? ___69 degrees___

2. How much colder is it in San Francisco, California than in Bogotá, Columbia? ___18 degrees___

3. How much warmer is it in Tampa, Florida than in Montreal, Canada? ___39 degrees___

4. Arthur is 53 inches tall. His 3-year-old brother, Andrew, is 25 inches tall. How much taller is Arthur than Andrew? ___28 inches___

5. Bill made 34 oatmeal cookies for the art club's bake sale. Kathie made 18 gingerbread cookies. How many more cookies did Bill make than Kathie? ___16 cookies___

6. Justin exercised for 42 minutes on Friday and 33 minutes on Saturday. How many more minutes did he exercise on Friday? ___9 minutes___

Exploring Subtracting 3-Digit Numbers

1. Find the difference of 148 and 92.

a. Draw place-value blocks in the space below to show 148 − 92.

b. Do you need to regroup? Explain.

Yes; To subtract 9 tens from 4 tens I must regroup 1 hundred for 10 tens.

c. What is the difference of 148 and 92? ___56___

2. Would you have to regroup to find 233 − 183? Explain.

Yes; To subtract 8 tens from 3 tens I must regroup 1 hundred for 10 tens.

3. Would you have to regroup to find the difference of 364 and 136? Explain.

Yes; To subtract 6 ones from 4 ones I must regroup 1 ten for 10 ones.

4. Johanna says, "To find 323 − 142, you need to regroup a hundred." Do you agree? Explain.

Yes; You need to regroup 1 hundred for 10 tens.

5. Suppose you had 2 hundreds blocks, 3 tens blocks, and 8 ones blocks. Could you subtract 56 without regrouping? Explain.

No; You would have to regroup 1 hundred for 10 tens.

Subtracting 3-Digit Numbers

Technology When we hear the word technology, we often think of computers. However, technology can mean many things. Drawbridges are an example of technology. Drawbridges are special bridges that can be raised, lowered, or drawn aside so that boats can pass under them.

1. The Arthur Kill drawbridge connecting New York and New Jersey is 558 feet long and is the longest drawbridge in the United States. The Second Narrows bridge in Vancouver, British Columbia is the longest drawbridge in Canada and is 493 feet long. How much longer is the Arthur Kill drawbridge than the Second Narrows drawbridge? ___65 feet___

2. Two of the largest drawbridges in the United States are in Florida. They are the Main Street bridge in Jacksonville, at 386 feet and the St. Andrew's Bay bridge in Panama City, at 327 feet. What is the difference in length of the two drawbridges? ___59 feet___

3. The Marine Parkway drawbridge in New York City is 540 feet long. The Martinez railroad drawbridge in California is 328 feet long. How much shorter is the Martinez bridge than the Marine Parkway bridge? ___212 feet___

4. There are 219 students in the 4th grade at Tammy's school. There are 188 students in the 3rd grade. How many more students are in the 4th grade than in the 3rd grade? ___31___

5. The rug in Theresa's living room is 116 inches long and 74 inches wide. What is the difference between the rug's length and width? ___42 inches___

6. Ryan has read a total of 365 pages in his book. Yesterday he had read to page 229. How many pages did he read today? ___136 pages___

Subtracting with 2 Regroupings

1. How many more students are there in the 3rd grade than in the 4th grade? __54__

2. How many fewer students are there in 1st grade than in the 2nd grade? __68__

3. If there are 249 girls in the 3rd grade, how many boys are in the 3rd grade? __173__

Students at County Elementary School	
1st grade	347
2nd grade	415
3rd grade	422
4th grade	368

4. What is the total number of students in all four grades? __1,552 students__

5. Suppose 14 new students will be entering the third grade next year and none of the current students leave. How many students will there be in the third grade?

   __429 students__

6. Janine had 213 thumb tacks. She has 176 left. How many did she use?

   __37__

7. Aaron was in school 176 days last year. How many days was Aaron not in school? (Remember: 1 year = 365 days)

   __189 days__

8. **Choose a strategy** Farmer Joe has 551 animals on his farm. He only has cows and pigs. There are 394 cows on the farm. How many pigs are on the farm?

   a. What strategy would you use to solve the problem?

   __Possible answers: Guess and Check__

   b. Answer the problem. __157 pigs__

   - Use Objects/Act It Out
   - Draw a Picture
   - Look for a Pattern
   - Guess and Check
   - Use Logical Reasoning
   - Make an Organized List
   - Make a Table
   - Solve a Simpler Problem
   - Work Backward

Subtracting Across 0

Health The table shows the amount of calories in certain foods. Use the chart to solve the problems.

Food	Calories	Food	Calories
Apple juice, 1 cup	120	Lentil soup, 1 cup	606
Beef stew, 1 cup	260	Lobster, 1 cup	105
Chocolate malted milk	502	Macaroni and cheese, $\frac{1}{2}$ cup	215
Flounder, baked, 1 serving	204	Wild rice, cooked, $\frac{2}{3}$ cup	103

1. Ted had 1 cup of apple juice. Paula had a chocolate malted milk. How many more calories did Paula have? __382 calories__

2. Maleek had baked flounder for dinner. Jerome had lobster. How many more calories did Maleek have? __99 calories__

3. What is the difference in calories between 1 cup of beef stew and $\frac{1}{2}$ cup of macaroni and cheese? __45 calories__

4. Carly decided to have $\frac{2}{3}$ cup of wild rice with her dinner instead of 1 cup of lentil soup. How many fewer calories did she have? __503 calories__

Solve the problems.

5. Dina burned 360 calories playing volleyball for one hour. Pam burned 288 calories bowling. How many more calories did Dina burn than Pam? __72 calories__

6. Scrubbing floors burns 360 calories per hour. Walking fast burns 480. How many more calories does walking fast burn? __120 calories__

Subtracting 4-Digit Numbers: Choose a Calculation Method

Geography Cities across the United States are different in many ways. For example, the temperature in January can be very cold in New York City while it is very warm in Los Angeles, California. Some cities are surrounded by mountains, like Denver, Colorado and some cities are next to lakes, like Chicago, Illinois. Think about how far these cities are from one another, and what differences you might see between them.

1. Between 1962 and 1991, Florida had a total of 1,590 tornadoes. During the same period of time, Nebraska had 1,118 tornadoes. How many fewer tornadoes did Nebraska have than Florida? __472 tornadoes__

2. Iowa had 1,079 tornadoes from 1962 to 1991, and Texas had 4,174. How many more tornadoes did Texas have than Iowa? __3,095 tornadoes__

3. Kansas had 1,198 tornadoes, and Oklahoma had 1,412. How many more did Oklahoma have? __214 tornadoes__

4. There are 3,291 ants in the ant colony at the State University. There are 1,583 ants in the ant colony at City College. How many more ants are in the colony at the State University than at City College? __1,708 ants__

5. Ms. Atkins is shopping for a new computer for her business. She has narrowed her choices down to two computers. One costs $3,465 and the other costs $2,870. What is the difference in the two prices? __$595__

GPS PROBLEM 5, STUDENT PAGE 185

Joy hiked in Bryce Canyon for an hour. She took one 10-minute rest and one 13-minute rest. How many minutes did she walk?

— Understand —

1. How many minutes are in one hour? __60 minutes__

2. About how long did Joy rest? __About 20 minutes__

3. Which of these is a reasonable answer to the question?

   A. about 60 min   B. about 20 min   C. about 40 min   D. about 30 min

— Plan —

4. What steps will you take to solve the problem?

   __Add the time Joy spent resting, then subtract from 60.__

— Solve —

5. Write number sentences to solve.

   __10 + 13 = 23; 60 − 23 = 37__

6. Joy walked __37__ minutes.

— Look Back —

7. Does your answer make sense? How do you know?

   __Possible answer: Yes; 37 is close to my estimate of 40.__

SOLVE ANOTHER PROBLEM

Maddie has $12. Jim has $3 less than Maddie. How much more money does Jim need to buy a theme park admission ticket that costs $20?

__$11__

Mental Math

Recreation Ice hockey began in Canada in the mid-1800s. The National Hockey League was formed in 1916 and has been in operation ever since. It is made up of teams from the United States and Canada.

1. There was a disagreement between the players and the owners at the beginning of the 1994–1995 hockey season. The season was only 48 games rather than the usual 84. How many fewer games did they play?   **36**

2. During the 1994–1995 season, the Boston Bruins won 27 games and lost 18 games. How many more games did they win than lose?   **9**

3. In the 1994–1995 season, there were 26 teams in the NHL with 19 teams in the United States. The other teams were from Canada. How many teams were from Canada?   **7**

4. In the year 2,000, how many years old will the National Hockey League be?   **84 years old**

5. Hawaii is the only state made up entirely of islands. There are 122 Hawaiian islands. People live on 7 of the islands. How many islands do not have people living on them?   **115**

6. In 1788, Maryland became the seventh state to enter into the Union, which later became known as the United States. How many years ago was that?   **Check students' answers.**

7. In 1997 there were 30 countries in Europe. 15 of them belonged to the European Union. How many did not?   **15**

8. 9 countries applied to join the European Union. If they all joined, how many countries would be members?   **24**

Subtracting Money

Careers This advertisement shows regular and sale prices. Use the advertisement to answer the questions.

Strong's Annual August Sale		
	Regular	Sale
Twin sheet (flat or fitted)	$18.50	$12.99
Full sheet (flat or fitted)	$24.49	$15.89
Queen sheet (flat or fitted)	$28.65	$18.98
Standard pillowcases (2)	$14.39	$12.99
King pillowcases (2)	$18.79	$14.99
Down comforter (any size)	$150 – $280	$129.99

1. A salesperson sold a queen sheet in July. How much less would he have charged the customer in August?   **$9.67**

2. If the regular price of a comforter is $220, how much less is the sale price?   **$90.01**

3. What is the difference between the regular prices of standard pillowcases and king pillowcases?   **$4.40**

4. By how much did the store manager reduce 2 king pillowcases for the August sale?   **$3.80**

5. Which costs more? _____ **b**

   a. 2 full sheets at the regular price

   b. 2 queen sheets and 2 king pillowcases at the sale price

6. The sale price of jeans that regularly sell for $42.00 is $28.99. What is the price difference?   **$13.01**

7. Sunglasses are on sale for $12.49 instead of $15.98. What is the price difference?   **$3.49**

GPS PROBLEM 5, STUDENT PAGE 192

Amy, Santiago, and their mother and father are in line for the ferry to the Statue of Liberty. Amy is the only person between her mother and father. Santiago is directly behind his mother. Who is first in line?

— Understand —

1. What does the problem ask you to find?
   Who is first in line

2. How many people in the family are waiting in line? ____ **4**

— Plan —

3. Use counters to act out the problem. What will the counters show?
   Possible answer: One counter for each person in line

— Solve —

4. Draw a picture on a separate sheet of paper to show how you can use counters to solve this problem.   **Check students' drawings.**

5. Who is first in line?   **Father**

— Look Back —

6. What other strategy could you use to solve this problem?
   Possible answers: Make an Organized List.

SOLVE ANOTHER PROBLEM

Amy and her family are talking to a man, woman, and teenager while they are standing in line. The man is in front of Amy's father. The teenager is the only person between Santiago and the woman. Who is last in line?
   The woman

Exploring Equal Groups

Write the next three numbers in each pattern. Then write the rule used to make the pattern.

1. 2, 4, 6, 8, __**10**__, __**12**__, __**14**__
   Rule: **Add 2.**

2. 5, 10, 15, 20, __**25**__, __**30**__, __**35**__
   Rule: **Add 5.**

3. 3, 6, 9, 12, __**15**__, __**18**__, __**21**__
   Rule: **Add 3.**

4. 4, 8, 12, 16, __**20**__, __**24**__, __**28**__
   Rule: **Add 4.**

5. 6, 12, 18, 24, __**30**__, __**36**__, __**42**__
   Rule: **Add 6.**

6. 7, 14, 21, 28, __**35**__, __**42**__, __**49**__
   Rule: **Add 7.**

7. 9, 18, 27, 36, __**45**__, __**54**__, __**63**__
   Rule: **Add 9.**

8. 10, 20, 30, 40, __**50**__, __**60**__, __**70**__
   Rule: **Add 10.**

9. Do you see a pattern as you answer each question and state each rule?
   Each pattern begins with the number that is added in the rule.

Writing Multiplication Sentences

Careers A worker is packing juice boxes.
Juice boxes come 3 to a pack.

1. The worker puts 4 packs in a container.
How many boxes of juice is that?

12 boxes

2. The worker puts 5 packs in a container. How many
boxes of juice is that?

15 boxes

3. Suppose juice boxes cost $1.19 a pack. How
much would 2 packs cost?

$2.38

4. What operations could you use to solve the problems above?

Addition or multiplication

Use the table for **4–7.**

Apple Cider Sale	
1 Half-Gallon	$2.50
1 Gallon	$4.00
2 half-gallons = 1 gallon	

4. How many gallons of cider can you buy for $8? **2 gallons**

5. How much would $1\frac{1}{2}$ gallons of cider cost? **$6.50**

6. Suppose you have $3. How much cider could you buy?

1 half-gallon

7. Suppose you want 1 gallon of cider. Which would you
buy: 2 half-gallons or 1 gallon? Explain.

1 gallon of cider; 2 half-gallons cost $5, but 1 gallon only

costs $4, so you would save $1.

Exploring Multiplication Stories

Look at each picture. Decide if you can write a multiplication
story about it. For yes, write a multiplication story that goes
with the picture. For no, explain.

1.

Yes; Look for 3 groups of 6; 18

2.

No; There are 4 groups that are not equal so you can't multiply.

3.

Yes; Look for 5 groups of 6 or 6 groups of 5; 30

4.

Yes; Look for 3 groups of 4; 12

---

2 as a Factor

Art Use the recipe to answer **1–2.**

Modeling Dough Recipe

1 cup salt
2 cups hot water
4 cups flour

Makes about 5 cups of modeling dough.

1. Lee wants to make twice as much dough. He multiplies each
ingredient by 2.

a. How much salt does he need? **2 cups**

b. How much water does he need? **4 cups**

c. How much flour does he need? **8 cups**

d. How much dough would he make? **About 10 cups**

2. Suppose each person in your class wants 1 cup of
dough. How many cups of dough would you need? **Cups of dough**

should equal the number of students in the class.

Marisol makes friendship bracelets. She sells them
for $2 each.

3. She sold 3 bracelets. How much money did
she make?

$6

4. She made 4 bracelets Friday, 5 bracelets Saturday,
and 7 bracelets on Monday. How many did she
make in all?

16 bracelets

5. Each bracelet costs $0.65 to make. How much
does it cost to make 2 bracelets?

$1.30

---

5 as a Factor

Careers A gardener is planning a garden. She divides it into
8 squares. Each square will have 5 lettuce plants.

1. How many plants are in the top part of the garden? **20 plants**

2. How many plants will she have in all? **40 plants**

3. Suppose the garden had only 6 squares. How
many plants would the gardener have? **30 plants**

Use the table for **4–7.**

Seed Pack Sale	
flower seeds	2 for $1
vegetable seeds	3 for $1

4. How many flower seed packs can you buy for $1? **2 packs**

5. How many vegetable seed packs can you buy for $5? **15 packs**

6. Suppose you have $2. What could you buy?

4 packs of flower seeds, 2 packs of flower seeds and 3

packs of vegetable seeds, or 6 packs of vegetable seeds

7. Which costs less: flower seeds or vegetable seeds?
Explain. **Vegetable seeds; Possible answer:**

You get more seed packets for $1.

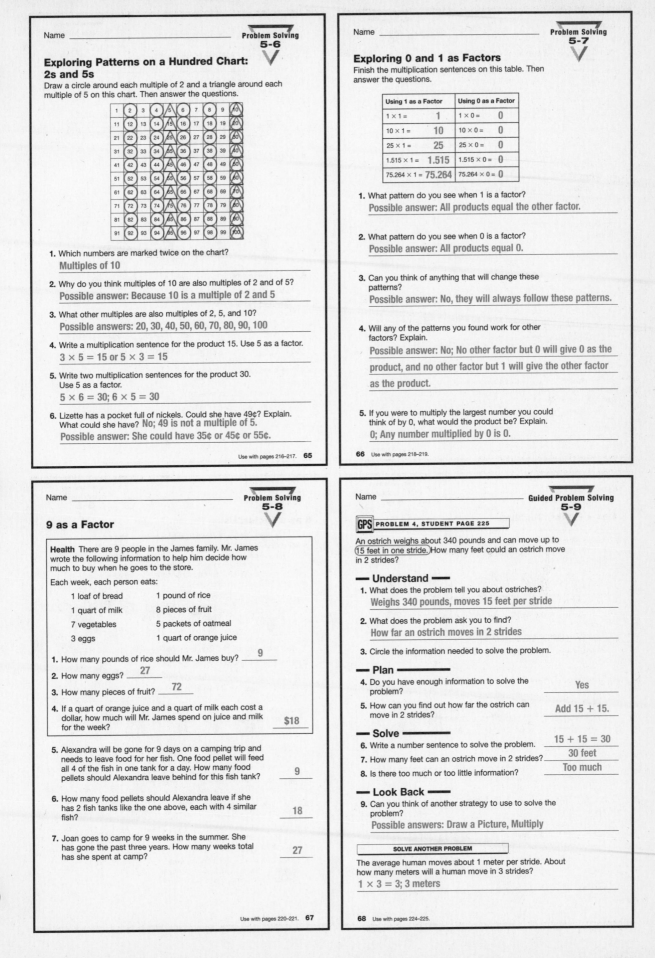

Exploring Patterns on a Hundred Chart: 2s and 5s

Draw a circle around each multiple of 2 and a triangle around each multiple of 5 on this chart. Then answer the questions.

1. Which numbers are marked twice on the chart?
   Multiples of 10

2. Why do you think multiples of 10 are also multiples of 2 and of 5?
   Possible answer: Because 10 is a multiple of 2 and 5

3. What other multiples are also multiples of 2, 5, and 10?
   Possible answers: 20, 30, 40, 50, 60, 70, 80, 90, 100

4. Write a multiplication sentence for the product 15. Use 5 as a factor.
   3 × 5 = 15 or 5 × 3 = 15

5. Write two multiplication sentences for the product 30. Use 5 as a factor.
   5 × 6 = 30; 6 × 5 = 30

6. Lizette has a pocket full of nickels. Could she have 49¢? Explain. What could she have? **No; 49 is not a multiple of 5.**
   Possible answer: She could have 35¢ or 45¢ or 55¢.

Exploring 0 and 1 as Factors

Finish the multiplication sentences on this table. Then answer the questions.

Using 1 as a Factor	Using 0 as a Factor
1 × 1 = **1**	1 × 0 = **0**
10 × 1 = **10**	10 × 0 = **0**
25 × 1 = **25**	25 × 0 = **0**
1.515 × 1 = **1.515**	1.515 × 0 = **0**
75.264 × 1 = **75.264**	75.264 × 0 = **0**

1. What pattern do you see when 1 is a factor?
   Possible answer: All products equal the other factor.

2. What pattern do you see when 0 is a factor?
   Possible answer: All products equal 0.

3. Can you think of anything that will change these patterns?
   Possible answer: No, they will always follow these patterns.

4. Will any of the patterns you found work for other factors? Explain.
   Possible answer: No; No other factor but 0 will give 0 as the product, and no other factor but 1 will give the other factor as the product.

5. If you were to multiply the largest number you could think of by 0, what would the product be? Explain.
   0; Any number multiplied by 0 is 0.

---

9 as a Factor

Health There are 9 people in the James family. Mr. James wrote the following information to help him decide how much to buy when he goes to the store.

Each week, each person eats:

1 loaf of bread	1 pound of rice
1 quart of milk	8 pieces of fruit
7 vegetables	5 packets of oatmeal
3 eggs	1 quart of orange juice

1. How many pounds of rice should Mr. James buy? **9**

2. How many eggs? **27**

3. How many pieces of fruit? **72**

4. If a quart of orange juice and a quart of milk each cost a dollar, how much will Mr. James spend on juice and milk for the week? **$18**

5. Alexandra will be gone for 9 days on a camping trip and needs to leave food for her fish. One food pellet will feed all 4 of the fish in one tank for a day. How many food pellets should Alexandra leave behind for this fish tank? **9**

6. How many food pellets should Alexandra leave if she has 2 fish tanks like the one above, each with 4 similar fish? **18**

7. Joan goes to camp for 9 weeks in the summer. She has gone the past three years. How many weeks total has she spent at camp? **27**

GPS PROBLEM 4, STUDENT PAGE 225

An ostrich weighs about 340 pounds and can move up to 15 feet in one stride. How many feet could an ostrich move in 2 strides?

Understand

1. What does the problem tell you about ostriches?
   Weighs 340 pounds, moves 15 feet per stride

2. What does the problem ask you to find?
   How far an ostrich moves in 2 strides

3. Circle the information needed to solve the problem.

Plan

4. Do you have enough information to solve the problem? **Yes**

5. How can you find out how far the ostrich can move in 2 strides? **Add 15 + 15.**

Solve

6. Write a number sentence to solve the problem. **15 + 15 = 30**

7. How many feet can an ostrich move in 2 strides? **30 feet**

8. Is there too much or too little information? **Too much**

Look Back

9. Can you think of another strategy to use to solve the problem?
   Possible answers: Draw a Picture, Multiply

SOLVE ANOTHER PROBLEM

The average human moves about 1 meter per stride. About how many meters will a human move in 3 strides?
1 × 3 = 3; 3 meters

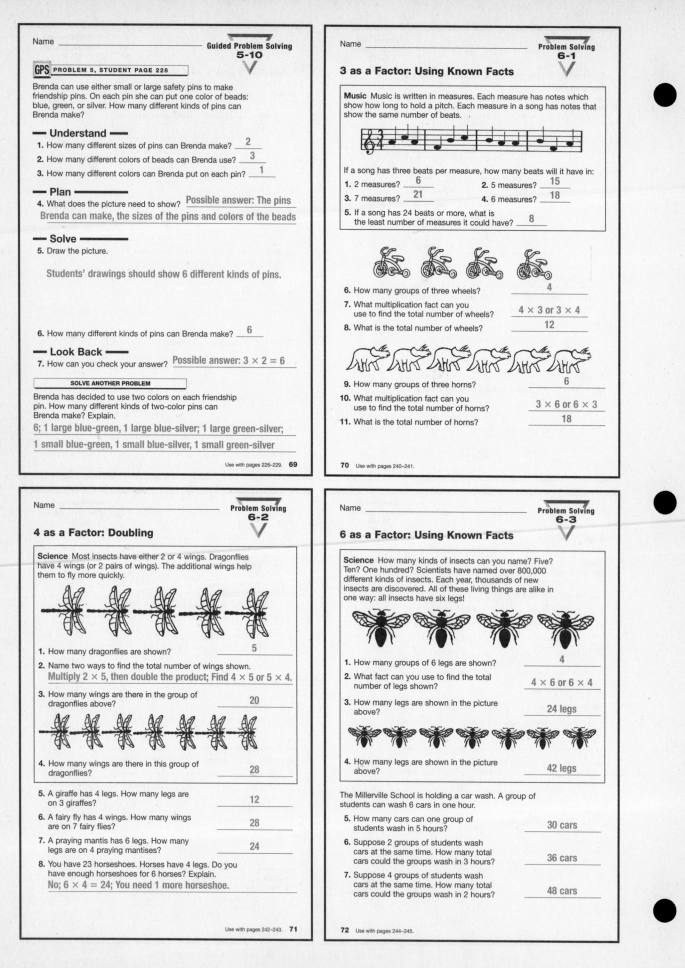

Panel 1 (top-left)

Name _____

GPS PROBLEM 5, STUDENT PAGE 228

Brenda can use either small or large safety pins to make friendship pins. On each pin she can put one color of beads: blue, green, or silver. How many different kinds of pins can Brenda make?

Understand

1. How many different sizes of pins can Brenda make? __2__

2. How many different colors of beads can Brenda use? __3__

3. How many different colors can Brenda put on each pin? __1__

Plan

4. What does the picture need to show? Possible answer: The pins Brenda can make, the sizes of the pins and colors of the beads

Solve

5. Draw the picture.

Students' drawings should show 6 different kinds of pins.

6. How many different kinds of pins can Brenda make? __6__

Look Back

7. How can you check your answer? Possible answer: 3 × 2 = 6

SOLVE ANOTHER PROBLEM

Brenda has decided to use two colors on each friendship pin. How many different kinds of two-color pins can Brenda make? Explain.

6; 1 large blue-green, 1 large blue-silver; 1 large green-silver; 1 small blue-green, 1 small blue-silver, 1 small green-silver

Use with pages 226–229. **69**

Panel 2 (top-right)

Name _____

3 as a Factor: Using Known Facts

Music Music is written in measures. Each measure has notes which show how long to hold a pitch. Each measure in a song has notes that show the same number of beats.

If a song has three beats per measure, how many beats will it have in:

1. 2 measures? __6__   2. 5 measures? __15__

3. 7 measures? __21__   4. 6 measures? __18__

5. If a song has 24 beats or more, what is the least number of measures it could have? __8__

6. How many groups of three wheels? __4__

7. What multiplication fact can you use to find the total number of wheels? __4 × 3 or 3 × 4__

8. What is the total number of wheels? __12__

9. How many groups of three horns? __6__

10. What multiplication fact can you use to find the total number of horns? __3 × 6 or 6 × 3__

11. What is the total number of horns? __18__

70 Use with pages 240–241.

Panel 3 (bottom-left)

Name _____

4 as a Factor: Doubling

Science Most insects have either 2 or 4 wings. Dragonflies have 4 wings (or 2 pairs of wings). The additional wings help them to fly more quickly.

1. How many dragonflies are shown? __5__

2. Name two ways to find the total number of wings shown.
Multiply 2 × 5, then double the product; Find 4 × 5 or 5 × 4.

3. How many wings are there in the group of dragonflies above? __20__

4. How many wings are there in this group of dragonflies? __28__

5. A giraffe has 4 legs. How many legs are on 3 giraffes? __12__

6. A fairy fly has 4 wings. How many wings are on 7 fairy flies? __28__

7. A praying mantis has 6 legs. How many legs are on 4 praying mantises? __24__

8. You have 23 horseshoes. Horses have 4 legs. Do you have enough horseshoes for 6 horses? Explain.
No; 6 × 4 = 24; You need 1 more horseshoe.

Use with pages 242–243. **71**

Panel 4 (bottom-right)

Name _____

6 as a Factor: Using Known Facts

Science How many kinds of insects can you name? Five? Ten? One hundred? Scientists have named over 800,000 different kinds of insects. Each year, thousands of new insects are discovered. All of these living things are alike in one way: all insects have six legs!

1. How many groups of 6 legs are shown? __4__

2. What fact can you use to find the total number of legs shown? __4 × 6 or 6 × 4__

3. How many legs are shown in the picture above? __24 legs__

4. How many legs are shown in the picture above? __42 legs__

The Millerville School is holding a car wash. A group of students can wash 6 cars in one hour.

5. How many cars can one group of students wash in 5 hours? __30 cars__

6. Suppose 2 groups of students wash cars at the same time. How many total cars could the groups wash in 3 hours? __36 cars__

7. Suppose 4 groups of students wash cars at the same time. How many total cars could the groups wash in 2 hours? __48 cars__

72 Use with pages 244–245.

7 and 8 as Factors

Health Our bodies need calcium for strong teeth and bones. The Recommended Daily Allowance (RDA) tells how much calcium our bodies need in one day. Each of the items below would give a student the RDA of calcium.

Foods that Provide the Recommended Daily Allowance of Calcium			
4 slices cheese	3 cups spinach	6 cups broccoli	8 pieces tofu

1. If Patrick ate 4 slices of cheese per day, how many slices would he eat in one week?   **28 slices**

2. If you ate enough broccoli each day to get the RDA of calcium, how many cups would you eat in eight days?   **48 cups**

3. If you ate enough tofu each day to get the RDA of calcium, how many pieces would you eat in one week? in 5 days?   **56; 40**

Mia is decorating sweatshirts for a craft fair. She sews 8 buttons and 7 fabric squares on each sweatshirt.

4. How many buttons and fabric squares will Mia sew on 6 sweatshirts?
48 buttons and 42 fabric squares

5. How many buttons and fabric squares will Mia sew on 9 sweatshirts?
72 buttons and 63 fabric squares

Decision Making

A scout troop is going on an overnight camping trip. Two adults and eight scouts will be on the trip. You have been asked to create a menu for the campers. You need to choose a breakfast, lunch, and dinner that can be cooked over a camp fire. Use the food pyramid on page 250 of your book to help plan the meals.

1. Name three things that you know.
How many campers on the trip, how many many meals to plan, how many servings of each type of food are needed

2. What do you need to decide?
What meals they will have

3. What kinds of food should the campers have 9 servings of?
Breads, cereals, rice and pasta

4. What kinds of food should the campers have 3 servings of?
Fruit

5. Write your menu. **Menus will vary.**
Breakfast _____

_____

Lunch _____

Dinner _____

6. Share your menu with the class. Check that you have the appropriate number of servings per food group and that these foods can be cooked over a camp fire.

Exploring Patterns on a Hundred Chart: 3s and 6s

1	2	3	4	5	6	7	8	9	10
11	12	13	14	15	16	17	18	19	20
21	22	23	24	25	26	27	28	29	30
31	32	33	34	35	36	37	38	39	40
41	42	43	44	45	46	47	48	49	50

Use basic facts and patterns to find all the multiples of 3 and 6 on the chart above. Shade each multiple of 3 red. Shade each multiple of 6 blue.

1. What are the purple (red and blue) numbers called?
Multiples of 6

2. What pattern do you see in the shaded squares? **Possible answer: The shaded squares make diagonal stripes.**

3. Are there any boxes that are only blue? Why or why not?
No; Because all multiples of 6 are also multiples of 3

4. What other patterns do you see in the chart?
Possible answers: There are 2 unshaded boxes between each shaded box; shaded boxes form diagonal patterns; as you follow the path of a diagonal stripe, the ones digits decrease by one and the tens digits increase by one; every other multiple of 3 is a multiple of 6.

5. Describe how one pattern you see will help you remember the basic facts for 3 or 6.
Possible answer: I can find any basic fact for 6 by doubling a basic fact for 3. 6 × 4 is the same as twice 3 × 4.

Exploring Patterns on a Fact Table

Check students' shading.

Use the fact table to help you answer the questions.

1. Shade all the multiples of 3 yellow. What pattern do you see?
Possible answer: The multiples of 3 make 8 strips on the page—the 3, 6, 9, and 12 columns and rows.

2. Shade all the multiples of 6 red. What patterns do you see?
Possible answer: Multiples of 6 and 12 are shaded orange.

3. The multiples of 12 are what color? Why?
Orange; Because they are multiples of both 6 and 3

4. 0, 1, 4, 9, 16, 25, 36, 49, 64, 81, 100, 121, 144
This sequence of numbers appears in the table.
   a. Draw a blue line to connect this sequence of numbers.
   b. Shade in these numbers whenever they appear in the table.
   c. What patterns do you see? **Possible answer: The shaded numbers are in the same positions on both sides of the diagonal line.**
   d. What do these numbers have in common?
   They are all products of a number multiplied by itself.

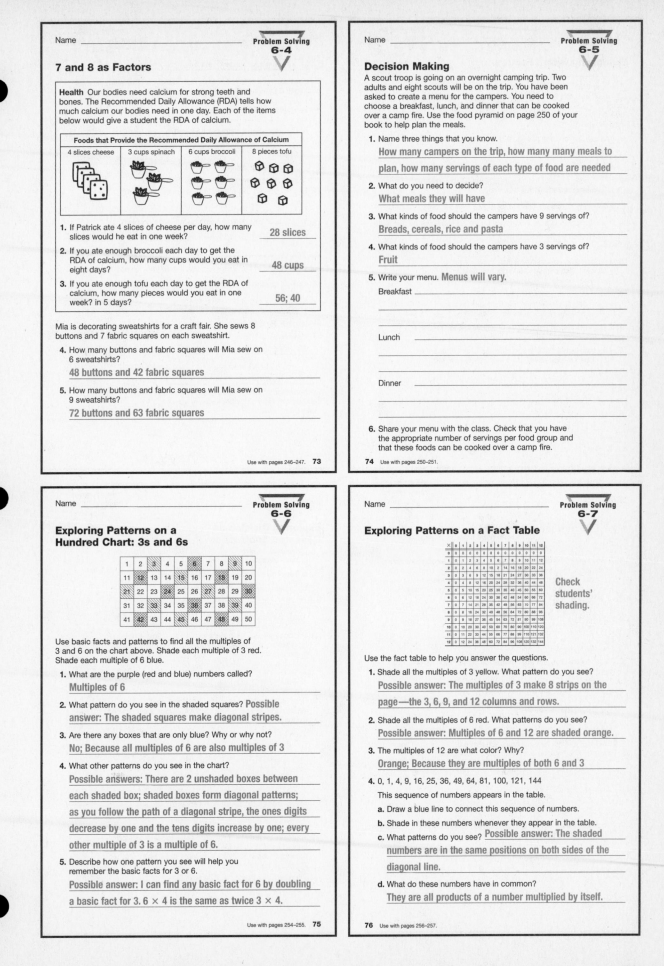

Multiplying with 3 Factors

Physical Education Your school is building a new gymnasium. Each floor of the gym will have a basketball court. For each new basketball court they build, the school needs to buy 2 hoops. For each new hoop, they need 6 basketballs.

1. Your school decides to build a gym with 2 floors.

   a. How many hoops will they need? __4__

   b. How many basketballs? __24__

2. If your school builds a gym with 3 floors, how many basketballs will they need? __36__

3. How many hoops are needed for a gym with 5 floors? __10__

4. If a 4-floor gym is built, how many hoops and balls will be needed?
   __8 hoops, 48 basketballs__

5. Suppose you make oatmeal raisin cookies for 3 people. Each person gets 3 cookies. Each cookie has 5 raisins. How many raisins will you need? __45__

6. You make ham sandwiches for 2 people. Each person gets 2 sandwiches. Each sandwich has 2 slices of ham. How many ham slices will you need? __8__

7. You give 4 friends 2 packages of markers. Each package has 6 markers in it. How many markers do you give? __48__

8. 3 friends each purchase 3 sheets of stickers. There are 8 stickers on each sheet. How many stickers in all? __72__

GPS PROBLEM 2, STUDENT PAGE 263

One package of pita bread makes 6 sandwiches. How many packages do you need to make 45 sandwiches?

— Understand —

1. How many sandwiches can you make with one package of pita bread? __6 sandwiches__

2. What do you need to find out? The number of packages needed to make 45 sandwiches

— Plan —

3. How could you use a pattern to solve the problem?
   Possible answer: Make a Table

4. What could you draw to help you solve the problem?
   Possible answer: A picture of the packages of pita bread

— Solve —

5. Choose one of the strategies. Show how you solved the problem.
   Check students' work.

6. What is the answer? __8 packages__

— Look Back —

7. How can you check your answer? You can check your answer by using another strategy to solve the problem.

SOLVE ANOTHER PROBLEM

One package of English muffins makes 6 egg sandwiches. How many packages do you need to make 20 sandwiches? __4 packages__

Exploring Division as Sharing

Draw a picture to show how you can solve these problems. Then write your answer.

1. A Boys and Girls club is on a special trip to an amusement park. There are 15 children in the club. Everyone wants to ride the giant roller coaster. Each car of the roller coaster has room for 3 people. How many cars will be needed if all 15 children go on the ride?
   __5 cars__

2. 12 of the children want to ride the log flume. Each log will hold 4 people. How many logs will be needed?
   __3 logs__

3. The log flume ride was so much fun that 8 of the children want to ride it again. This time, how many logs will be needed?
   __2 logs__

4. 14 children want to ride the ferris wheel. Each car holds 2 passengers. How many cars will be needed?
   __7 cars__

Exploring Division as Repeated Subtraction

1. Carlos has 14 envelopes. He has to deliver 2 envelopes to each classroom.

   a. How many classrooms will Carlos visit? __7 classrooms__

   b. Explain how you solved the problem.
   Possible answer: Used counters to represent the 14 envelopes. Took away 7 groups of 2.

2. Suppose you had 6 flowers to put into 2 flower pots. How would you solve this problem? How many flowers in each pot?
   Possible answer: Draw 6 flowers and 2 pots. Cross out each flower as it is planted. Each pot gets 3 flowers.

3. Bonnie Lee puts 2 bows on each package. Can she decorate 8 packages with 15 bows? Draw a picture and explain.

   No, Bonnie Lee needs 1 more bow. Drawing should show 7 packages each with 2 bows and 1 package with 1 bow.

4. You have 24 sheets of paper to put into folders. Each folder needs to have the same number of sheets of paper in it. How many folders could there be? (Hint: There's more than 1 answer.)
   Possible answers: 1, 2, 3, 4, 6, 8, 12, or 24

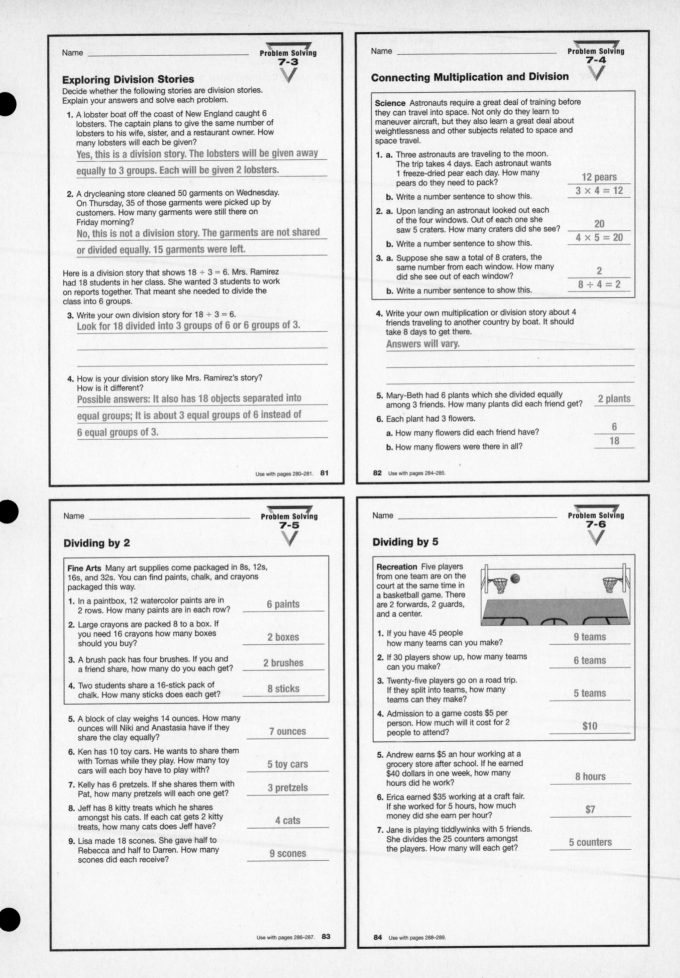

Exploring Division Stories

Decide whether the following stories are division stories.
Explain your answers and solve each problem.

1. A lobster boat off the coast of New England caught 6 lobsters. The captain plans to give the same number of lobsters to his wife, sister, and a restaurant owner. How many lobsters will each be given?

   Yes, this is a division story. The lobsters will be given away

   equally to 3 groups. Each will be given 2 lobsters.

2. A drycleaning store cleaned 50 garments on Wednesday. On Thursday, 35 of those garments were picked up by customers. How many garments were still there on Friday morning?

   No, this is not a division story. The garments are not shared

   or divided equally. 15 garments were left.

Here is a division story that shows 18 ÷ 3 = 6. Mrs. Ramirez had 18 students in her class. She wanted 3 students to work on reports together. That meant she needed to divide the class into 6 groups.

3. Write your own division story for 18 ÷ 3 = 6.

   Look for 18 divided into 3 groups of 6 or 6 groups of 3.

4. How is your division story like Mrs. Ramirez's story? How is it different?

   Possible answers: It also has 18 objects separated into

   equal groups; It is about 3 equal groups of 6 instead of

   6 equal groups of 3.

Connecting Multiplication and Division

Science Astronauts require a great deal of training before they can travel into space. Not only do they learn to maneuver aircraft, but they also learn a great deal about weightlessness and other subjects related to space and space travel.

1. a. Three astronauts are traveling to the moon. The trip takes 4 days. Each astronaut wants 1 freeze-dried pear each day. How many pears do they need to pack?

   12 pears
   3 × 4 = 12

   b. Write a number sentence to show this.

2. a. Upon landing an astronaut looked out each of the four windows. Out of each one she saw 5 craters. How many craters did she see?

   20
   4 × 5 = 20

   b. Write a number sentence to show this.

3. a. Suppose she saw a total of 8 craters, the same number from each window. How many did she see out of each window?

   2
   8 ÷ 4 = 2

   b. Write a number sentence to show this.

4. Write your own multiplication or division story about 4 friends traveling to another country by boat. It should take 8 days to get there.

   Answers will vary.

5. Mary-Beth had 6 plants which she divided equally among 3 friends. How many plants did each friend get?   **2 plants**

6. Each plant had 3 flowers.

   a. How many flowers did each friend have?   **6**

   b. How many flowers were there in all?   **18**

Dividing by 2

Fine Arts Many art supplies come packaged in 8s, 12s, 16s, and 32s. You can find paints, chalk, and crayons packaged this way.

1. In a paintbox, 12 watercolor paints are in 2 rows. How many paints are in each row?   **6 paints**

2. Large crayons are packed 8 to a box. If you need 16 crayons how many boxes should you buy?   **2 boxes**

3. A brush pack has four brushes. If you and a friend share, how many do you each get?   **2 brushes**

4. Two students share a 16-stick pack of chalk. How many sticks does each get?   **8 sticks**

5. A block of clay weighs 14 ounces. How many ounces will Niki and Anastasia have if they share the clay equally?   **7 ounces**

6. Ken has 10 toy cars. He wants to share them with Tomas while they play. How many toy cars will each boy have to play with?   **5 toy cars**

7. Kelly has 6 pretzels. If she shares them with Pat, how many pretzels will each one get?   **3 pretzels**

8. Jeff has 8 kitty treats which he shares amongst his cats. If each cat gets 2 kitty treats, how many cats does Jeff have?   **4 cats**

9. Lisa made 18 scones. She gave half to Rebecca and half to Darren. How many scones did each receive?   **9 scones**

Dividing by 5

Recreation Five players from one team are on the court at the same time in a basketball game. There are 2 forwards, 2 guards, and a center.

1. If you have 45 people how many teams can you make?   **9 teams**

2. If 30 players show up, how many teams can you make?   **6 teams**

3. Twenty-five players go on a road trip. If they split into teams, how many teams can they make?   **5 teams**

4. Admission to a game costs $5 per person. How much will it cost for 2 people to attend?   **$10**

5. Andrew earns $5 an hour working at a grocery store after school. If he earned $40 dollars in one week, how many hours did he work?   **8 hours**

6. Erica earned $35 working at a craft fair. If she worked for 5 hours, how much money did she earn per hour?   **$7**

7. Jane is playing tiddlywinks with 5 friends. She divides the 25 counters amongst the players. How many will each get?   **5 counters**

Dividing by 3 and 4

Physical Education Your gym class is having a jump rope-a-thon after school to help raise money for a local charity. Students jump rope for as long as they can. People agree to give them a certain amount of money per minute that they jump. For example, Mrs. Hughes sponsored Jennifer for 1¢ per minute she jumps. Students compete in teams of 3 for prizes for the most money raised.

1. After the jump rope-a-thon, Larry collected 36¢ from Mr. Jackson. If Mr. Jackson pledged 4¢ per minute, how many minutes did Larry jump rope? _____ **9 minutes**

2. Caitlin jumped rope for 3 minutes. If she collected 21¢ from Mr. Fernandez, how much did he pledge per minute? _____ **7¢**

3. Antonio, Martha, and Ming are all on one team.

   a. If each person on the team earns $5 from their pledges, how much did the entire team earn? _____ **$15**

   b. If the entire team earned $24, and each team member earned the same amount, how much did each member earn? _____ **$8**

4. Ana brought 12 apples to the picnic. If 4 people are at the picnic, how many apples can each person eat?
   3 apples

5. Your class is working with computers. There are 18 students in your class and 3 students are working at each computer. How many computers are in the classroom?
   6 computers

Exploring Dividing With 0 and 1
You can find patterns when you divide with 0 and 1.

1. **a.** What pattern do you see when 0 is divided by a number?
   0 divided by a number is 0.

   b. How can you find the answer to 0 ÷ 98? Explain.
   Since 0 divided by a number is 0, 0 ÷ 98 = 0.

2. **a.** What pattern do you see when a number is divided by 1?
   A number divided by 1 is that number.

   b. How can you find the answer to 2,952 ÷ 1? Explain.
   Since a number divided by 1 is that number,
   2,952 ÷ 1 = 2,952.

3. **a.** What pattern do you see when a number (except zero) is divided by itself?
   A number divided by itself is 1.

   b. How can you find the answer to 423 ÷ 423? Explain.
   Since a number divided by itself is 1, 423 ÷ 423 = 1.

4. Write a word problem showing division by 1.
   Check students' problems.

5. Write a word problem showing a number being divided by itself.
   Check students' problems.

GPS PROBLEM 5, STUDENT PAGE 297

Suppose Bonnie bought a 5-pound bag of cat food for $4.95. She also bought a 3-pound bag of bird seed for $1.50. How much money did she spend?

— Understand —
1. Draw X's through numbers in the problem you do not need. **5 and 3**
2. What do you need to find out?
   The total amount that Bonnie spent

— Plan —
3. How much did Bonnie spend on cat food? _____ **$4.95**
4. How much did Bonnie spend on bird seed? _____ **$1.50**
5. What operation would you choose to solve the problem? _____ **C**

   A. Multiplication **B.** Division **C.** Addition **D.** Subtraction

— Solve —
6. Write the number sentence and solve the problem.
   $4.95 + $1.50 = $6.45. Bonnie spent $6.45.

— Look Back —
7. Explain how you can check to make sure your answer is reasonable.
   Possible answer: I will estimate. $4.95 is close to $5, $1.50 is close to $2, $5 + $2 = $7; $7 is close to $6.45, so my answer is reasonable.

SOLVE ANOTHER PROBLEM

Alex buys 6 cartons of milk for $12. If all of the cartons cost the same amount, how much does each carton cost? _____ **$2**

Dividing by 6 and 7

Music A symphony orchestra consists of 4 different sections: the string section, the woodwind section, the percussion section, and the brass section. Each section contains several instruments and can vary in size. The conductor of the orchestra organizes the seating of each group in order to achieve a particular sound.

1. If the string section has 24 violinists and the conductor seats them in 6 rows, how many violinists are in each row? _____ **4**

2. If there are 18 musicians in the brass section and 6 musicians in each row, how many rows are there in the brass section? _____ **3**

3. The entire orchestra has 63 musicians. If the conductor wants to arrange them in 7 rows, how many musicians would be in each row? _____ **9**

4. Alice has 24 pencils to share with her friends. If she gives an equal number of pencils to 6 friends, how many pencils will each friend receive? _____ **4**

5. Alice wants to buy bean bag dolls for her collection. Each doll costs $5.00. How much will she spend for 6 dolls? _____ **$30.00**

6. **a.** Alice wants to line up her doll collection. She wants to put 28 dolls in 7 equal rows. How many dolls will be in each row? _____ **4**

   b. If she places the dolls in 6 equal rows how many will be left over? _____ **4**

7. **a.** Emma arranges her 56 books in 7 equal rows. How many are in each row? _____ **8**

   b. If she arranges them in rows of 6, how many will be in each row, and how many will be left over?
   9; 2 left over

Problem Solving
7-11

Dividing by 8 and 9

Science The eagle is the national bird of the United States. It is one of the largest birds in the world.

1. An eagle's nest is called an *eyrie*. If 8 eyries had a total measurement of 32 feet across, how wide is each eyrie?

   4 feet

2. 9 eagle eggs are laid end to end. The total length is 27 inches. How long is each egg?

   3 inches

3. 8 eagles have a total weight of 64 pounds. How much does each eagle weigh?

   8 pounds

4. Golden eagles are about 32 inches long and have a wingspan of about 7 feet. How much greater is their wingspan than their length?

   4 feet, 4 inches

5. a. Arthur spends 72¢ on a pack of 8 sports trading cards. How much does each card cost?

   _9¢_

   b. Arthur loses one card. How much are his cards worth now?

   _63¢_

6. Arthur buys 5 more cards for 40¢. How much does each of these cards cost?

   _8¢_

7. Arthur keeps 3 cards and divides the remaining 9 cards among 9 friends. How many cards does each friend get?

   1 card

Problem Solving
7-12

Exploring Even and Odd Numbers

Cut a 10 × 10 grid into five 2 × 10 arrays. From these arrays cut out models of the even numbers 2, 4, 6, 8, and 10. Also cut out models of the odd numbers 3, 5, 7, and 9. Shade or color the even number models.

1. Add two even numbers by joining the models. What do you notice about the sum?

   It is an even number.

2. Add an even and an odd number by joining the models. What do you notice about the sum?

   It is an odd number.

3. Add two odd numbers using the models. What do you notice about the sum?

   You always get an even number.

4. Conduct experiments finding differences. Write even or odd to describe each difference.

   a. Subtract an even number from an even number.

   The difference is _even_.

   b. Subtract an even number from an odd number.

   The difference is _odd_.

   c. Subtract an odd number from an even number.

   The difference is _odd_.

   d. Subtract an odd number from an odd number.

   The difference is _even_.

5. Kirsten is packing puzzle cubes into different size boxes. Each box must have an even number of puzzle cubes. She has twelve cubes.

   a. Can she pack her twelve cubes?

   Yes

   b. She can't pack 3 of them because they are broken. Can she pack all of the rest?

   _No_

   c. She finds she must pack another nine cubes. Can she pack all of her non-broken cubes?

   Yes

Guided Problem Solving
7-13

GPS PROBLEM 3, STUDENT PAGE 309

Kate wants to take a picture of 20 students in the band. She wants the students to stand in equal rows. What are all the ways she can arrange them?

— Understand —

1. How many students are in the band? _20_

2. How does Kate want the students to stand? _In equal rows_

— Plan —

3. Make a table of all the ways Kate could arrange the rows. What number will always be in the total column?

   _20_

— Solve —

4. Complete the table.

Rows	Students in Each Row	Total
1	20	20
2	10	20
4	5	20
5	4	20
10	2	20
20	1	20

   a. How many different arrangements of rows are in the list? _6_

   b. List the different ways Kate can arrange the students.

   1 row of 20, 2 rows of 10, 4 rows of 5, 5 rows of 4, 10 rows of 2, 20 rows of 1

— Look Back —

5. How do you know your answer is reasonable? _Possible answer: All the factors of 20 are listed._

SOLVE ANOTHER PROBLEM

Kate is also taking a picture of the nature club which has 28 members. What are all the ways she can arrange the students in equal rows?

1 row of 28, 2 rows of 14, 4 rows of 7, 7 rows of 4, 14 rows of 2, 28 rows of 1

Problem Solving
7-14

Exploring Algebra: Balancing Scales

Here is an addition chart for the digits 0–9. Some of the sums have been filled in for you.

1. Complete the chart by filling in the missing sums.

2. How many times does the sum of 3 appear on the chart?

   _4_

+	0	1	2	3	4	5	6	7	8	9
0	0	1	2	3	4	5	6	7	8	9
1	1	2	3	4	5	6	7	8	9	10
2	2	3	4	5	6	7	8	9	10	11
3	3	4	5	6	7	8	9	10	11	12
4	4	5	6	7	8	9	10	11	12	13
5	5	6	7	8	9	10	11	12	13	14
6	6	7	8	9	10	11	12	13	14	15
7	7	8	9	10	11	12	13	14	15	16
8	8	9	10	11	12	13	14	15	16	17
9	9	10	11	12	13	14	15	16	17	18

3. Is there a pattern to these 3s?

   They are in a diagonal line.

4. Find all the different ways numbers can be added to total 3. Make an organized list to show all the ways.

   _3 + 0; 2 + 1; 1 + 2; 0 + 3_

5. How does the addition chart help in finding the ways to total 3? Explain.

   It shows all the addends; It shows the 4 possible ways.

6. How many different ways are there to total 5? _6_

7. Box A has 3 cubes inside. Use the addition chart to list how many cubes can be in boxes B and C.

B	0	1	2	3
C	3	2	1	0

8. Each box A has 4 cubes inside. Use the addition chart to list how many cubes can be in boxes B and C.

B	0	1	2	3	4	5	6	7	8
C	8	7	6	5	4	3	2	1	0

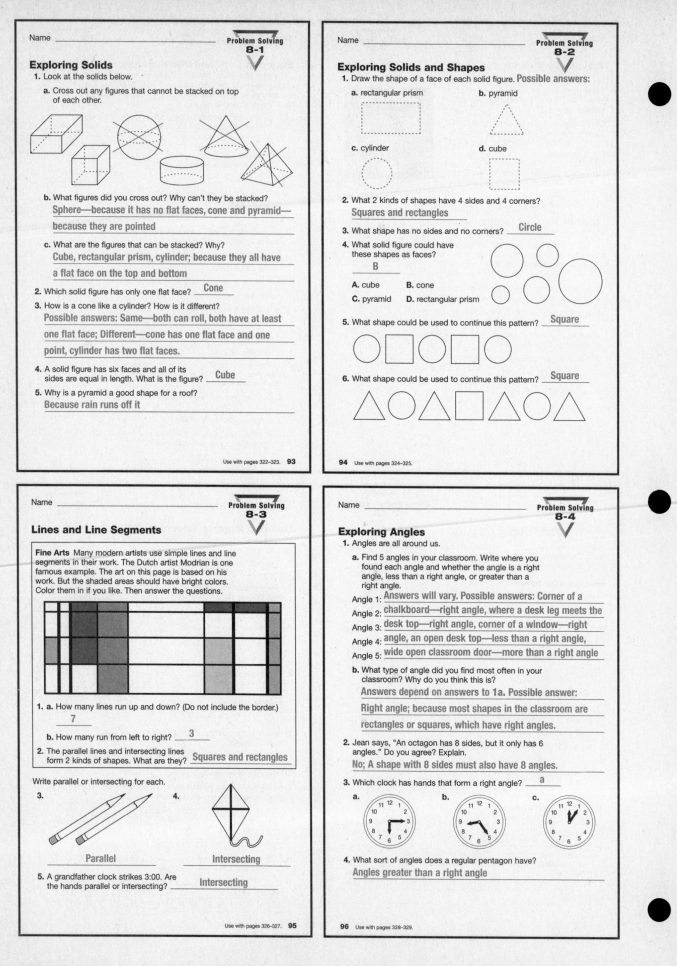

Name _____

Exploring Solids

1. Look at the solids below.

   a. Cross out any figures that cannot be stacked on top of each other.

   b. What figures did you cross out? Why can't they be stacked?
   Sphere—because it has no flat faces, cone and pyramid—because they are pointed

   c. What are the figures that can be stacked? Why?
   Cube, rectangular prism, cylinder; because they all have a flat face on the top and bottom

2. Which solid figure has only one flat face? **Cone**

3. How is a cone like a cylinder? How is it different?
   Possible answers: Same—both can roll, both have at least one flat face; Different—cone has one flat face and one point, cylinder has two flat faces.

4. A solid figure has six faces and all of its sides are equal in length. What is the figure? **Cube**

5. Why is a pyramid a good shape for a roof?
   Because rain runs off it

Name _____

Exploring Solids and Shapes

1. Draw the shape of a face of each solid figure. Possible answers:

   a. rectangular prism   b. pyramid

   c. cylinder   d. cube

2. What 2 kinds of shapes have 4 sides and 4 corners?
   Squares and rectangles

3. What shape has no sides and no corners? **Circle**

4. What solid figure could have these shapes as faces?
   B

   A. cube   B. cone
   C. pyramid   D. rectangular prism

5. What shape could be used to continue this pattern? **Square**

6. What shape could be used to continue this pattern? **Square**

Name _____

Lines and Line Segments

Fine Arts Many modern artists use simple lines and line segments in their work. The Dutch artist Modrian is one famous example. The art on this page is based on his work. But the shaded areas should have bright colors. Color them in if you like. Then answer the questions.

1. a. How many lines run up and down? (Do not include the border.)
   7

   b. How many run from left to right? **3**

2. The parallel lines and intersecting lines form 2 kinds of shapes. What are they? **Squares and rectangles**

Write parallel or intersecting for each.

3.   4.

   Parallel   **Intersecting**

5. A grandfather clock strikes 3:00. Are the hands parallel or intersecting? **Intersecting**

Name _____

Exploring Angles

1. Angles are all around us.

   a. Find 5 angles in your classroom. Write where you found each angle and whether the angle is a right angle, less than a right angle, or greater than a right angle.

   Angle 1: **Answers will vary. Possible answers: Corner of a**
   Angle 2: **chalkboard—right angle, where a desk leg meets the**
   Angle 3: **desk top—right angle, corner of a window—right**
   Angle 4: **angle, an open desk top—less than a right angle,**
   Angle 5: **wide open classroom door—more than a right angle**

   b. What type of angle did you find most often in your classroom? Why do you think this is?
   Answers depend on answers to 1a. Possible answer:
   Right angle; because most shapes in the classroom are rectangles or squares, which have right angles.

2. Jean says, "An octagon has 8 sides, but it only has 6 angles." Do you agree? Explain.
   No; A shape with 8 sides must also have 8 angles.

3. Which clock has hands that form a right angle? **a**

   a.   b.   c.

4. What sort of angles does a regular pentagon have?
   Angles greater than a right angle

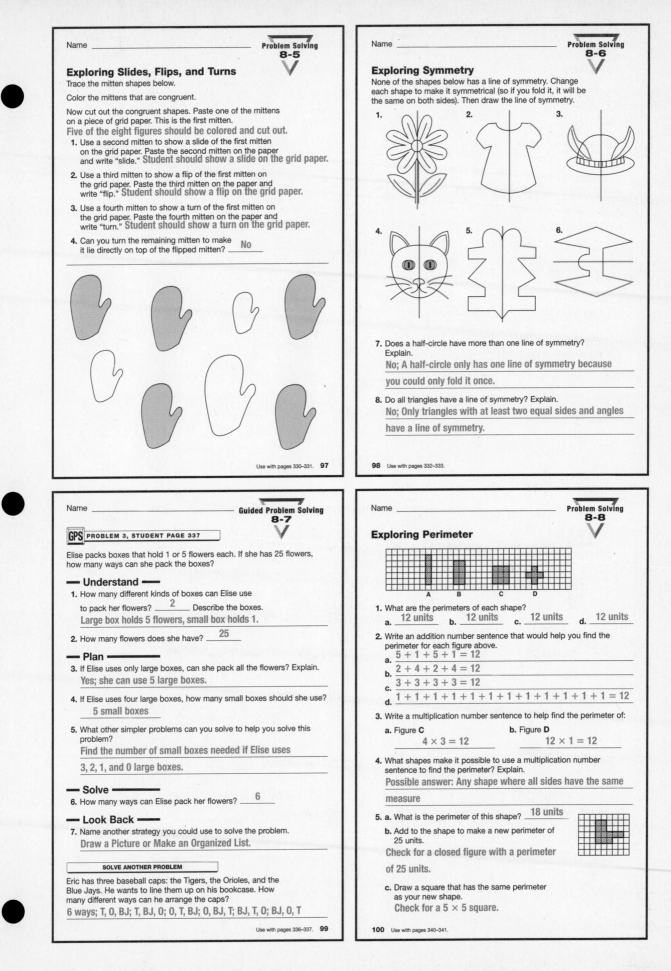

8-5

Name _____

Exploring Slides, Flips, and Turns

Trace the mitten shapes below.

Color the mittens that are congruent.

Now cut out the congruent shapes. Paste one of the mittens on a piece of grid paper. This is the first mitten.

Five of the eight figures should be colored and cut out.

1. Use a second mitten to show a slide of the first mitten on the grid paper. Paste the second mitten on the paper and write "slide." **Student should show a slide on the grid paper.**

2. Use a third mitten to show a flip of the first mitten on the grid paper. Paste the third mitten on the paper and write "flip." **Student should show a flip on the grid paper.**

3. Use a fourth mitten to show a turn of the first mitten on the grid paper. Paste the fourth mitten on the paper and write "turn." **Student should show a turn on the grid paper.**

4. Can you turn the remaining mitten to make it lie directly on top of the flipped mitten? **No**

Name _____

Exploring Symmetry

None of the shapes below has a line of symmetry. Change each shape to make it symmetrical (so if you fold it, it will be the same on both sides). Then draw the line of symmetry.

1.   2.   3.

4.   5.   6.

7. Does a half-circle have more than one line of symmetry? Explain.
   No; A half-circle only has one line of symmetry because you could only fold it once.

8. Do all triangles have a line of symmetry? Explain.
   No; Only triangles with at least two equal sides and angles have a line of symmetry.

Name _____

GPS **PROBLEM 3, STUDENT PAGE 337**

Elise packs boxes that hold 1 or 5 flowers each. If she has 25 flowers, how many ways can she pack the boxes?

— Understand —

1. How many different kinds of boxes can Elise use to pack her flowers? **2** Describe the boxes.
   Large box holds 5 flowers, small box holds 1.

2. How many flowers does she have? **25**

— Plan —

3. If Elise uses only large boxes, can she pack all the flowers? Explain.
   Yes; she can use 5 large boxes.

4. If Elise uses four large boxes, how many small boxes should she use?
   5 small boxes

5. What other simpler problems can you solve to help you solve this problem?
   Find the number of small boxes needed if Elise uses 3, 2, 1, and 0 large boxes.

— Solve —

6. How many ways can Elise pack her flowers? **6**

— Look Back —

7. Name another strategy you could use to solve the problem.
   Draw a Picture or Make an Organized List.

SOLVE ANOTHER PROBLEM

Eric has three baseball caps: the Tigers, the Orioles, and the Blue Jays. He wants to line them up on his bookcase. How many different ways can he arrange the caps?
6 ways; T, O, BJ; T, BJ, O; O, T, BJ; O, BJ, T; BJ, T, O; BJ, O, T

Name _____

Exploring Perimeter

A   B   C   D

1. What are the perimeters of each shape?
   a. **12 units** b. **12 units** c. **12 units** d. **12 units**

2. Write an addition number sentence that would help you find the perimeter for each figure above.
   a. **5 + 1 + 5 + 1 = 12**
   b. **2 + 4 + 2 + 4 = 12**
   c. **3 + 3 + 3 + 3 = 12**
   d. **1 + 1 + 1 + 1 + 1 + 1 + 1 + 1 + 1 + 1 + 1 + 1 = 12**

3. Write a multiplication number sentence to help find the perimeter of:
   a. Figure C **4 × 3 = 12** b. Figure D **12 × 1 = 12**

4. What shapes make it possible to use a multiplication number sentence to find the perimeter? Explain.
   Possible answer: Any shape where all sides have the same measure

5. a. What is the perimeter of this shape? **18 units**
   b. Add to the shape to make a new perimeter of 25 units.
   Check for a closed figure with a perimeter of 25 units.
   c. Draw a square that has the same perimeter as your new shape.
   Check for a 5 × 5 square.

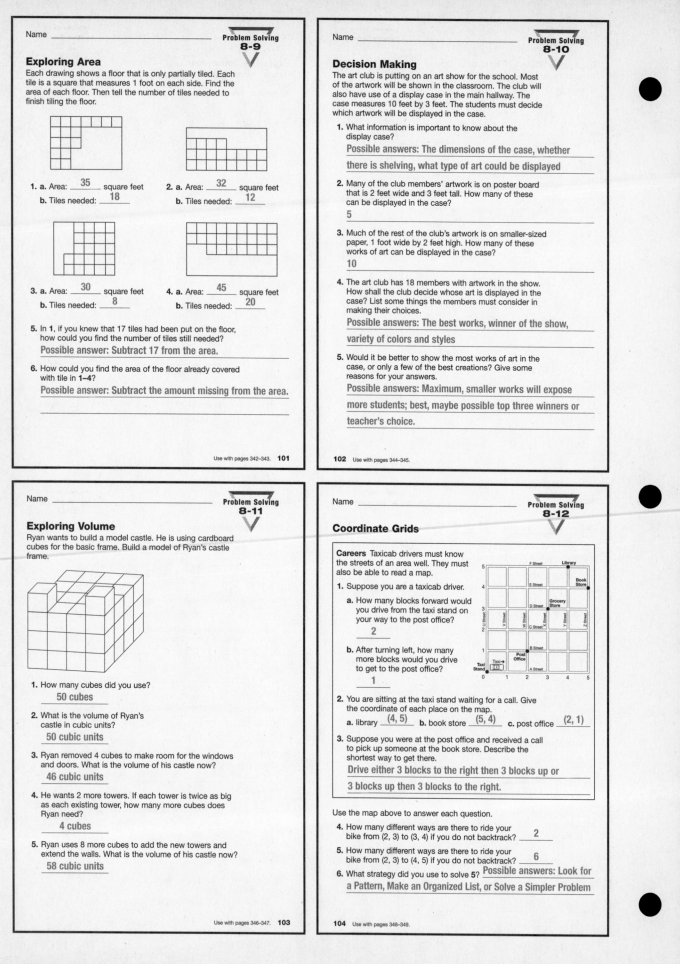

Exploring Area

Each drawing shows a floor that is only partially tiled. Each tile is a square that measures 1 foot on each side. Find the area of each floor. Then tell the number of tiles needed to finish tiling the floor.

1. a. Area: __35__ square feet
   b. Tiles needed: __18__

2. a. Area: __32__ square feet
   b. Tiles needed: __12__

3. a. Area: __30__ square feet
   b. Tiles needed: __8__

4. a. Area: __45__ square feet
   b. Tiles needed: __20__

5. In **1**, if you knew that 17 tiles had been put on the floor, how could you find the number of tiles still needed?
   Possible answer: Subtract 17 from the area.

6. How could you find the area of the floor already covered with tile in **1–4**?
   Possible answer: Subtract the amount missing from the area.

Decision Making

The art club is putting on an art show for the school. Most of the artwork will be shown in the classroom. The club will also have use of a display case in the main hallway. The case measures 10 feet by 3 feet. The students must decide which artwork will be displayed in the case.

1. What information is important to know about the display case?
   Possible answers: The dimensions of the case, whether there is shelving, what type of art could be displayed

2. Many of the club members' artwork is on poster board that is 2 feet wide and 3 feet tall. How many of these can be displayed in the case?
   5

3. Much of the rest of the club's artwork is on smaller-sized paper, 1 foot wide by 2 feet high. How many of these works of art can be displayed in the case?
   10

4. The art club has 18 members with artwork in the show. How shall the club decide whose art is displayed in the case? List some things the members must consider in making their choices.
   Possible answers: The best works, winner of the show, variety of colors and styles

5. Would it be better to show the most works of art in the case, or only a few of the best creations? Give some reasons for your answers.
   Possible answers: Maximum, smaller works will expose more students; best, maybe possible top three winners or teacher's choice.

Exploring Volume

Ryan wants to build a model castle. He is using cardboard cubes for the basic frame. Build a model of Ryan's castle frame.

1. How many cubes did you use?
   50 cubes

2. What is the volume of Ryan's castle in cubic units?
   50 cubic units

3. Ryan removed 4 cubes to make room for the windows and doors. What is the volume of his castle now?
   46 cubic units

4. He wants 2 more towers. If each tower is twice as big as each existing tower, how many more cubes does Ryan need?
   4 cubes

5. Ryan uses 8 more cubes to add the new towers and extend the walls. What is the volume of his castle now?
   58 cubic units

Coordinate Grids

Careers Taxicab drivers must know the streets of an area well. They must also be able to read a map.

1. Suppose you are a taxicab driver.
   a. How many blocks forward would you drive from the taxi stand on your way to the post office?
   2
   b. After turning left, how many more blocks would you drive to get to the post office?
   1

2. You are sitting at the taxi stand waiting for a call. Give the coordinate of each place on the map.
   a. library __(4, 5)__ b. book store __(5, 4)__ c. post office __(2, 1)__

3. Suppose you were at the post office and received a call to pick up someone at the book store. Describe the shortest way to get there.
   Drive either 3 blocks to the right then 3 blocks up or 3 blocks up then 3 blocks to the right.

Use the map above to answer each question.

4. How many different ways are there to ride your bike from (2, 3) to (3, 4) if you do not backtrack? __2__

5. How many different ways are there to ride your bike from (2, 3) to (4, 5) if you do not backtrack? __6__

6. What strategy did you use to solve **5**? Possible answers: Look for a Pattern, Make an Organized List, or Solve a Simpler Problem

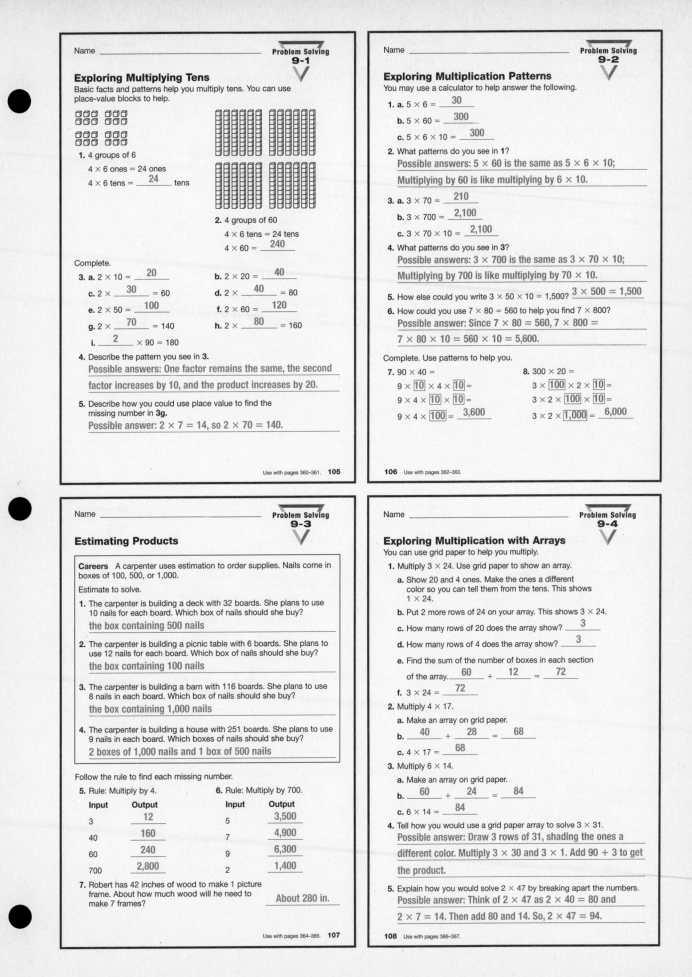

Name _____

Exploring Multiplying Tens

Basic facts and patterns help you multiply tens. You can use place-value blocks to help.

1. 4 groups of 6

4×6 ones = 24 ones

4×6 tens = ___24___ tens

2. 4 groups of 60

4×6 tens = 24 tens

$4 \times 60 =$ ___240___

Complete.

3. a. $2 \times 10 =$ ___20___   **b.** $2 \times 20 =$ ___40___

c. $2 \times$ ___30___ $= 60$ **d.** $2 \times$ ___40___ $= 80$

e. $2 \times 50 =$ ___100___   **f.** $2 \times 60 =$ ___120___

g. $2 \times$ ___70___ $= 140$ **h.** $2 \times$ ___80___ $= 160$

i. ___2___ $\times 90 = 180$

4. Describe the pattern you see in **3**.

Possible answers: One factor remains the same, the second factor increases by 10, and the product increases by 20.

5. Describe how you could use place value to find the missing number in **3g**.

Possible answer: $2 \times 7 = 14$, so $2 \times 70 = 140$.

Name _____

Exploring Multiplication Patterns

You may use a calculator to help answer the following.

1. a. $5 \times 6 =$ ___30___

b. $5 \times 60 =$ ___300___

c. $5 \times 6 \times 10 =$ ___300___

2. What patterns do you see in **1**?

Possible answers: 5×60 is the same as $5 \times 6 \times 10$;

Multiplying by 60 is like multiplying by 6×10.

3. a. $3 \times 70 =$ ___210___

b. $3 \times 700 =$ ___2,100___

c. $3 \times 70 \times 10 =$ ___2,100___

4. What patterns do you see in **3**?

Possible answers: 3×700 is the same as $3 \times 70 \times 10$;

Multiplying by 700 is like multiplying by 70×10.

5. How else could you write $3 \times 50 \times 10 = 1,500$? ___$3 \times 500 = 1,500$___

6. How could you use $7 \times 80 = 560$ to help you find 7×800?

Possible answer: Since $7 \times 80 = 560$, $7 \times 800 =$

$7 \times 80 \times 10 = 560 \times 10 = 5,600$.

Complete. Use patterns to help you.

7. $90 \times 40 =$

$9 \times \boxed{10} \times 4 \times \boxed{10} =$

$9 \times 4 \times \boxed{10} \times \boxed{10} =$

$9 \times 4 \times \boxed{100} =$ ___3,600___

8. $300 \times 20 =$

$3 \times \boxed{100} \times 2 \times \boxed{10} =$

$3 \times 2 \times \boxed{100} \times \boxed{10} =$

$3 \times 2 \times \boxed{1,000} =$ ___6,000___

Name _____

Estimating Products

Careers A carpenter uses estimation to order supplies. Nails come in boxes of 100, 500, or 1,000.

Estimate to solve.

1. The carpenter is building a deck with 32 boards. She plans to use 10 nails for each board. Which box of nails should she buy?

the box containing 500 nails

2. The carpenter is building a picnic table with 6 boards. She plans to use 12 nails for each board. Which box of nails should she buy?

the box containing 100 nails

3. The carpenter is building a barn with 116 boards. She plans to use 8 nails in each board. Which box of nails should she buy?

the box containing 1,000 nails

4. The carpenter is building a house with 251 boards. She plans to use 9 nails in each board. Which boxes of nails should she buy?

2 boxes of 1,000 nails and 1 box of 500 nails

Follow the rule to find each missing number.

5. Rule: Multiply by 4.

Input	Output
3	12
40	160
60	240
700	2,800

6. Rule: Multiply by 700.

Input	Output
5	3,500
7	4,900
9	6,300
2	1,400

7. Robert has 42 inches of wood to make 1 picture frame. About how much wood will he need to make 7 frames?

About 280 in.

Name _____

Exploring Multiplication with Arrays

You can use grid paper to help you multiply.

1. Multiply 3×24. Use grid paper to show an array.

a. Show 20 and 4 ones. Make the ones a different color so you can tell them from the tens. This shows 1×24.

b. Put 2 more rows of 24 on your array. This shows 3×24.

c. How many rows of 20 does the array show? ___3___

d. How many rows of 4 does the array show? ___3___

e. Find the sum of the number of boxes in each section of the array. ___60___ + ___12___ = ___72___

f. $3 \times 24 =$ ___72___

2. Multiply 4×17.

a. Make an array on grid paper.

b. ___40___ + ___28___ = ___68___

c. $4 \times 17 =$ ___68___

3. Multiply 6×14.

a. Make an array on grid paper.

b. ___60___ + ___24___ = ___84___

c. $6 \times 14 =$ ___84___

4. Tell how you would use a grid paper array to solve 3×31.

Possible answer: Draw 3 rows of 31, shading the ones a different color. Multiply 3×30 and 3×1. Add $90 + 3$ to get the product.

5. Explain how you would solve 2×47 by breaking apart the numbers.

Possible answer: Think of 2×47 as $2 \times 40 = 80$ and $2 \times 7 = 14$. Then add 80 and 14. So, $2 \times 47 = 94$.

Multiplying: Partial Products

Recreation The height of a pony or horse is measured from the ground to the top of its back. Instead of being measured in centimeters or inches, the animal is measured in *hands*. Each hand equals about 4 inches.

1. Juwan's pony is 13 hands high.
   How tall is it in inches? **52 in.**

2. Sadie's horse is 16 hands high.
   How tall is it in inches? **64 in.**

3. Matt's pony is 48 inches high. How tall is it in hands? **12 hands**

4. Lynn's pony is 80 inches high. How tall is it in hands? **20 hands**

5. Keri is training for a race that takes place in 7 weeks. If she runs 24 miles a week, how many miles will she run before the race? **168 miles**

6. Mr. Duff needs 150 apples to sell the day of the race. A case contains 36 apples. If he buys 4 cases, will he have enough apples? **No; $4 \times 36 = 144$**

7. Mr. Duff also needs 150 oranges for the runners to eat. The oranges come in boxes of 24. If he buys 7 boxes, will he have enough oranges? **Yes; $7 \times 24 = 168$**

8. There are 8 groups of runners. Each group has 34 people. How many runners in all? **272 runners**

Multiplying 2-Digit Numbers

New York, New York! It's a great place for a vacation.

1. The ferry tickets to visit the Statue of Liberty cost 12 dollars each. How much money will we need to buy tickets for 6 people? **$72**

2. How about a show? If there are 4 shows every day, including weekends, at Radio City Music Hall, how many shows are there in March? (Hint: March has 31 days.) **124 shows**

3. New York City has 5 *boroughs* (or parts). If each borough has 25 libraries, about how many libraries are in New York City? **125 libraries**

4. New York City is known for its skyscrapers. If 4 new skyscrapers are built this year and each one has 98 floors, how many new floors are there in all? **392 floors**

5. You will be spending 12 days in New York. If you plan 3 activities each day, how many activities will you have planned for the entire trip? **36**

6. **Choose a strategy** A family of 4 want to ride 17 rides at Coney Island Amusement Park. If each ride costs 2 tickets, how many tickets will they need to buy?

   • Use Objects/Act It Out
   • Draw a Picture
   • Look for a Pattern
   • Guess and Check
   • Use Logical Reasoning
   • Make an Organized List
   • Make a Table
   • Solve a Simpler Problem
   • Work Backward

   a. What strategy would you use to solve the problem?
   Possible answer: Use Objects/Act It Out or Find a Pattern.

   b. Answer the problem. **136 tickets**

Multiplying 3-Digit Numbers

Science Human beings are *primates*. So are gorillas, chimps, orangutans, baboons, and lemurs!

The World's Largest Primates	
Primate	Average weight
Gorilla	485 pounds
Human	170 pounds
Orangutan	165 pounds
Chimpanzee	110 pounds

Use the chart to help you solve each problem.

1. How much would 4 gorillas weigh? **1,940 pounds**

2. How much would half a dozen chimpanzees weigh? **660 pounds**

3. The elevator sign says "Limit 1,000 pounds." Which group could not ride together: 8 chimpanzees, 7 orangutans, or 5 humans? Explain.
   7 orangutans could not ride together; $165 \times 7 = 1,155$; $1,155 > 1,000$

4. The Statue of Liberty is 151 feet high. If another statue were 3 times higher, how tall would it be? **453 feet**

5. The drama club presented a play on Thursday, Friday, Saturday, and Sunday. Each night the play was sold out. If there are 128 seats in the auditorium, how many people saw the play all together? **512 people**

6. If 122 people can travel in 1 train car, how many people could travel on a train with 7 cars? **854**

Multiplying Money

Literature In the 19th century, Charles Dickens wrote a famous book called *A Tale of Two Cities*. The book is still very popular and the library is purchasing several new copies. They can buy a hardcover edition of the book for $9.95, or a paperback edition for $3.95.

1. How much would 3 hardcover editions cost?
   $29.85

2. How much would 5 paperback editions cost?
   $19.75

3. How much would 2 hardcover editions and 2 paperback editions cost?
   $19.90 + $7.90 = $27.80

4. A soccer ball costs $14.95. Your school needs to buy 9 new ones. How much will they cost? **$134.55**

5. A package of D-batteries costs $3.99. How much would 3 packages of D-batteries cost? **$11.97**

6. A single floppy disk costs $1.29. A box of 9 floppy disks costs $10.95. Which is less expensive: 9 single disks or a box? Explain.
   The box; 9 single disks costs $11.61 ($1.29 × 9), compared to only $10.95 for the box.

7. A package of 3 t-shirts costs $6.95. A package of 4 t-shirts costs $7.95. How much would it cost to purchase 10 t-shirts? Explain.
   $21.85; $6.95 × 2 = $13.90; $13.90 + $7.95 = $21.85

Mental Math

Science Swans are large, beautiful birds which sometimes live in city parks. Male swans weigh about 41 pounds. Female swans weigh about 37 pounds.

Use mental math to solve these problems.

1. How much would 4 male swans weigh?   164 pounds

2. How much would 2 female swans weigh?   74 pounds

3. How much would two pairs of swans weigh, 2 males and 2 females?   156 pounds

Snack	Calories
1 fresh apple	61 calories
1 graham cracker	58 calories
1 cup of popcorn	41 calories

4. The table shows the number of calories in each of the following snacks. Find the total number of calories in:

a. 2 fresh apples   122 calories

b. 4 cups of popcorn   164 calories

c. 3 graham crackers   174 calories

d. 1 apple, 2 cups of popcorn, and 5 graham crackers   433 calories

5. There are 27 books on each shelf of a 9-shelf bookcase. How many books are in the entire bookcase?   243 books

---

GPS PROBLEM 5, STUDENT PAGE 387

There are 63 apartments in a building. After 1 month, 7 apartments were rented. After 2 months, 14 were rented. After 3 months, 21 were rented. If the pattern continues, how long will it take for all of the apartments to be rented?

— Understand —

1. What do you know?

7 rented in 1 month; 14 in 2 months; and 21 in 3 months

2. What do you need to find out?

Number of months it will take for all 63 to be rented

— Plan —

3. Complete the table. Fill in what you know.

Month	1	2	3	4	5	6	7	8	9
Apartments Rented	7	14	21	28	35	42	49	56	63

— Solve —

4. Find a pattern and complete the table. What is your answer?

9 months

— Look Back —

5. How could you have solved the problem in another way?

Possible answer: I could divide 63 by 7 to get 9 months.

SOLVE ANOTHER PROBLEM

The fire alarms in all the apartments must be inspected. After one week, the fire marshal has inspected 9 alarms. After 2 weeks, she has inspected 18 alarms. How long will it take her to inspect all 63 alarms?   7 weeks

---

Exploring Division Patterns

Write the basic fact that you can use to solve these problems. Then, solve each problem.

	Basic Fact	Quotient
1. $140 \div 2$	$14 \div 2 = 7$	70
2. $30 \div 3$	$3 \div 3 = 1$	10
3. $40 \div 2$	$4 \div 2 = 2$	20
4. $600 \div 3$	$6 \div 3 = 2$	200
5. $80 \div 2$	$8 \div 2 = 4$	40
6. $800 \div 4$	$8 \div 4 = 2$	200
7. $900 \div 3$	$9 \div 3 = 3$	300
8. $120 \div 6$	$12 \div 6 = 2$	20
9. $500 \div 5$	$5 \div 5 = 1$	100
10. $70 \div 7$	$7 \div 7 = 1$	10

11. Sam picks out a videotape that is 90 minutes long. His mother says he may watch it in 3 parts.

a. If Sam wants each part to be equal, how long will each part be?

30 minutes

b. How could you use a basic fact to find the answer?

Possible answer: $9 \div 3 = 3$, so 9 tens $\div 3 = 3$ tens, or 30.

12. An insect is 120 centimeters long. It has three body parts of nearly equal length.

a. About how long is each body part?   40 centimeters

b. How could you use a basic fact to find the answer?

Possible answer: $12 \div 3 = 4$, so 12 tens $\div 3 = 4$ tens, or 40.

Estimating Quotients

Physical Education Every day at baseball camp, a different number of players show up! Estimate how many teams can be made each day. (Hint: there are 9 players on a baseball team.) Complete the table.

	Day	Number of Players	Number of Teams
1.	Monday	73	8 teams
2.	Tuesday	37	4 teams
3.	Wednesday	82	9 teams
4.	Thursday	55	6 teams
5.	Friday	46	5 teams

6. How many baseball games can be played at the same time on Monday?   4 games

7. You have $9 and need to buy presents for 4 people. You want to spend the money equally. About how much can you spend on each person?   About $2

8. Your class is studying the solar system. You must divide the 26 students into groups. Each group will research one of the nine planets. About how many students will be in each group?   About 3 students

9. Your web browser lists 57 web sites about paper recycling in your area. You want to visit them all in 7 days. About how many web sites should you visit each day?   About 8 web sites

10. There are 65 students visiting a museum. If they are divided into 8 tour groups, about how many students are in each group?   8 students

Exploring Division with Remainders

Mari bought 22 bananas at the fruit market. She wants to make some banana bread for the school party.

The recipe for Old Time Banana Bread uses 4 bananas per loaf. The recipe for Fab–Fab Banana Bread uses 3 bananas per loaf. Mari needs to decide which recipe to use.

Answer each question. You may use the bananas to help you.

1. Suppose Mari makes as much Old Time Banana Bread as possible.

   a. How many bananas for each loaf? __4__

   b. How many loaves all together? __5__

   c. How many bananas left over? __2__

2. What if Mari makes as much Fab–Fab Banana Bread as possible.

   a. How many bananas for each loaf? __3__

   b. How many loaves all together? __7__

   c. How many bananas left over? __1__

3. How did you find out how many bananas were left over?

   Possible answer: Circled groups of bananas, then counted the remainder.

4. How will dividing and finding leftovers help Mari decide what kind of banana bread to make? Possible answer: She can choose the recipe that will make the most loaves or the one that leaves her more bananas to eat.

Dividing

Geography The United States of America has 50 states. Did you know that Mexico has 29 states?

Your class wants to study Mexico. The class will work in groups. Each group will study the same number of Mexican states and give a report to the class. How many states would each group study if the class was divided into:

1. 3 groups? __9__ states with __2__ left over

2. 4 groups? __7__ states with __1__ left over

3. 5 groups? __5__ states with __4__ left over

4. 6 groups? __4__ states with __5__ left over

5. 7 groups? __4__ states with __1__ left over

6. 8 groups? __3__ states with __5__ left over

7. 9 groups? __3__ states with __2__ left over

8. Into how many groups would you divide the class? How many states would each group study? Explain your reasoning.

   Possible answer: Make 7 groups, 6 groups study 4 states and 1 group studies 5 states. When the students are assigned groups, the largest group studies 5 states. This way every group will have about the same amount of work.

9. If a 25-foot rope is used to make 3 jump ropes of equal length, how long will each jump rope be? How much rope will be left over?

   8 feet, 1 foot left over

10. A cross-country race is 12 miles long and has 4 equal "legs" (or parts). How long is each leg?   3 miles

---

Decision Making

Your community is planning a Walk Against Hunger and they have asked you to help. First, you must plan a route. It must be 12 miles long, finish at the town hall, and go through the park.

Draw your route on the grid paper below. Let each square represent 1 mile. **Check students' maps.**

Your Town

Key:
- river
- bridge
- town hall

1. You want to put a snack table every three miles on the route. How many will you need?   4

Mark your snack tables on the map.

2. There should be 1 snack per walker at each table. You are expecting 30 walkers this year. How many snacks will you need?   120

3. You want to put some juice stands on the route as well. At what intervals do you think they should be? Remember, the walkers will be thirsty!

   Possible answer: Every 2 miles.

4. How many juice stands will you have? Mark them on the map.   Possible answer: 6

5. If every walker needs 1 glass of juice at each stand, how many glasses of juice will you need in total?

   Possible answer: 180

6. 1 juice bottle serves 5 people. How many bottles will you need for the walk?

   Possible answer: 36 bottles

Exploring Equal Parts

Use the clock to answer each question.

1. You can divide the clock into 2 equal parts by drawing a line from 12 to 6. You can also draw a line from 1 to 7 that divides the clock into 2 equal parts.

   a. In what other ways can you divide the clock into 2 equal parts? Show them on the clock.

      Possible answers: Draw lines from 2 to 8, 3 to 9, 4 to 10, 5 to 11.

   b. What pattern do you notice in the pairs of numbers?

      Possible answer: The difference of each pair of numbers is 6.

2. You can divide the clock into 3 equal parts. You can draw lines from the center to 1, 5 and 9.

   a. What other lines can you draw to divide the clock into 3 equal parts? Show them on the clock.

      Possible answers: Center to 2, 6, and 10; center to 3, 7 and 11, center to 4, 8, and 12.

   b. What pattern do you notice in the sets of 3 numbers?

      Possible answer: If you add 4 to the first number you get the second number, and if you add 4 to the second number you get the third number.

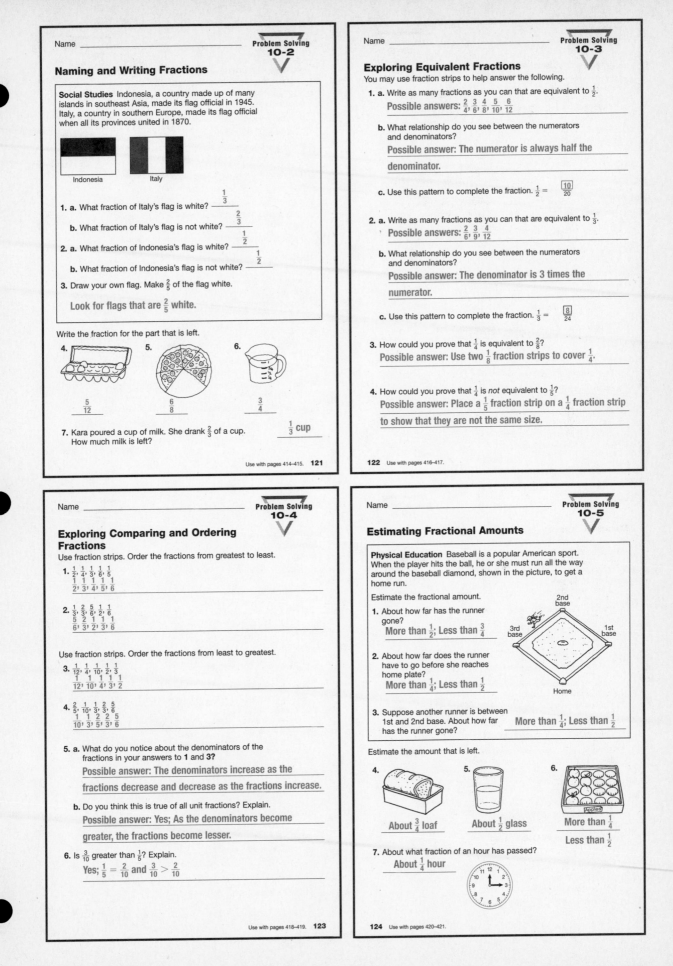

Naming and Writing Fractions

Social Studies Indonesia, a country made up of many islands in southeast Asia, made its flag official in 1945. Italy, a country in southern Europe, made its flag official when all its provinces united in 1870.

Indonesia   Italy

1. a. What fraction of Italy's flag is white? $\frac{1}{3}$

b. What fraction of Italy's flag is not white? $\frac{2}{3}$

2. a. What fraction of Indonesia's flag is white? $\frac{1}{2}$

b. What fraction of Indonesia's flag is not white? $\frac{1}{2}$

3. Draw your own flag. Make $\frac{2}{5}$ of the flag white.

Look for flags that are $\frac{2}{5}$ white.

Write the fraction for the part that is left.

4.   **5.**   **6.**

$\frac{5}{12}$ $\frac{6}{8}$ $\frac{3}{4}$

7. Kara poured a cup of milk. She drank $\frac{2}{3}$ of a cup. How much milk is left? $\frac{1}{3}$ cup

Exploring Equivalent Fractions

You may use fraction strips to help answer the following.

1. a. Write as many fractions as you can that are equivalent to $\frac{1}{2}$.
Possible answers: $\frac{2}{4}, \frac{3}{6}, \frac{4}{8}, \frac{5}{10}, \frac{6}{12}$

b. What relationship do you see between the numerators and denominators?
Possible answer: The numerator is always half the denominator.

c. Use this pattern to complete the fraction. $\frac{1}{2} = \frac{10}{20}$

2. a. Write as many fractions as you can that are equivalent to $\frac{1}{3}$.
Possible answers: $\frac{2}{6}, \frac{3}{9}, \frac{4}{12}$

b. What relationship do you see between the numerators and denominators?
Possible answer: The denominator is 3 times the numerator.

c. Use this pattern to complete the fraction. $\frac{1}{3} = \frac{8}{24}$

3. How could you prove that $\frac{1}{4}$ is equivalent to $\frac{2}{8}$?
Possible answer: Use two $\frac{1}{8}$ fraction strips to cover $\frac{1}{4}$.

4. How could you prove that $\frac{1}{4}$ is *not* equivalent to $\frac{1}{5}$?
Possible answer: Place a $\frac{1}{5}$ fraction strip on a $\frac{1}{4}$ fraction strip to show that they are not the same size.

Exploring Comparing and Ordering Fractions

Use fraction strips. Order the fractions from greatest to least.

1. $\frac{1}{2}, \frac{1}{4}, \frac{1}{3}, \frac{1}{6}, \frac{1}{5}$
$\frac{1}{2}, \frac{1}{3}, \frac{1}{4}, \frac{1}{5}, \frac{1}{6}$

2. $\frac{1}{3}, \frac{2}{3}, \frac{5}{6}, \frac{1}{2}, \frac{1}{6}$
$\frac{5}{6}, \frac{2}{3}, \frac{1}{2}, \frac{1}{3}, \frac{1}{6}$

Use fraction strips. Order the fractions from least to greatest.

3. $\frac{1}{12}, \frac{1}{4}, \frac{1}{10}, \frac{1}{2}, \frac{1}{3}$
$\frac{1}{12}, \frac{1}{10}, \frac{1}{4}, \frac{1}{3}, \frac{1}{2}$

4. $\frac{2}{5}, \frac{1}{10}, \frac{1}{3}, \frac{2}{3}, \frac{5}{6}$
$\frac{1}{10}, \frac{1}{3}, \frac{2}{5}, \frac{2}{3}, \frac{5}{6}$

5. a. What do you notice about the denominators of the fractions in your answers to **1** and **3**?
Possible answer: The denominators increase as the fractions decrease and decrease as the fractions increase.

b. Do you think this is true of all unit fractions? Explain.
Possible answer: Yes; As the denominators become greater, the fractions become lesser.

6. Is $\frac{3}{10}$ greater than $\frac{1}{5}$? Explain.
Yes; $\frac{1}{5} = \frac{2}{10}$ and $\frac{3}{10} > \frac{2}{10}$

Estimating Fractional Amounts

Physical Education Baseball is a popular American sport. When the player hits the ball, he or she must run all the way around the baseball diamond, shown in the picture, to get a home run.

Estimate the fractional amount.

1. About how far has the runner gone?
More than $\frac{1}{2}$; Less than $\frac{3}{4}$

2. About how far does the runner have to go before she reaches home plate?
More than $\frac{1}{4}$; Less than $\frac{1}{2}$

3. Suppose another runner is between 1st and 2nd base. About how far has the runner gone?
More than $\frac{1}{4}$; Less than $\frac{1}{2}$

Estimate the amount that is left.

4.   **5.**   **6.**

About $\frac{3}{4}$ loaf   About $\frac{1}{2}$ glass   More than $\frac{1}{4}$
                                                  Less than $\frac{1}{2}$

7. About what fraction of an hour has passed?
About $\frac{1}{4}$ hour

Fractions and Sets

Careers Mrs. Gomez is a school cafeteria manager. She plans lunch for hundreds of students every day!

Look at this week's lunch menu to answer each question.

Lunch Menu					
	Monday	**Tuesday**	**Wednesday**	**Thursday**	**Friday**
Hot dish	Pizza	Turkey Stew	Pizza	Veggie Burger	Fish Sticks
Side dish	Fruit Salad	Fruit Salad	Garden Salad	Spinach Salad	Cole Slaw
Sandwich	Tuna Fish	Veggie Roll	Egg Salad	Veggie Roll	Cheese

1. On what fraction of the days this week will the cafeteria serve

   a. fruit salad? $\frac{2}{5}$ **b.** cole slaw? $\frac{1}{5}$

   c. tuna sandwiches? $\frac{1}{5}$ **d.** veggie rolls? $\frac{2}{5}$

2. The cafeteria will serve pizza on Monday and Wednesday. On what fraction of these "pizza days" will they also serve a garden salad? $\frac{1}{2}$

3. What fraction of the 15 menu items are fish dishes? $\frac{2}{15}$

Answer each question.

4. What fraction of a year is one month? $\frac{1}{12}$

5. Alyssa has 5 sisters. 2 of them are younger. What fraction of her sisters are older than her? $\frac{3}{5}$

6. Randall has $\frac{1}{5}$ of his garden planted. Terry has $\frac{1}{6}$ of his garden planted. Who has planted more of his garden? **Randall**

Exploring Finding a Fraction of a Number

Use counters to solve each problem.

1. Alex had 20 crackers. He ate $\frac{1}{4}$ of them. How many crackers did he eat? 5

   How many counters did you use to solve the problem? 20

   How many groups did you make? 4

2. The soccer team sold 12 t-shirts at the fair. Kenny sold $\frac{1}{3}$ of them. How many t-shirts did he sell? 4

   How many counters did you use to solve the problem? 12

   How many groups did you make? 3

3. The math team scored 25 points at the championship. Linda scored $\frac{1}{5}$ of them herself. How many points did she score? 5

   How many counters did you use to solve the problem? 25

   How many groups did you make? 5

4. This is a picture of a garden. Complete the picture to show the following.

   a. $\frac{1}{4}$ of the plants are sunflowers.

   b. $\frac{1}{2}$ of the plants have flowers.

   c. $\frac{1}{8}$ of the plants are trees.

   4. **a.** 2 plants should be sunflowers.

   b. 4 plants should have flowers.

   c. 1 plant should be a tree.

Mixed Numbers

Health Eating well is an important part of staying healthy. We need to eat different kinds of foods every day to give our bodies what they need.

1. Calcium is important for healthy bones and nerves. To get one day's worth of calcium, you could drink:

   whole milk   or   skim milk

   Which kind of milk has more calcium? **Skim milk**

2. Protein is important for healthy muscles and blood. To get one day's worth of protein, you could eat:

   salmon   or   tuna

   Which canned fish has more protein? **Salmon**

3. Vitamin C helps bones stay strong and wounds to heal. To get one day's worth of Vitamin C, you could eat:

   melon   or   grapefruit

   Which fruit has more Vitamin C? **Grapefruit**

4. Draw a picture to show each mixed number.

   a. $1\frac{4}{5}$ **b.** $2\frac{1}{3}$

   a. Check that wholes are divided into equal groups of 5.
   b. Check that wholes are divided into equal groups of 3.

5. If you cut pies into 6 slices each and gave away $1\frac{1}{6}$ pies, how many slices is that? 7

Exploring Adding and Subtracting Numbers

1. Add fractions by drawing pictures.

   a. Draw $\frac{1}{4}$.

   b. Add $\frac{2}{4}$ to your drawing.

   c. $\frac{1}{4} + \frac{2}{4} =$ $\frac{3}{4}$

2. Subtract fractions by drawing pictures.

   a. Draw $\frac{5}{6}$.

   b. Take away $\frac{2}{6}$ from your drawing.

   c. $\frac{5}{6} - \frac{2}{6} =$ $\frac{3}{6}$

3. **a.** What portion of the pizza will remain after 4 more slices are eaten? $\frac{1}{4}$ or $\frac{2}{8}$

   b. Write a number sentence to show the problem you solved. $\frac{6}{8} - \frac{4}{8} = \frac{2}{8}$

4. **a.** What portion of a cup will there be if $\frac{1}{3}$ of a cup of water is added? $\frac{2}{3}$

   b. Write a number sentence to show the problem you solved. $\frac{1}{3} + \frac{1}{3} = \frac{2}{3}$

5. **a.** How much will $\frac{3}{4}$ yard of fabric cost? $9

   b. Describe how you solved the problem.

   Possible answer: $\frac{1}{4} + \frac{1}{4} + \frac{1}{4} = \frac{3}{4}$, so the fabric will cost $3 + $3 + $3 = $9.

Decision Making

You're in charge of the holiday party for the 10-member gymnastics team and must decide what to serve. Here is a list of the foods you can offer:

Pizza: 8 slices per pizza

Fruit salad: 6 servings per jar

Granola bars: 9 granola bars per box

Apple juice: 8 glasses per bottle

Milk: 4 glasses per carton

1. What do you know?
   Number of team members; The number of servings for each party food

2. What do you need to decide?
   Which foods to serve; How many of each item you will need

3. How many people will you serve? ___10___

4. Which foods will you choose?
   Students may choose some or all of the foods.

5. How many servings will each team member get?
   Students give number of servings per player for each food.

Fill in this chart to show your plan. **Check students' answers.**

Food	Amount Needed for 1 Gymnast	Amount Needed for 10 Gymnasts	Amount to Order
Pizza			Pizzas
Fruit Salad			Jars
Granola Bars			Boxes
Apple Juice			Bottles
Milk			Cartons

Exploring Length

1. Draw a line to show 5 inches.
   Check length for accuracy.

2. Look at your line. Then look around your classroom. Name five items that you think have a length of about 5 inches. List the items in the table. Then use a ruler to check your predictions. Record the actual length of each item in the table.

Item	Length in Inches
a.	
b.	
c.	
d.	
e.	

Possible answers: Pencil, board eraser, notepad, marker, crayon

3. Is the length of your nose greater or less than 5 inches?
   Less than 5 inches

4. Is the width of your desk greater or less than 5 inches?
   Greater than 5 inches

5. Write the following list of items in the table in order from longest to shortest. Then measure to the nearest inch. Write the actual measurements in the table.

pencil   width of paper   eraser

Item	Actual Measure
a.	
b.	
c.	

Answers and measurements will vary.

Measuring to the Nearest $\frac{1}{2}$ Inch and $\frac{1}{4}$ Inch

Social Studies People who lived in ancient Rome and Greece had their own systems of measurement. Both systems had a unit called the cubit. The Greek cubit was a little more than $18\frac{1}{4}$ inches. The Roman cubit measured $17\frac{1}{2}$ inches. This difference caused problems for merchants!

1. Suppose you lived in ancient Greece. You want to buy 2 cubits of cloth. How many inches of cloth do you want? $36\frac{1}{2}$ in.

2. Suppose the cloth seller used Roman cubits to measure his cloth. Would he give you more or less than 2 Greek cubits? Explain.
   Less; The Roman cubit is $\frac{3}{4}$ inch less than the Greek cubit.

3. If a cubit was based on the length of a body part, such as the distance from the elbow to the tip of the finger, do you think an average Greek or Roman was larger? Explain.
   Possible answer: Greek, since their cubit was longer.

Ricki is making bracelets. She uses the following beads.

4. Ricki made a bracelet with beads arranged from smallest to largest. Draw the beads in order.

5. Ricki put one white bead on a bracelet. Next, she wants to add grey beads that have the same total length as one white bead. How many grey beads should she use?   **3 grey beads**

Exploring Length in Feet and Inches

1. Work with a partner to measure height.   **Answers will vary.**

   a. Estimate your height in feet and inches. Then estimate your partner's height. Record your estimates in the table.

   b. Stand against a wall. Have your partner put a piece of tape on the wall even with the top of your head. Switch places and mark your partner's height.

   c. Use a ruler to measure from the tape to the floor.

Complete the table.

Name	Estimated Height	Actual Height (in feet and inches)	Actual Height (in inches)

2. Why do you think height is usually given in feet and inches rather than just feet?
   Possible answer: Feet and inches are more exact than just feet.

Write whether each object should be measured in feet or inches.

3. a dog's tail   4. the height of a tree   5. the length of your arm
   Inches   **Feet**   **Feet or inches**

6. Which object in 3–5 would be better to measure in feet *and* inches?
   Possible answer: The length of my arm; Using feet and inches would give a more accurate measurement.

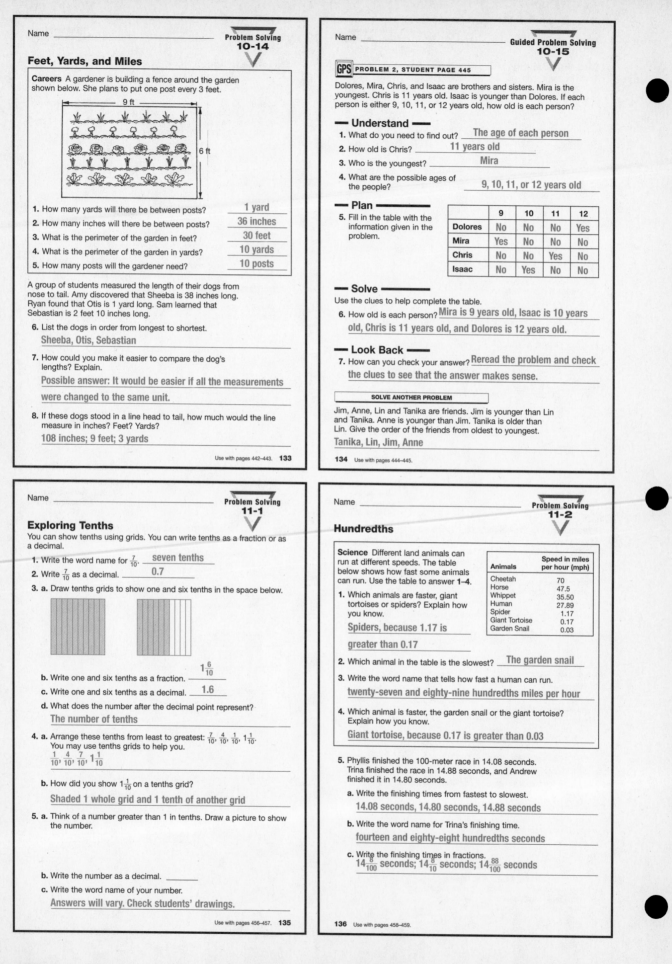

Feet, Yards, and Miles

Careers A gardener is building a fence around the garden shown below. She plans to put one post every 3 feet.

9 ft

6 ft

1. How many yards will there be between posts? **1 yard**
2. How many inches will there be between posts? **36 inches**
3. What is the perimeter of the garden in feet? **30 feet**
4. What is the perimeter of the garden in yards? **10 yards**
5. How many posts will the gardener need? **10 posts**

A group of students measured the length of their dogs from nose to tail. Amy discovered that Sheeba is 38 inches long. Ryan found that Otis is 1 yard long. Sam learned that Sebastian is 2 feet 10 inches long.

6. List the dogs in order from longest to shortest.

   Sheeba, Otis, Sebastian

7. How could you make it easier to compare the dog's lengths? Explain.

   Possible answer: It would be easier if all the measurements were changed to the same unit.

8. If these dogs stood in a line head to tail, how much would the line measure in inches? Feet? Yards?

   108 inches; 9 feet; 3 yards

GPS PROBLEM 2, STUDENT PAGE 445

Dolores, Mira, Chris, and Isaac are brothers and sisters. Mira is the youngest. Chris is 11 years old. Isaac is younger than Dolores. If each person is either 9, 10, 11, or 12 years old, how old is each person?

Understand

1. What do you need to find out? **The age of each person**
2. How old is Chris? **11 years old**
3. Who is the youngest? **Mira**
4. What are the possible ages of the people? **9, 10, 11, or 12 years old**

Plan

5. Fill in the table with the information given in the problem.

	9	10	11	12
Dolores	No	No	No	Yes
Mira	Yes	No	No	No
Chris	No	No	Yes	No
Isaac	No	Yes	No	No

Solve

Use the clues to help complete the table.

6. How old is each person? **Mira is 9 years old, Isaac is 10 years old, Chris is 11 years old, and Dolores is 12 years old.**

Look Back

7. How can you check your answer? **Reread the problem and check the clues to see that the answer makes sense.**

SOLVE ANOTHER PROBLEM

Jim, Anne, Lin and Tanika are friends. Jim is younger than Lin and Tanika. Anne is younger than Jim. Tanika is older than Lin. Give the order of the friends from oldest to youngest.

Tanika, Lin, Jim, Anne

Exploring Tenths

You can show tenths using grids. You can write tenths as a fraction or as a decimal.

1. Write the word name for $\frac{7}{10}$. **seven tenths**
2. Write $\frac{7}{10}$ as a decimal. **0.7**
3. a. Draw tenths grids to show one and six tenths in the space below.

   $1\frac{6}{10}$

   b. Write one and six tenths as a fraction. $1\frac{6}{10}$
   c. Write one and six tenths as a decimal. **1.6**
   d. What does the number after the decimal point represent?

   The number of tenths

4. a. Arrange these tenths from least to greatest: $\frac{7}{10}, \frac{4}{10}, \frac{1}{10}, 1\frac{1}{10}$. You may use tenths grids to help you.

   $\frac{1}{10}, \frac{4}{10}, \frac{7}{10}, 1\frac{1}{10}$

   b. How did you show $1\frac{1}{10}$ on a tenths grid?

   Shaded 1 whole grid and 1 tenth of another grid

5. a. Think of a number greater than 1 in tenths. Draw a picture to show the number.

   b. Write the number as a decimal.
   c. Write the word name of your number.

   Answers will vary. Check students' drawings.

Hundredths

Science Different land animals can run at different speeds. The table below shows how fast some animals can run. Use the table to answer 1–4.

Animals	Speed in miles per hour (mph)
Cheetah	70
Horse	47.5
Whippet	35.50
Human	27.89
Spider	1.17
Giant Tortoise	0.17
Garden Snail	0.03

1. Which animals are faster, giant tortoises or spiders? Explain how you know.

   Spiders, because 1.17 is greater than 0.17

2. Which animal in the table is the slowest? **The garden snail**

3. Write the word name that tells how fast a human can run.

   twenty-seven and eighty-nine hundredths miles per hour

4. Which animal is faster, the garden snail or the giant tortoise? Explain how you know.

   Giant tortoise, because 0.17 is greater than 0.03

5. Phyllis finished the 100-meter race in 14.08 seconds. Trina finished the race in 14.88 seconds, and Andrew finished it in 14.80 seconds.

   a. Write the finishing times from fastest to slowest.

   14.08 seconds, 14.80 seconds, 14.88 seconds

   b. Write the word name for Trina's finishing time.

   fourteen and eighty-eight hundredths seconds

   c. Write the finishing times in fractions.

   $14\frac{8}{100}$ seconds; $14\frac{8}{10}$ seconds; $14\frac{88}{100}$ seconds

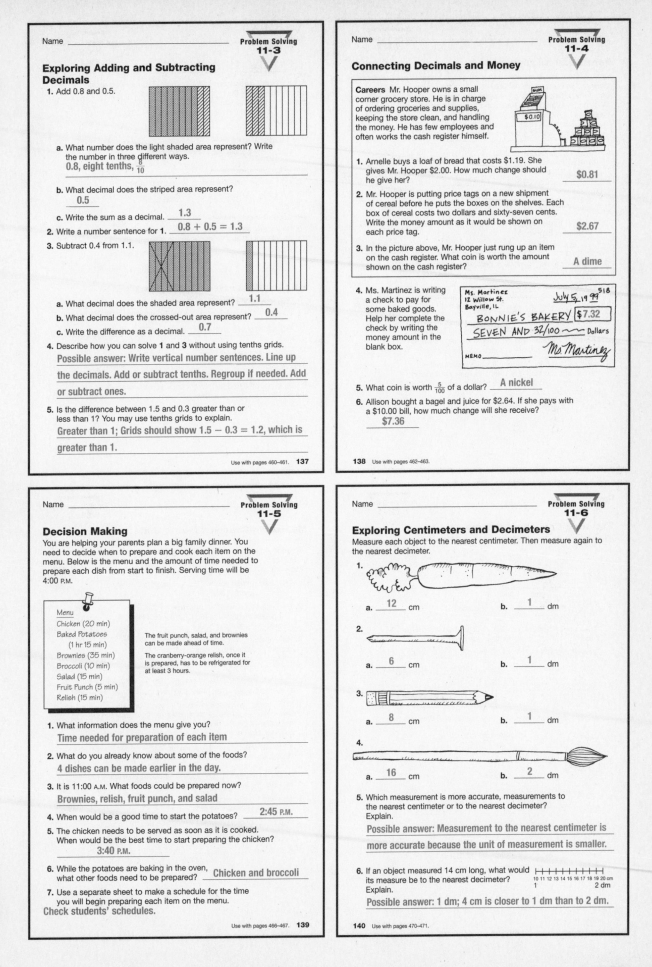

Exploring Adding and Subtracting Decimals

1. Add 0.8 and 0.5.

   a. What number does the light shaded area represent? Write the number in three different ways.
   0.8, eight tenths, $\frac{8}{10}$

   b. What decimal does the striped area represent?
   0.5

   c. Write the sum as a decimal. 1.3

2. Write a number sentence for 1. 0.8 + 0.5 = 1.3

3. Subtract 0.4 from 1.1.

   a. What decimal does the shaded area represent? 1.1

   b. What decimal does the crossed-out area represent? 0.4

   c. Write the difference as a decimal. 0.7

4. Describe how you can solve 1 and 3 without using tenths grids.
   Possible answer: Write vertical number sentences. Line up the decimals. Add or subtract tenths. Regroup if needed. Add or subtract ones.

5. Is the difference between 1.5 and 0.3 greater than or less than 1? You may use tenths grids to explain.
   Greater than 1; Grids should show 1.5 − 0.3 = 1.2, which is greater than 1.

Use with pages 460–461. **137**

Connecting Decimals and Money

Careers Mr. Hooper owns a small corner grocery store. He is in charge of ordering groceries and supplies, keeping the store clean, and handling the money. He has few employees and often works the cash register himself.

1. Arnelle buys a loaf of bread that costs $1.19. She gives Mr. Hooper $2.00. How much change should he give her? $0.81

2. Mr. Hooper is putting price tags on a new shipment of cereal before he puts the boxes on the shelves. Each box of cereal costs two dollars and sixty-seven cents. Write the money amount as it would be shown on each price tag. $2.67

3. In the picture above, Mr. Hooper just rung up an item on the cash register. What coin is worth the amount shown on the cash register? A dime

4. Ms. Martinez is writing a check to pay for some baked goods. Help her complete the check by writing the money amount in the blank box.

   Ms. Martinez
   12 Willow St.
   Bayville, IL
   July 5, 1999 518
   BONNIE'S BAKERY $7.32
   SEVEN AND 32/100 ——— Dollars
   MEMO _____
   Ms. Martinez

5. What coin is worth $\frac{5}{100}$ of a dollar? A nickel

6. Allison bought a bagel and juice for $2.64. If she pays with a $10.00 bill, how much change will she receive? $7.36

138 Use with pages 462–463.

Decision Making

You are helping your parents plan a big family dinner. You need to decide when to prepare and cook each item on the menu. Below is the menu and the amount of time needed to prepare each dish from start to finish. Serving time will be 4:00 P.M.

Menu
Chicken (20 min)
Baked Potatoes (1 hr 15 min)
Brownies (35 min)
Broccoli (10 min)
Salad (15 min)
Fruit Punch (5 min)
Relish (15 min)

The fruit punch, salad, and brownies can be made ahead of time.

The cranberry-orange relish, once it is prepared, has to be refrigerated for at least 3 hours.

1. What information does the menu give you?
   Time needed for preparation of each item

2. What do you already know about some of the foods?
   4 dishes can be made earlier in the day.

3. It is 11:00 A.M. What foods could be prepared now?
   Brownies, relish, fruit punch, and salad

4. When would be a good time to start the potatoes? 2:45 P.M.

5. The chicken needs to be served as soon as it is cooked. When would be the best time to start preparing the chicken?
   3:40 P.M.

6. While the potatoes are baking in the oven, what other foods need to be prepared? Chicken and broccoli

7. Use a separate sheet to make a schedule for the time you will begin preparing each item on the menu.
   Check students' schedules.

Use with pages 466–467. **139**

Exploring Centimeters and Decimeters

Measure each object to the nearest centimeter. Then measure again to the nearest decimeter.

1.
   a. 12 cm   b. 1 dm

2.
   a. 6 cm   b. 1 dm

3.
   a. 8 cm   b. 1 dm

4.
   a. 16 cm   b. 2 dm

5. Which measurement is more accurate, measurements to the nearest centimeter or to the nearest decimeter? Explain.
   Possible answer: Measurement to the nearest centimeter is more accurate because the unit of measurement is smaller.

6. If an object measured 14 cm long, what would its measure be to the nearest decimeter? Explain.
   Possible answer: 1 dm; 4 cm is closer to 1 dm than to 2 dm.

140 Use with pages 470–471.

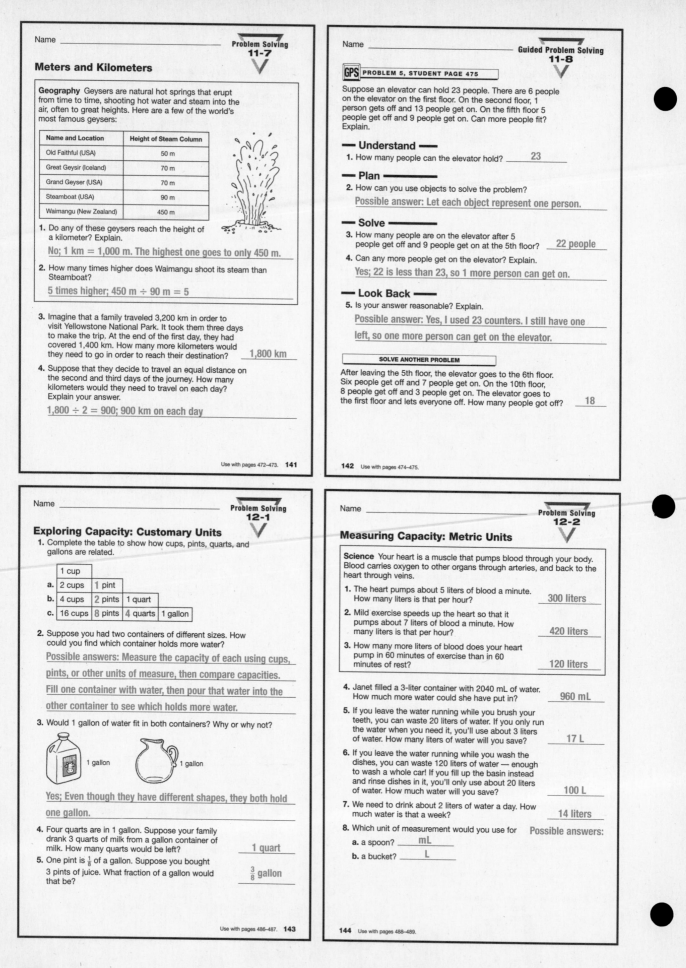

Meters and Kilometers

Geography Geysers are natural hot springs that erupt from time to time, shooting hot water and steam into the air, often to great heights. Here are a few of the world's most famous geysers:

Name and Location	Height of Steam Column
Old Faithful (USA)	50 m
Great Geysir (Iceland)	70 m
Grand Geyser (USA)	70 m
Steamboat (USA)	90 m
Waimangu (New Zealand)	450 m

1. Do any of these geysers reach the height of a kilometer? Explain.

No; 1 km = 1,000 m. The highest one goes to only 450 m.

2. How many times higher does Waimangu shoot its steam than Steamboat?

5 times higher; 450 m ÷ 90 m = 5

3. Imagine that a family traveled 3,200 km in order to visit Yellowstone National Park. It took them three days to make the trip. At the end of the first day, they had covered 1,400 km. How many more kilometers would they need to go in order to reach their destination?   1,800 km

4. Suppose that they decide to travel an equal distance on the second and third days of the journey. How many kilometers would they need to travel on each day? Explain your answer.

1,800 ÷ 2 = 900; 900 km on each day

Guided Problem Solving

GPS PROBLEM 5, STUDENT PAGE 475

Suppose an elevator can hold 23 people. There are 6 people on the elevator on the first floor. On the second floor, 1 person gets off and 13 people get on. On the fifth floor 5 people get off and 9 people get on. Can more people fit? Explain.

— Understand —
1. How many people can the elevator hold? ____ 23

— Plan —
2. How can you use objects to solve the problem?

Possible answer: Let each object represent one person.

— Solve —
3. How many people are on the elevator after 5 people get off and 9 people get on at the 5th floor?   22 people

4. Can any more people get on the elevator? Explain.

Yes; 22 is less than 23, so 1 more person can get on.

— Look Back —
5. Is your answer reasonable? Explain.

Possible answer: Yes, I used 23 counters. I still have one

left, so one more person can get on the elevator.

> SOLVE ANOTHER PROBLEM

After leaving the 5th floor, the elevator goes to the 6th floor. Six people get off and 7 people get on. On the 10th floor, 8 people get off and 3 people get on. The elevator goes to the first floor and lets everyone off. How many people got off?   18

Exploring Capacity: Customary Units

1. Complete the table to show how cups, pints, quarts, and gallons are related.

	1 cup			
	1 cup			
a.	2 cups	1 pint		
b.	4 cups	2 pints	1 quart	
c.	16 cups	8 pints	4 quarts	1 gallon

2. Suppose you had two containers of different sizes. How could you find which container holds more water?

Possible answers: Measure the capacity of each using cups,

pints, or other units of measure, then compare capacities.

Fill one container with water, then pour that water into the

other container to see which holds more water.

3. Would 1 gallon of water fit in both containers? Why or why not?

1 gallon   1 gallon

Yes; Even though they have different shapes, they both hold

one gallon.

4. Four quarts are in 1 gallon. Suppose your family drank 3 quarts of milk from a gallon container of milk. How many quarts would be left?   1 quart

5. One pint is $\frac{1}{8}$ of a gallon. Suppose you bought 3 pints of juice. What fraction of a gallon would that be? $\frac{3}{8}$ gallon

---

Measuring Capacity: Metric Units

Science Your heart is a muscle that pumps blood through your body. Blood carries oxygen to other organs through arteries, and back to the heart through veins.

1. The heart pumps about 5 liters of blood a minute. How many liters is that per hour?   300 liters

2. Mild exercise speeds up the heart so that it pumps about 7 liters of blood a minute. How many liters is that per hour?   420 liters

3. How many more liters of blood does your heart pump in 60 minutes of exercise than in 60 minutes of rest?   120 liters

4. Janet filled a 3-liter container with 2040 mL of water. How much more water could she have put in?   960 mL

5. If you leave the water running while you brush your teeth, you can waste 20 liters of water. If you only run the water when you need it, you'll use about 3 liters of water. How many liters of water will you save?   17 L

6. If you leave the water running while you wash the dishes, you can waste 120 liters of water — enough to wash a whole car! If you fill up the basin instead and rinse dishes in it, you'll only use about 20 liters of water. How much water will you save?   100 L

7. We need to drink about 2 liters of water a day. How much water is that a week?   14 liters

8. Which unit of measurement would you use for   Possible answers:

a. a spoon? ____ mL

b. a bucket? ____ L

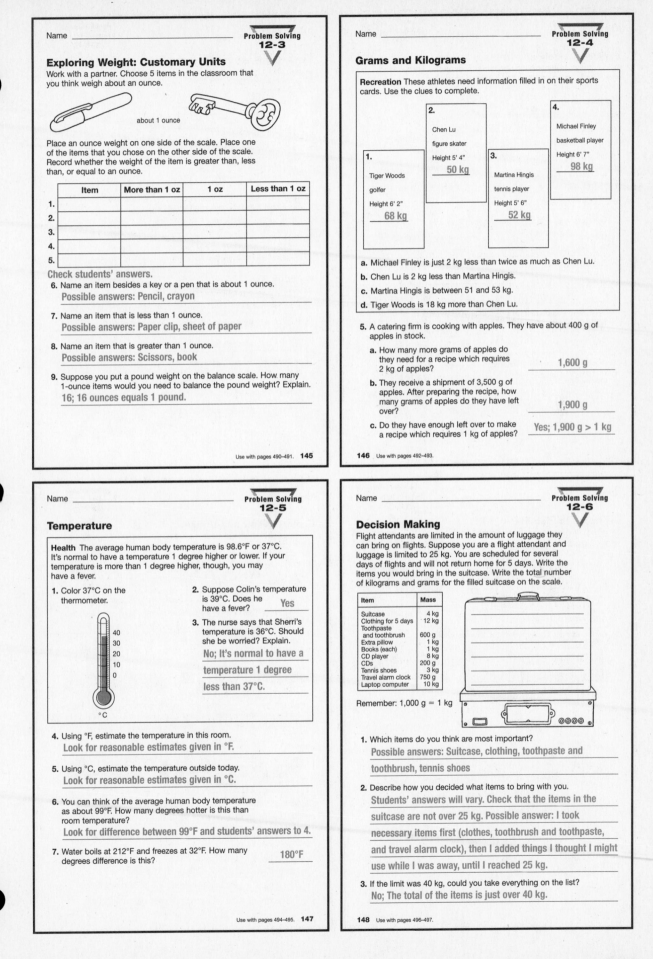

Exploring Weight: Customary Units

Work with a partner. Choose 5 items in the classroom that you think weigh about an ounce.

about 1 ounce

Place an ounce weight on one side of the scale. Place one of the items that you chose on the other side of the scale. Record whether the weight of the item is greater than, less than, or equal to an ounce.

	Item	More than 1 oz	1 oz	Less than 1 oz
1.				
2.				
3.				
4.				
5.				

Check students' answers.

6. Name an item besides a key or a pen that is about 1 ounce.
   Possible answers: Pencil, crayon

7. Name an item that is less than 1 ounce.
   Possible answers: Paper clip, sheet of paper

8. Name an item that is greater than 1 ounce.
   Possible answers: Scissors, book

9. Suppose you put a pound weight on the balance scale. How many 1-ounce items would you need to balance the pound weight? Explain.
   16; 16 ounces equals 1 pound.

Grams and Kilograms

Recreation These athletes need information filled in on their sports cards. Use the clues to complete.

2. Chen Lu figure skater Height 5' 4" — 50 kg

4. Michael Finley basketball player Height 6' 7" — 98 kg

1. Tiger Woods golfer Height 6' 2" — 68 kg

3. Martina Hingis tennis player Height 5' 6" — 52 kg

a. Michael Finley is just 2 kg less than twice as much as Chen Lu.

b. Chen Lu is 2 kg less than Martina Hingis.

c. Martina Hingis is between 51 and 53 kg.

d. Tiger Woods is 18 kg more than Chen Lu.

5. A catering firm is cooking with apples. They have about 400 g of apples in stock.

a. How many more grams of apples do they need for a recipe which requires 2 kg of apples? — 1,600 g

b. They receive a shipment of 3,500 g of apples. After preparing the recipe, how many grams of apples do they have left over? — 1,900 g

c. Do they have enough left over to make a recipe which requires 1 kg of apples? — Yes; 1,900 g > 1 kg

Temperature

Health The average human body temperature is 98.6°F or 37°C. It's normal to have a temperature 1 degree higher or lower. If your temperature is more than 1 degree higher, though, you may have a fever.

1. Color 37°C on the thermometer.

2. Suppose Colin's temperature is 39°C. Does he have a fever? **Yes**

3. The nurse says that Sherri's temperature is 36°C. Should she be worried? Explain.
   No; It's normal to have a temperature 1 degree less than 37°C.

4. Using °F, estimate the temperature in this room.
   Look for reasonable estimates given in °F.

5. Using °C, estimate the temperature outside today.
   Look for reasonable estimates given in °C.

6. You can think of the average human body temperature as about 99°F. How many degrees hotter is this than room temperature?
   Look for difference between 99°F and students' answers to 4.

7. Water boils at 212°F and freezes at 32°F. How many degrees difference is this? — 180°F

Decision Making

Flight attendants are limited in the amount of luggage they can bring on flights. Suppose you are a flight attendant and luggage is limited to 25 kg. You are scheduled for several days of flights and will not return home for 5 days. Write the items you would bring in the suitcase. Write the total number of kilograms and grams for the filled suitcase on the scale.

Item	Mass
Suitcase	4 kg
Clothing for 5 days	12 kg
Toothpaste and toothbrush	600 g
Extra pillow	1 kg
Books (each)	1 kg
CD player	8 kg
CDs	200 g
Tennis shoes	3 kg
Travel alarm clock	750 g
Laptop computer	10 kg

Remember: 1,000 g = 1 kg

1. Which items do you think are most important?
   Possible answers: Suitcase, clothing, toothpaste and toothbrush, tennis shoes

2. Describe how you decided what items to bring with you.
   Students' answers will vary. Check that the items in the suitcase are not over 25 kg. Possible answer: I took necessary items first (clothes, toothbrush and toothpaste, and travel alarm clock), then I added things I thought I might use while I was away, until I reached 25 kg.

3. If the limit was 40 kg, could you take everything on the list?
   No; The total of the items is just over 40 kg.

Exploring Likely and Unlikely

Each sentence is about something that is possible. For each one, write a related sentence that is likely and a related sentence that is unlikely.

Example

Some students will be absent tomorrow.

Likely: More than one student will be absent tomorrow.

Unlikely: All students will be absent tomorrow. **Possible answers are shown.**

1. Several kinds of birds are at the park this afternoon.

   a. Likely: Wrens, sparrows, and robins are at the park this afternoon.

   b. Unlikely: Dinosaurs are at the park this afternoon.

2. Our class will go on a field trip this year.

   a. Likely: Our class will go on a field trip to a museum this year.

   b. Unlikely: Our class will go on a field trip to Africa this year.

3. Some students in our school have their birthdays in March.

   a. Likely: One out of 12 students in our school has a birthday in March.

   b. Unlikely: More than half the students in our school have their birthdays in March.

4. Our basketball team will win tomorrow's game.

   a. Likely: Our basketball team will win tomorrow's game by 8 points.

   b. Unlikely: Our basketball team will win tomorrow's game by 1,000 points.

Exploring Predictions

Duane has a lot of T-shirts. He stores them in a drawer in random order. The table shows how many shirts of each color Duane has.

Shirt color	Number
Blue	15
White	10
Green	9
Red	6
Yellow	3

1. All of Duane's shirts are in his drawer. He reaches in to get a shirt. What are the possible outcomes?
   Blue, white, green, red, and yellow

2. Each morning, Duane takes the first shirt he comes to, without choosing any special one. On the first day, what color is he most likely to wear? Why do you think so?
   Blue; There are more blue shirts than there are shirts of any other color.

3. After wearing a shirt once, Duane throws it in the wash. Three days in a row, Duane wears a yellow shirt. Do you think he will wear a yellow shirt again on the fourth day? Why?
   No; He has already taken out all the yellow shirts.

4. In the past 10 days, Duane has worn 6 blue shirts, 2 red ones, and 2 green ones. What color is he most likely to wear on the eleventh day? Explain.
   White; There are only 9 blue shirts left, so the chances of taking out a white one are greater.

Exploring Probability

Circle the spinner that matches the description.

1. On this spinner, the probability of spinning dots is $\frac{2}{5}$.

2. On this spinner, the probability of spinning stripes is $\frac{1}{3}$.

3. On this spinner, the probability of spinning a 7 is $\frac{3}{10}$.

4. On this spinner, the probability of spinning fish is $\frac{1}{6}$.

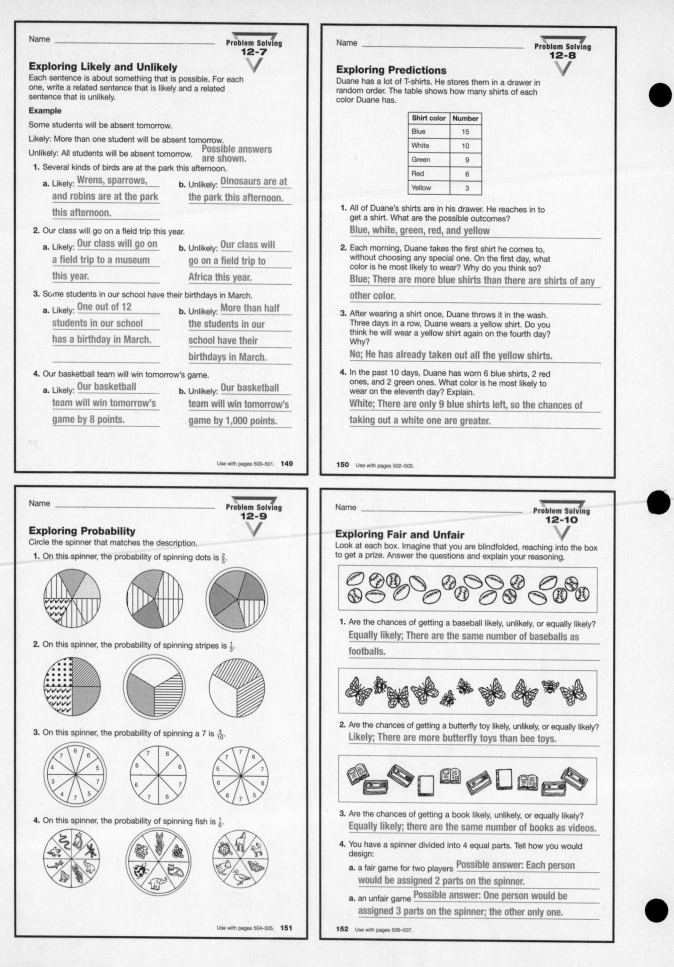

Exploring Fair and Unfair

Look at each box. Imagine that you are blindfolded, reaching into the box to get a prize. Answer the questions and explain your reasoning.

1. Are the chances of getting a baseball likely, unlikely, or equally likely?
   Equally likely; There are the same number of baseballs as footballs.

2. Are the chances of getting a butterfly toy likely, unlikely, or equally likely?
   Likely; There are more butterfly toys than bee toys.

3. Are the chances of getting a book likely, unlikely, or equally likely?
   Equally likely; there are the same number of books as videos.

4. You have a spinner divided into 4 equal parts. Tell how you would design:

   a. a fair game for two players Possible answer: Each person would be assigned 2 parts on the spinner.

   a. an unfair game Possible answer: One person would be assigned 3 parts on the spinner; the other only one.

Name _____

GPS | PROBLEM 3, STUDENT PAGE 511

Sandy likes number riddles. She picked a number to start with. Then she added 16, subtracted 4, and added 5. If Sandy ended up with 45, what number did she start with?

── **Understand** ──

1. What do you need to find out? __The number Sandy started with__

2. List the things that Sandy did to the number. __+16; −4; +5__

── **Plan** ──

3. When you work backwards, you undo steps. How do you undo adding 5?

   __Subtract 5.__

── **Solve** ──

4. Begin with 45. Work backward to find the number that Sandy started with.

   __28__

── **Look Back** ──

5. a. Could you use the Guess and Check strategy to solve this problem?

   __Yes__

   b. Would it be as easy as the Work Backward strategy? Explain.

   __No; With Guess and Check, you might have to work the__

   __problem several times.__

| SOLVE ANOTHER PROBLEM |

Polly runs 10 miles every week. On Monday, she runs half of the total distance. On Wednesday, she ran 2 miles. If Polly runs the remaining distance on Friday, how far will she run?   __3 miles__